From left to right: Eric de Grolier, Phyllis Richmond, S. R. Ranganathan, Rasmus Molgaard'H, Pauline Atherton (now Cochrane), Dan Fink, and Georges Toman.

Photo taken at FID/CR Conference on *Classification Research* in 1964 (Sept. 14-18), Elsinore Denmark

Saving the Time of the Library User
Through Subject Access Innovation

Papers in Honor of
Pauline Atherton Cochrane

Edited by William J. Wheeler

Table of Contents

Introduction

with a Note from Marcia J. Bates

✦ William J. Wheeler ✦

auline Atherton Cochrane has been contributing to library and information science for fifty years. Think of it—from mid-century to the millennium, from ENIAC (practically) to Internet II (almost here). What a time to be in our field! Her work on indexing, subject access, and the user-oriented approach had immediate and sustained impact, and she continues to be one of our most heavily cited authors (see *JASIS, 49*[4], 327-55) and most beloved personages. This introduction includes a few words about my own experiences with Pauline as well as a short summary of the contributions that make up this tribute.

A review of the curriculum vita provided at the end of this publication shows that Pauline Cochrane has been involved in a wide variety of work. As Marcia Bates points out in her note (see below), Pauline was (and *is*) a role model, but I will always think of her as simply the best teacher I ever had. In 1997, I entered the University of Illinois Graduate School of Library and Information Science as a returning mid-life student; my previous doctorate had not led to a full-time job and I was re-tooling. I was not sure what I would find in library school, and the introductory course attended by more than 100 students from widely varied backgrounds had not yet convinced me I was in the right place. Then, one day, Pauline gave a guest lecture on the digital library in my introductory class. I still remember it. She put up some notes—a few words clustered on the blackboard with some circles and directional arrows—and then she gave a free, seemingly extemporaneous, but riveting narrative. She set out a vision for ideal information exchange in the digital environment but noted a host of practical concerns, issues, and potential problems that required (demanded!) continued human intervention. The lecture brought that class and the entire semester's work into focus; it created tremendous excitement for the future of librarianship. I saw that librarians and libraries would play an active role. I was in the right place.

I took two classes from Pauline—Indexing and Abstracting and Cataloging. In both, she was always able to move easily between the two poles of theory and practice. In indexing and abstracting class, we carefully analyzed the very abstract work of Robert Fugmann (along with others) and shared interpretations of the most theoretical nature about models for indexing systems. But Pauline would also assign the most practical tasks: "Here, take this book, read Chapter 3, assign index terms, now check the index—how many terms do you and the book indexer agree on—who's right?" Or, for a longer paper, she would ask us to create an indexing system for some collection (one person indexed circus newsletters, another proposed a model for complementary human and machine indexing). In cataloging class, she showed the same ability to think and describe expansively the issues of cataloging while focusing in on the most mundane. Pauline obtained pre-conference copies of papers given at the International Conference on the Principles and Future Development of AACR held in Toronto (1998) which we analyzed in class, discussing especially the concepts of Work, Expression, Manifestation, and Item. I later saw the Committee on Cataloging: Description and Access at the 1999 ALA Annual meeting continue these discussions and make final recommendations. What we had argued about in class more than a year ago was now close to being acted on—some of the same discussions we had in class (and the same misunderstandings) came up in this ALA committee session. Balancing these theoretical concerns with more practical tasks, Pauline would come in with a stack of CDs or a stack of interesting books, hand them out, and ask us to catalog them. We also worked as interns with the public schools to help them get their collections online. Always and in every class, students were treated as practitioners *and* theorists—we learned from each other, we respected each other, we shared information—all facilitated by Pauline. We were becoming professionals, we were treated as professionals, and we were experiencing professionalism rather than just doing "class work."

These are the characteristics of a truly outstanding teacher—the ability to provide structure without limiting the student, the ability to shape a world view for the student while leaving room for the student to re-create and modify it, the ability to move easily and comfortably between the airy reaches of theory and the muddy depths of practicality. Pauline has something few teachers, colleagues, or researchers have—an ability to bring out the best in people, to make people *want* to go above and beyond (and enjoy it). I believe she revels in the mud *and* the ether, in the humanity *and* the machine, in the chaos *and* the organization. She recognizes the beauty and necessity of both improvisation *and* precision in the organization of knowledge.

The papers in this book run the gamut on subject access issues and are contributed by some of the most influential scholars in the field. Some worked closely with Pauline in the early years, others were students of hers at Syracuse or work closely with her now at Illinois. You will see that subject access encompasses a wide range of issues and that people don't agree on the solution. Two papers in particular are central in this book and represent nearly diametrically opposed viewpoints: while Robert Fugmann can be seen as the champion of the human equation in indexing, Karen Drabenstott argues we should let the machines do what they do best. I believe Eric Johnson's model presents the best alternative for combining human work with sophisticated machine intelligence, but I leave that for the reader to decide. Here is a brief summary of the contents in order of appearance.

Robert Fugmann in "Obstacles to Progress in Mechanized Subject Access and the Necessity of a Paradigm Change" provides a detailed and convincing argument for renewed attention to human indexing. He champions the position few have been courageous enough to speak—that free-text natural language searching is not living up to its claims and never will. Beyond merely stating this, however, Fugmann goes on to show in detail the reasons why this endeavor is doomed from the beginning due to the nature of language, and he suggests that the field of library and information science needs to re-think its empiricist underpinnings.

Bjorn Tell in "On MARC and Natural Text Searching: A Review of Pauline Cochrane's Inspirational Thinking Grafted onto a Swedish Spy on Library Matters" provides an interesting Swedish perspective on the development of the MARC record and its dissemination to developing countries. Noting that it should not be made such a difficult task to provide a basic organizational structure through the catalog, he wonders if perhaps we have needlessly complicated some activities and prevented access.

Donald King in "Blazing New Trails: In Celebration of an Audacious Career" gives a history of early projects on information retrieval evaluation that he and Pauline worked on including the AUDACIOUS and SUPARS projects. Issues addressed then of accuracy, relevance, user input, and system output are still with us (and hotly debated) today.

Raya Fidel in "The User Centered Approach: How We Got Here" reviews some of the contributions Pauline made to the user-centered approach and goes on to survey the kinds of studies that have been done and the methods available for user study.

Linda Smith in "Subject Access in Interdisciplinary Research" presents an overview of the problems associated with interdisciplinary research and subject access to library collections. She reviews work on mapping between vocabularies and suggests that further work on mapping between indexing languages and between indexing and user query language is needed.

Karen Drabenstott in "Web Search Strategies" provides a user-oriented guide to searching the Internet that links early models of information retrieval with modifications that can be more effective on the Web. An opposing viewpoint to Fugmann's, her perspective argues that, with the natural language capabilities of the new search engines, we need to forget some of the details of previous models and enable the machines to do what they do best.

Vinh-The Lam in "Enhancing Subject Access to Monographs in Online Public Access Catalogs: Table of Contents Added to Bibliographic Records" provides a historical perspective on one very clear subject access alternative: adding tables of contents to cataloging records. After reviewing more than thirty years of work in the area (which, of course, involved Pauline), he goes on to tell about current research in the area and gives sample data from a small survey he conducted between two Canadian libraries.

Eric Johnson in "Objects for Distributed Heterogeneous Information Retrieval" presents an exciting possibility enabled by object-oriented thinking that will allow sophisticated subject searching across distributed databases. He describes the experimental IODyne system under development at the University of Illinois that allows the kind of user-oriented searching and mapping across databases that we all want. His work cuts across old paradigms with new alternative solutions that promise high rewards. Human indexing remains important in this scheme of things, but there is no necessity of a single indexing language, and there is the freedom to switch between the most complex indexing systems and the simplest.

Each of the papers here addresses a critical element of subject access. In some we see the roots of issues we still debate, in others are the glimmers of solution. Taken together, they inform historically, discuss the present state of affairs, and project into the future, and as such cover ground in one volume that has not before been so clearly articulated. They are a true scholarly tribute to one of our leading thinkers whose influence will be felt into the next century. Happy 70th birthday Pauline!

Acknowledgments

I would like to thank Leigh Estabrook, Dean of the Graduate School of Library & Information Science, who supported this project from the moment I suggested it, the Publications Office who got the manuscripts ready, and Sandy Roe who produced the index (gratis!). It was truly an honor and a pleasure to work with the outstanding scholars, all friends of Pauline, who contributed to this book—I am especially cognizant of their hard work and patience.

A Note from Marcia J. Bates

Pauline Atherton Cochrane has been a pioneer in many ways in her life. She had a significant role in developing the foundational theory and practice of scientific indexing early in her career, then of online catalogs and, later, online information retrieval. The writers in this volume will celebrate her research through their own contributions. It happened that I was unable to contribute a chapter to this Festschrift at the time Will Wheeler was organizing it, but I do wish to write a brief, more personal, note about Pauline.

When I started out as a doctoral student in information science, Pauline Atherton (now Cochrane) was one of few women researchers in the field. Her friendliness and support were evident from the very beginning, and I always felt I could talk with her.

It is hard to remember nowadays how difficult it was in the late 1960s and early 1970s for substantial numbers of women to enter academia and other research environments. Graduate admissions were frequently biased against women—a professor I talked with in one (non-librarianship) program told me I would have to be "twice as smart" as any male applicant to be admitted to graduate school—and hiring and promoting of women in faculty positions was rare.

I went through undergraduate education at a private college and a master's and doctorate in librarianship at the University of California at Berkeley without once being taught by a woman holding a doctorate in a tenure-track position. In fact, the first woman I knew personally with a doctorate was a high school girlfriend who received hers before I got mine.

In such an environment, I hungered for professional women in the field who could be models for me as a researcher. In the 1950s and 1960s, women who worked were commonly portrayed in the media as mannish unhappy creatures, obvious failures because they were not at home taking care of husband and children. We did not have mothers or friends of our mothers as examples to see how one should act in the professional world. Neither of my parents had a college education, so it was all new to me.

Some women who did make it under such harsh conditions turned on young newcomers to their fields, sometimes being tougher on these women than even the men were. Somehow Pauline avoided all those dangers. She had a natural professional manner, and made it seem easy to earn the respect of the largely male worlds she worked in. She had become one of only two women presidents of the American Society for Information Science during its first forty years of existence.

At several key points in my career, Pauline provided the support and encouragement I needed to move forward. When I was starting out, she found grant money to hire me to develop some ideas that appeared in several later publications of mine. Another time she helped me get an article published that had been turned down, it seemed, because of the new ideas in it. There is much in common in our research interests, and we have talked on numerous occasions. I value deeply our professional relationship.

The research and academic worlds can be very competitive. Pauline Cochrane is one researcher who has never forgotten that research should be exciting, fun, and collegial. Whether I was a junior person just coming on, or a more mature and confident scholar, she has always been a true colleague and friend to me, and I will treasure that always.

Marcia J. Bates
Department of Information Studies
University of California at Los Angeles

Obstacles to Progress in Mechanized Subject Access and the Necessity of a Paradigm Change

✦ Robert Fugmann ✦

1. Introduction

Contemporary information systems, both the private and the commercially available ones, have often been blamed for their low effectiveness in terms of precision and recall, especially when they have reached considerable size with respect to file volume and use frequency (see, for example, Belkin, 1980;[1] Blair, 1996, p. 19; Desai, 1997; Drabenstott, 1996; Knorz, 1998). Saracevic (1989), after having reviewed the contemporary design of online subject access, calls "for radically different design principles and implementation" (p. 107). Van Rijsbergen (1990) writes: "The keywords approach with statistical techniques has reached its theoretical limit and further attempts for improvement are considered a waste of time" (p. 111). Lancaster (1992) deplores that very little really significant literature on subject indexing has been published in the last thirty or so years. In her preface to the Proceedings of the Sixth International Study Conference on Classification Research in 1997, McIlwaine (1997) writes, "many were surprised to find that the problems with which they wrestle today are not greatly different from those that have been occupying the minds of specialists in the field for over a generation, and probably a great deal longer" (p. v).

It has often been deplored that lack of theory prevails and that an erratic approach by trial and error has been pursued. For example, the literature swarms with contradictory statements concerning the capabilities and limitations of intellectual indexing on the one hand and of free text searching on the other—i.e., any approach that renunciates indexing (see, for example, Boyce & McLain, 1989). This chaos is also reflected in Lancaster's 1991 book (also see Fugmann, 1992a).

It is true, information technology has made magnificent progress in the last decades. We can communicate worldwide, fast, and at low cost. We have easy access to millions of documents at the desktop, provided we know the correct address, as is often the case in known-item searches. But it is also true that little has changed for the better in the case of subject access and of searches for topics. Here, the achievement of information technology is largely restricted to providing the unsatisfactory set of responses from the search files faster, in better print, and cheaper to the searcher. We must often be content with intolerably numerous irrelevant responses among the retrievals and with the highly incomplete responses.

When we review four decades of information research and practice, we can realize a number of obstacles that have substantially impeded progress in the direction of drastically improved mechanized information supply. Several reasons for this stagnation have already aptly been compiled in Neill's 1992 book. In this article, the negative influence of positivistic-empiricistic philosophy is being traced. The problem is also viewed in the light of indeterminacy, predictability, definability, user fallibility, and misplaced jurisdictional claims of information technology.

The impediments to better book indexing are not treated in detail in this article. Again, we realize a misplaced claim of information technology (section 4) which promises the mechanized compilation of book indexes with a minimum of intellectual work. These people confuse an index with a concordance—i.e., an alphabetical list of text words. We also encounter parsimoniousness on the part of publishers who often provide too little space for the printed index and impose too little time on the indexer for his/her work.

Problems of user evaluation (section 2.5 in this article) also recur in book indexes. Too often publishers, book authors, and readers are content with indexes that do not really provide access to the book's subject contents. Book indexing needs substantially more than the use of the text marker and the knowledge of the alphabet, to mention only one widespread misconception of the book indexer's work. The indexers, on the other hand, often make too little use of thesaurus routines for structuring their index vocabulary. Well considered employment of advanced information technology could help to overcome some of these impediments to the better (Fugmann, 1997).

Traditionally, a gap has existed between book indexing on the one hand and database indexing on the other. This has constituted an obstacle to progress in database indexing. An example is the widespread omission of subheadings in database indexing, although they could constitute a fairly effective substitute for index language grammar here, especially for the syntax of such a grammar.

Subheadings display the context in which the concept of interest is treated at the location in the book as specified by heading and locator. Thus, they constitute a special type of natural language syntax. They facilitate and accelerate the visual search for the concept of interest in its desired embedment.

It is inherent in uncontrolled natural language that the employment of its various syntactical devices (for example, pronouns, relative sentences, word sequence, noun phrases, attributive phrases, and so on) is unpredictable. Therefore, natural language syntax cannot effectively be addressed through search statements in the mechanized search. It is the domain of artificial index languages to provide this predictability and to make possible syntactical search statements of sufficient effectiveness. Representing the syntactical relations between indexing terms has early been recommended (see, for example, Meincke & Atherton, 1976, p. 19).

This type of syntax has not become common in databases mainly because of the user unfriendliness which such a syntax necessarily displays due to its artificiality and also because of the additional effort incurred in input and maintenance. This has constituted an obstacle to the operational employment of index language syntax and has also constituted a source of much imprecision in the representation of topics and, consequently, of the search results in databases.

This lack of index language syntax in databases could, at least in part, be compensated for, if in database indexing, subheadings (or "text modifications" as they are also often called) were also assigned, in addition to descriptor and locator. Database indexing and searching could be made more effective in this way because the search results in the print out could visually be scanned for the fulfillment of the syntactical requirements that the searcher has in mind. The look-up of the original document texts, which is necessary for this clarification and which may well be (or soon become) intolerably time consuming, could then be dispensed with. Thus, database indexing could learn much for its advancement from book indexing (see Fugmann, 1997).

Concentrating in database indexing now, it is useful to draw a line between two types of obstacles to progress. On the one hand we find obstacles that can be surmounted, although, in part, only at considerably increased effort (see section 2). On the other hand, there is an obstacle which cannot be overcome in some fields, and which we must put up with in our profession (section 3) if the terminology of these fields continues to display a high degree of vagueness.

A substantial obstacle to progress is seen in the dominance of a fundamentally inadequate philosophy on which most of research and evaluation seems to have been based so far and which, in the opinion of the author, has contributed much to the imperfection of our contemporary information systems. Can this obstacle be surmounted in the not too distant future? This question is left open.

2. Surmountable Obstacles

Many of the obstacles to advanced subject access are of the type which can be overcome through the better use of existing knowledge and through the readiness to invest more time and expertise into subject analysis. Overcoming these surmountable obstacles is no utopia, as is shown in the example in section 4, which was launched in a discipline in which professional information supply prospers.

2.1 The Dominance of the Positivistic View in Information Science

The field of information science and technology has more or less latently been dominated by a markedly positivistic philosophy. Its detrimental influence on progress has repeatedly been criticized, for example, by Budd (1995), Hjorland (1997, pp. 61, 133), Kiel (1994, p. 148), and by Svenonius (1992).[2] Soergel (1994),[3] without expressly referring to positivism or empiricism, also warns against drawing conclusions from ill-designed experiments.

In the positivistic view, reality of phenomena is only acknowledged if they are observable. From what escapes observation, exclusively mathematics and pure logics are acknowledged. This philosophy flourished until the second and third decades of this century. But, for its obvious inadequacy, it has been abandoned, at least in the natural sciences. Ernst Mach, one of the most prominent representatives of German positivism in the beginning of this century, even rejected the idea of atoms and molecules because they could not be observed. Positivism is not far from the long abandoned philosophy of naïve realism, which had recognized all and only what is perceived through the senses, thus rendering them the source of ultima ratio in our understanding of the world.

In this article, empiricism is also traced as the root of a variety of misconceptions and unfounded generalizations. Pure empiricism would, for example, have supported the ancient statement of the direct relation of weight and speed of free falling bodies. Ample empirical evidence for this thesis could be compiled by comparing stones on the one hand and feathers or balls of paper on the other. Galileo stated the opposite relationship, namely the independence of falling speed from weight. He could also present convincing observations in favor of his hypothesis, but this was restricted to massive falling bodies. Mere reasoning would have corroborated Galileo: Why should two stones, after having been joined (and having double weight), fall faster than one of them alone? Which of them would accelerate itself and the other one? Obviously, something is wrong with the empirical interpretation of the experiments with light bodies.

Empiricism leads us astray when we select the wrong experimental conditions or restrict ourselves to studying the wrong examples or to using the wrong instruments, namely to those that happen to be available (for a discussion of instrumentalism, see also Budd, 1995, p. 301; Kiel, 1994). It is easy and fast to put the purse on the balance and to take the purse's weight as a measure of the money it contains. Ample "evidence" could be supplied for the existence of a relationship between a purse's weight and the amount of money it contains if only those experimental conditions prevail or are chosen which are conducive to the statement.

In information science, we encounter several examples where we are mislead through the insistence on measurement and, in fact, of what is inherently unmeasurable—e.g., the phenomenon of information. But scepticism toward measurement and the avoiding of unrealistic experimental conditions requires some theoretical view—in Galileo's case, the hypothesis of the vacuum. It had not yet been discovered at that time and, consequently, the disturbing influence of air resistance in the experiments was not realized.

Empiricism neglects what cannot be observed (for example, the future of an information system) and cannot be measured. Hence, empirical "evidence" cannot constitute genuine evidence. The role of empirical investigations is restricted to supplying the raw material for critical reasoning and to supplying suggestions for a more advanced interpretation of reality, such that observed phenomena can be better explained and future phenomena can be better predicted.

In the information field and in a purely empirical approach, literally any intended evaluation result for an information system can be produced, and any opinion on the effectiveness of a type of information system can be corroborated through the choice of a suitable constellation of experimental conditions or through the selection of suitable examples, and in fact in a manner which seems perfectly convincing and unsuspicious (see Fugmann, 1984), just as is the case in the experimentation with falling bodies, if there is no critical contemplation on the experimental conditions. It is here that we badly need a drastic paradigm change in information science.

2.1.1 Full-Text Storage versus Indexing and Classification. Equivalence of full-text storage with intellectual indexing, the former inclusive of free text searching, has often been stated and empirically been "proved," for example, in the Cranfield experiments (Cleverdon, 1967). In fact, an equivalence (or sometimes even a superiority) seems to prevail but only if any distinction between individual concepts and general concepts is dispensed with.

In this reasoning, we must first clarify what is to be understood by a concept in our context of this article. According to Dahlberg (1976, 1994),[4] we define the concept as the (invisible) sum of the essential features of a referent and, in fact, irrespective of the mode of expression that happens to have been chosen for this sum by an author or searcher. Here, a referent is anything (of the material or immaterial nature) about which statements can be made. A general concept is one which is amenable to meaningful specification. Its set of conceptual features can be extended by meaningful additional features. For example, the concept of "fuel" can be subdivided into the solid, liquid, and gaseous types. In contrast, an individual concept is one to which no meaningful conceptual feature can be added. In other words, it is not amenable to meaningful specification—for example, a person, a town, a mountain, a specific metal, a specific book, and so on.

It is typical of general concepts that they can be (and often are) expressed in an infinite multitude of expressions, such as paraphrasing expressions. For example, perfectly equivalent to "thalassophobia" is the non-lexical expression "displayed a pathological anxiety towards entering any type of boat. . . ," and any other definition-like expression of this concept. During the emergence of a new concept, this mode of expression is even the only available one, and it is—for good reason—often retained by authors and questioner even after a neologism has been coined for the new concept (should this ever be the case). Do we have "oilplaning" or "leafplaning" in analogy to "aquaplaning"? Instead we have (still) an infinitely large number of non-lexical definition-like paraphrasing expressions for these important concepts to communicate about them but which are unpredictable in their wording. All these expressions should be retrieved in a search request for "slippery hazards in traffic."

In other words, it is unpredictable in which modes of expression a general concept may have entered the file in full-text or free-text storage (see, for example, Bates, 1998, pp. 1188, 1202). Correspondingly incomplete will necessarily be the set of search parameters with which a general concept would have to be addressed and correspondingly incomplete will also be the set of responses to such an incompletely phrased query. It is the lack of predictability[5] of these modes of expression which constitutes an insurmountable obstacle to the phrasing of a complete set of search statements. The larger the variation of expressions (for example, the larger the search file of uncontrolled natural language texts), the more incomplete will be the set of responses.

Here we encounter what has been called the "small systems' syndrome"—i.e., the phenomenon that small search files display properties that are fundamentally different from those of large files and that the mere growth of a small system may well lead to its decline and eventual break-down (see, for example, Bates, 1998, pp. 1186, 1196; Gey & Dabney, 1990).

Full-text searching is fairly successful only in the case of individual concepts because their names are fairly predictable and can easily be compiled completely through look-up in appropriate dictionaries due to their lexical nature, which is inherent in their representations. If there is no revelation of the types of query concepts in retrieval experiments, no meaningful conclusions can be drawn from them, especially not concerning recall values.

The statement of the equivalence of substantially different input and retrieval systems (for example, of the indexed and nonindexed ones in the Cranfield experiments) also only seems to be impirically proven, but only if the representations of (general) concepts in the search file are artificially made predictable. This happens (as another manifestation of the "small systems' syndrome") if one and the same (and unnaturally small) set of texts is processed again and again in a variety of experiments so that the searcher memorizes their wording. This has been pointed out, for example, by Milstead (1994, p. 579) in her criticism and by Blair (1996, p. 17). Under these unrealistic circumstances, human memory (still) functions as a substitute for the predictability of concept representations. The criterion of predictability, crucial for indexing quality and successful retrieval, is not put to the test under these circumstances.

Often, any distinction between word and concept has been neglected (as, for example, reported by Yee, 1991, p. 93 and has earlier been deplored by Meincke & Atherton, 1976, p. 19), and the search is naïvely seen as a process of merely finding those words which a questioner had used to describe the topic of interest. At most, synonymy is taken into consideration—i.e., the phenomenon that different words mean (almost) the same concept. In case of such a primitive goal, it is easy to achieve a user's "satisfaction" even with full-text storage and retrieval.

Here we encounter the failure to realize that the word in its use in natural language is not intended for use in isolation. It is only in its context that the word assumes its meaning and importance. Only in its context, a word or a phrase reveals what it more or less tacitly implies, obvious to the reader or to anyone who listens to speech. Hence, in colloquial discourse, any text requires (and subconsciously receives) interpretation (see, for example, Budd, 1995, pp. 307, 308).

Text interpretation yields reliable essence recognition (the importance of a concept depends on the context in which it is embedded), meaning disambiguation, paraphrase lexicalization (i.e., substituting a paraphrase in storage or retrieval by one of its lexical equivalents in natural or artificial language such as notations), establishing concept relationships, ellipses filling (i.e., making explicit what has only been implied in a text and must be inferred from it) (see, for example, Ranganathan, 1962,

p. 129; Green, 1992, p. 84; Fugmann, 1993, p. 70); "addition of terms not used in text" (Meincke & Atherton, 1976, p. 19); (near) synonym control, verbalization of nontextual information, all of which are typical achievements of good intellectual indexing. They are, however, renounced in searching noninterpreted full texts much to the detriment of search quality.

As far as context is concerned, it is always freely phrased and, hence, expressed in an unpredictable manner. Thus, it escapes inclusion in the query as a reliable additional interpretative statement.

In a special series of the Cranfield experiments, the searcher held a document in his hands, read the wording, and phrased a query (reported by Ellis, 1996, p. 25), certainly more or less tailored to the wording encountered in the target texts. Under such unrealistic circumstances, where predictability is circumvented, full-text storage and retrieval is bound to perform unnaturally and treacherously well.

In spite of all these limitations, most of our contemporary research concentrates on the processing of words—i.e., focuses on the verbal plane of the Indian school and neglects the idea plane (Ranganathan & Gopinath, 1967). A multitude of mathematical models has been developed, more or less distant from depicting reality and without success of reliably identifying the concepts that are meant through them. Here again a markedly positivistic-empiricistic view leaks through: Words of speech or in print can be observed, counted, compared with each other, their spatial vicinity in text can be explored, and so on, quite in contrast to concepts (as unobservable mental constructs) which cannot.

Accordingly, the problem of expression multiplicity has largely been seen in synonymy. This view has its roots in a definition in which the concept is considered as the meaning of a lexical unit such as a word or phrase. This definition may be useful in linguistics, but it is irrelevant to the information field.

It is one of the tasks of the knowledgeable and carefully working indexer to interpret and translate (i.e., to lexicalize) paraphrases into the expressions of the index language in order to make these concepts easily retrievable. The onomantic approach of Riggs (1996, p. 28), which aims at organizing concepts irrespective of their names (and of the existence of names), also deserves more attention.

The type of grammar in natural language text contributes much to its expressiveness and specificity. But this grammar is not useful for retrieval because of the unpredictability with which its various devices are employed by authors and questioners (see section 3.3.2). Specificity without predictability is useless for retrieval. Hence, in stating a superior specificity in an information system, especially that of a system in uncontrolled natural language, we must judge to what extent the highly specific expressions encountered there are predictable (see also section 2.2.2).

The problems in processing the infinitely large multitude of nonlexical expressions are insurmountable for any mechanism when the satisfactory autonomous processing of them is the goal—i.e., one which is not based on a predetermined selection of well known examples, and one which does not necessitate the subsequent intervention of a human for their improvement (see section 2.7). Hence, natural language will defy any satisfactory algorithmic processing (see section 2.3.2). That neural networks do not constitute a way out of this dilemma cannot be treated in the scope of this article.

There is still another pitfall in the empirical evaluation of retrieval experiments. Ironically, the less careful the experimenter is in tracing nonretrieved relevant documents, the more successful appears the search. There is no commonly accepted agreement concerning the desirable degree of effort in tracing information loss (Blair, 1996, p. 10). This raises the ethical question in information system evaluation.

Classification as a user's tool has been investigated earlier in the AUDACIOUS project, and it became obvious very early how much has to be undertaken to provide the inexperienced user with an easy-to-use system (Cochrane, 1982, p. 262).

2.1.2 The "Inverse Relationship between Precision and Recall." An apparently inverse relationship between precision and recall has also been observed in the Cranfield experiments: According to this "empirical law," neither precision nor recall can be improved without simultaneously and necessarily impairing each other. For decades this statement has constituted an excuse for inadequate information systems and, thus, has paralyzed their improvement, although this type of correlation has often been questioned (for example by Harter, 1990, pp. 136, 145; Green, 1992, p. 87; Soergel, 1985, p. 122; Svenonius, 1995, p. 247; Fugmann, 1994) or even found to be violated (Heine & Tague, 1991, p. 276).

The statement of the inverse relationship also neglects the fact that we know of information systems which work perfectly both at 100 percent precision and 100 percent recall, as is the case, for example, for the majority of chemical molecular structure searches (see section 4). This statement can easily be refuted in a simple "Gedankenexperiment"—experiment in the mind (Fugmann, 1993, p. 203).

What are the factors that exert an influence on the quality of the retrieval with respect to precision and recall? Representational fidelity controls precision, representational predictability controls recall (Fugmann, 1985, axioms 4 and 5). The quality of retrieval crucially depends on what degree of both fidelity and predictability have been achieved in storage. If both are made perfect, precision and recall in retrieval can be made close to 100 percent. This is the case in the example in section 4 and, for instance, in the telephone directory and in many other cases of data documentation.

But as for uncontrolled natural language text, the expressions for concepts inherently lack predictability, and gaps (ellipses) are common, particularly in the case of general concepts and topics, quite apart from the ambiguity of most natural language words. This obstructs good retrieval from natural language text files. It is the task of good indexing to overcome these shortcomings. Here, the essence of the documents is recognized and translated into the expressions of an index language, which makes them predictable at a foreseeable level of specificity.

Lack of representational fidelity and predictability prevails:

- if the index language lacks specificity (which enforces unspecific queries); and/or
- if the index language is used in an unreliable manner (which affects predictability); and/or
- if there is no index language in use at all.

Under these unfortunate circumstances, one has to find a way to the search statements and to their combinations through trial and error. In order to capture unforeseeable expressions (and to increase recall), the search idea is distorted through generalizations which necessarily provoke the correspondingly imprecise responses.

On the other hand, in order to increase precision, the search idea is distorted through the addition of restricting extraneous search parameters (such as year of publication, journal, Boolean negations, and so on) which necessarily provoke loss of relevant information. Hence, where an inverse relationship is observed:

- it is only a consequence of deficient, or a complete lack of, indexing, and
- occasionally, and in part, of the ambiguity of the terminology of the subject field.

The postulated "law" of the inverse relation is an example of the uncritical acceptance and distribution of a statement in the scientific community through hearsay.

Often, the special circumstances under which tests have been executed have not been revealed in reports. This concerns, for example, the type of test questions (individual versus general concepts), the time consumption for phrasing the test queries, the size and perspicuity of the vocabulary, and so on (as stated, for example, by Jordan, 1989).

It is true that the Cranfield experiments have initiated a period of rigorous information system evaluation, but they also constitute a model example of the purely positivistic-empiricistic approach. Hence, several of the conclusions drawn from these experiments have been grossly misleading and have necessitated contradiction (see, for example, Ellis, 1996, pp.

25-27; Fugmann, 1993, p. 203; Harter, 1996, p. 40; Soergel, 1985, p. 291; Svenonius, 1981, p. 91).

2.2 Wrong or Neglected Indexing Quality Criteria

If wrong goals are established and pursued, the true goal can never be achieved. Subject analysis and indexing do not constitute exceptions to this rule. A treacherous type of satisfaction will occur when wrong and true goals are in some vicinity (though markedly different) and when some progress in the direction of the wrong goal is being achieved or at least approximated[6]). Two treacherous quality criteria, heavy in use, are discussed here.

2.2.1 The Inadequacy of Consistency as an Indexing Quality Criterion

Traditionally, indexing consistency is recognized as a criterion for indexing quality, although this criterion has repeatedly been drawn into doubt (see, for example, Cooper, 1969). This statement neglects the fact that a mode of perfectly consistent indexing may well be consistently bad. An example is mechanically extracting keywords from natural language texts using a stopword list. Hence, striving at perfectly consistent indexing may well result in an entirely unusable information system.

On the other hand and intuitively, indexing consistency has something to do with indexing quality. If one and the same document is entirely differently indexed by different indexers (or differently indexed by the same indexer at different times), something seems wrong.

The solution to this puzzle is that only in the first step of indexing—that of essence selection—consistency is paramount. But here it is identical with predictability. In the second step of indexing, that of essence representation, only predictability is required (Fugmann, 1993, pp. 94-97). A concept may well have been (inconsistently) entered into the file with different expressions that can be looked up and are thus predictable. Then these expressions can be compiled as alternative search statements. For example, a substance may inconsistently be represented through different names, for example, through "vitamin C," "ascorbic acid," "cantan[R]," "the scurvy-preventing and scurvy healing substance in vegetables," and so on. But if we know these expressions, we can accurately retrieve the corresponding documents. Hence, what is required for good retrieval is not indexing consistency but, instead, an overall predictability of both essence selection and essence representation.

2.2.2 The Number of Access Points as a Criterion for Expected Retrieval Success

It has been assumed that the greater the number of access points, the better the retrievability of the text (see, for example, Lancaster, 1991, p. 197). But if this is true, full-text search files should be ideal for high recall values. We know that this is not the case (see, for example, Blair, 1996,

p. 19) because the words of the searcher for the topic of interest only rarely match the wording of the documents of interest, especially in the case of searches for general concepts and topics (that this is not merely a synonymy problem has been discussed in section 2.1.1).

Again, only those expressions can constitute an access point for retrieval which are phrased in a predictable mode. Therefore, indexing languages, with their predictable concept representations, may well be more specific in retrieval than an even more detailed and specific natural language text, especially in the case of searches for general concepts and topics.

2.2.3 Survival Power: The Neglected Criterion of Information System Quality

It is alien in the empiricist view to look into an information system's future because its future cannot be observed and because the system's future fate cannot empirically be demonstrated in the present. What is generally undertaken in information system evaluation is a snapshot-like analysis of the presently prevailing situation, in particular because such an analysis is fast and cheap. However, it should be important to an information system user to know if an information system is capable of continuing to serve its purpose in the future.

There may be various reasons to abandon an information system in the future after some time of having practiced it. The demands made on retrieval precision are steadily increasing during the growth of a mechanized information system, and the system may fail to provide a significantly higher search specificity. It may lose its value if it begins to produce hundreds or even thousands of responses from which the few relevant ones have to be sifted out through human inspection, a procedure which may well begin to cause an intolerably high expenditure of time and attention.

An information system may also lose its value because its vocabulary has become chaotic in the course of time. This renders the indexing procedure correspondingly unreliable, and the search results become increasingly incomplete as a consequence. This decrease in recall may remain hidden for quite a long time. But when this deficiency becomes apparent, perhaps through a correspondingly extended and careful investigation, an information system suddenly loses all of the appreciation that it had enjoyed so far. Most often, the reason for this failure is a misplaced parsimoniousness in the input step (see section 2.6). This type of positivistic and treacherous user satisfaction has often prevented a more advanced and durable information system from coming into existence or from surviving its initial stage.

The notion of information system survival power, although coined early in the history of our field (cited by Harmon, 1970 from Boulding 1956, p. 174), has not become popular in the contemporary information scientific literature, although this is one of the most important quality criteria for operational information systems.

2.3 Deficiencies in Index Languages

The use of index languages has often rendered unsatisfactory search results. Natural language ambiguity constitutes an almost insurmountable obstacle to advancement here (see section 3). But deficiencies in the index languages or their inadequate use (see section 2.4) may also be the reason. As to the index languages, we can distinguish between the deficiencies in their vocabularies and in their grammar.

2.3.1 Vocabulary Deficiencies. An index language vocabulary can serve its purpose to satisfaction only if it is reliably used by the indexer and if its capabilities are fully exploited by the questioner. If the indexer fails to select those terms from the vocabulary that most appropriately represent the concept of interest, the questioner's search statements, which will probably be the most appropriate ones, will not match. Loss of relevant information is the consequence.

A questioner, attempting to compensate for this inaccuracy, may include less appropriate vocabulary terms as alternative search statements. But then the correspondingly irrelevant documents will be retrieved. Hence, any successful search for the documents relevant to a topic of interest is—even if latently—preceded by a search in the vocabulary for the most appropriate terms.

The reason for the indexer's failure in the vocabulary search is often a lack of overview of the vocabulary and lack of time for the vocabulary search. This happens if the vocabulary is overly extended and has become chaotic in the course of time, in particular if vocabulary categorization has been dispensed with in the design of the vocabulary.

2.3.1.1 The Lack of Categorization. Semantic categories constitute the backbone of any expressive index language and can prevent a vocabulary from becoming chaotic. In particular, they constitute a guideline for:

- the definition of concepts in the view of the particular knowledge field,
- the decision on which types of concepts have to be represented in the vocabulary,
- creating order in the vocabulary,
- the division of the representational task between vocabulary and grammar (if there is any) especially for the resolution of precombinations (see section 2.3.1.2),
- the decision on which concepts of a text have to be selected for indexing and input,
- the decision on which type of search statements has to be avoided (because the corresponding concepts are not represented in the search file), and

- the choice of appropriate characteristics of subdivision (with the goal of avoiding precombinations).

Only few contemporary information systems have introduced categorization and facet formation of this type, much to the detriment of reliable and sufficiently specific indexing. The consequence is lack of vocabulary perspicuity and unreliable indexing, in particular through the abundance of precombinations in the vocabulary (Fugmann, 1993, p. 189). It is under these circumstances that an inverse relationship between precision and recall is observed to prevail (see section 2.1.2).

2.3.1.2 The Lack of Vocabulary Structure. In indexing for a database, precombinations[7] in its index language vocabulary are the cause of a large and incessantly growing network of concept relations and of an almost explosive growth of the vocabulary in the course of time. Under these circumstances, the search for the most appropriate vocabulary terms for a concept is impeded almost to impossibility in the course of time. Increasingly unreliable indexing is the consequence, with the additional consequence of increasingly defective search results (see section 2.3.1). However, the resolution of precombinations into their categorical constituents requires the use of index language grammar if substantial loss in representational fidelity is to be avoided (see section 2.3.2).

Using an index language vocabulary merely in the "controlled" mode does not result in adequately reliable indexing. Under these circumstances, the vocabulary terms are considered to be the merely permitted ones, and the search for the most appropriate terms is not made obligatory (see section 2.4).

In book indexing, grammar is largely restricted to that which manifests itself in the relationship of heading-subheading (Anderson, 1997, p. 22). In order to maintain an adequate degree of representational fidelity, and to make possible index searches at an adequate degree of precision, precombinations are indispensible here. Fortunately, the vocabulary is not subject to continual growth. Hence, good book indexing and pursuing the network of concept relations (marked by "see also references") is not substantially impeded through precombinations.

The structure of a vocabulary can drastically be improved and the search in the vocabulary be facilitated if characteristics of subdivision are employed as, for example, have been used by Aitchison and Gilchrist (1987, p. 89).

These devices for creating order in index language vocabularies are only rarely encountered in our contemporary index languages. A correspondingly defective manner of indexing and searching is the inevitable result.

2.3.1.3 The Lack of Notations for Nonlexicalized Concepts. For many important concepts, no lexical expressions have yet been formed in colloquial or technical language (see section 2.1.1). Only nonlexical para-phrasing expressions are in use for them. If the vocabulary is restricted to natural language terms, these nonlexicalized concepts can neither be indexed nor retrieved with these vocabularies. The way out is to assign them an artificial lexical unit in the shape of a notation as some type of neologism.

An advanced index language vocabulary should comprise both natu-ral language terms (typical of the thesaurus) and notations (typical of a classification), as is the case in Bhattacharyya's (1982) "classaurus." Nota-tions would make possible the lexicalization of concepts for which no natu-ral language terms have yet been coined. Several other advantages of no-tations could then be brought into play as well.

Contemporary indexing and retrieval practices have deliberately dis-pensed with such a powerful device, much to the disadvantage of the quality of indexing and searching. User friendliness has been the argument. But is it really user friendly if the bulk of new concepts remains unretrievable until natural language lexicalizes them? The first ten years of the litera-ture on AIDS research is almost unretrievable because this syndrome had not yet been lexicalized at that time.

2.3.2 The Lack of Index Language Grammar. Any type of language owes its expressiveness to the interplay between vocabulary and grammar, and in-dex languages do not constitute an exception. The type of grammar in natural language text is not useful for search because of the unpredictability with which its various devices are used (grammatical cases, the various types of pronouns, informative succcession of words, prepositions, attribute phrases, and so on) (see also section 2.1.1).

In spite of this, proximity operators have often been in use for natu-ral language text searching on a large scale. Here, the spatial adjacency in which search terms co-occur in the text is used as a search statement. But the distance in which the terms for closely connected concepts co-occur is unpredictable in natural language and depends on chance (see, for ex-ample, Schwarz, 1990, p. 408). Therefore, using proximity in natural lan-guage text as a search parameter necessarily provokes information loss.

As far as index language grammars are concerned, they have often not met the expectations made of them or they have even been aban-doned because of their observed ineffectiveness. This holds largely true, for example, for traditional "links." They have been used in indexing to connect terms which co-occur in the title of a document, in a sentence, or even in a paragraph.

The assumption is that, in view of the spatial proximity of terms in the text, the concepts expressed through them should also be conceptually related. But since these links are natural language based, they also have inherited the unpredictability of their employment. Even most closely connected concepts may be widely separated in the natural language text (Schwarz, 1990, p. 408) and, vice versa, unrelated concepts may well occur in immediate adjacency in a document. Hence, using links will inevitably cause both loss of relevant information and irrelevant responses.

As far as the traditional roles or role indicators are concerned (reviewed by Spang-Hansen, 1976), they lack specificity and are ill-defined. Therefore, their use has often been disappointing.

Promising grammatical-syntactical devices in index languages are, for example, the relation operators of PRECIS (Austin, 1984), the facet sequence in Colon classification (Ranganathan, 1967), and relation indicators (Fugmann, 1993, pp. 158-62), because their employment is predictable. But these grammatical-syntactical devices have not found the wide acceptance which they deserve. The reason may be that they have been considered unfriendly to users due to their artificiality (which, however, is just the reason and even condition for their effectiveness).

In the absence of an index language grammar, the vocabulary is burdened (and often overtaxed) with the task of representing the essence of a document to a sufficient degree of representational fidelity. This may well lead to continually growing and increasingly chaotic vocabularies. This is particularly due to the increasing dominance of precombinations (see section 2.5.2.3). These vocabularies increasingly defy reliable use on the part of indexers and users (see, for example, Soergel, 1994, p. 597, section 2.4). The consequence is correspondingly low ratios of precision and recall, which may well develop into intolerability during the continual growth of the systems (see also section 2.4).

What is generally lacking in our contemporary information systems is a well attuned, category-controlled balance between vocabulary and grammar (if there is any). What we encounter in the field of index languages is only some kind of primitive pidgin language, one which seriously lacks specificity of the predictable kind.

Where an index language grammar has been employed in a predictable manner, as is, for example, the case for the indexing of chemical molecules, the goal of extremely high ratios both of recall and precision has been attained, in company with extreme effectiveness and survival power (see section 4).

In book indexing, the relationship between heading and subheading constitutes a type of grammar but only one of the unpredictable type. This type of grammar is useful for the reader but it cannot be phrased as a parameter in a mechanized search. This is one of the reasons why merely making a conventional book index machine readable does not constitute that drastic advance which might be expected of its computerization.

2.4 Deficiencies in the Use of Index Languages

The mere existence of a good index language is no guarantee for good indexing. The vocabulary must also carefully be used both by indexer and searcher as has already repeatedly been mentioned. The most widespread use of such a vocabulary is the "controlled" mode: only the terms of this vocabulary are permitted in indexing. In other words, any term from this vocabulary which comes to the mind of the indexer or which happens to be encountered in browsing the vocabulary can be used. There is often no obligation to search for the most appropriate term from the vocabulary.

But often users cannot find the most appropriate terms in their vocabularies (Soergel, 1994, p. 597) due to a lack of vocabulary structure and due to excessive vocabulary size (see section 2.3.2). This impairs representational predictability and provokes loss of relevant information in retrieval. Under these circumstances, a query term will often not match with the term in the index and vice versa. On the other hand, noise will occur in the responses if the searcher, as a precaution, includes the less appropriate terms that the indexer may presumably have used.

It has only rarely expressly been made obligatory for the indexer to search for, and to use, only the most specific terms that are available in the vocabulary ("the indexing terms should be the most specific available" [Anderson, 1996, p. 12]), although this has been the common practice of the carefully working librarian since the times of Cutter more than a hundred years ago. Thus, the capabilities of intellectual indexing are far from being fully exploited, and it is not surprising for this reason (and not for an allegedly inherent ineffectiveness) that intellectual indexing has often not met the expectations of its users.

2.5 User Evaluation

Any indexing must aim to satisfy its users, not only in the present but especially in the future and under the changing requirements of the future. It is therefore paramount for an information system that the users be involved in the design of the system and in continually adapting the system to unforeseen new requirements.

2.5.1. Usefulness of User Evaluation. Users must render their opinion if the conceptual categories (section 2.3.1.1) of the system meet their requirements for searches and if navigation in the vocabulary is sufficiently easy and fast. They must also give feedback if the specificity of the vocabulary should be extended or reduced. They should also urge for timeliness of the input and for an appropriate speed in the execution of the searches. The searches should also be affordable, the responses should be easily and speedily accessible, and should display an appropriate ratio of precision and completeness (whereby the latter is difficult to assess and therefore mostly omitted). They should also care for the maintenance of an appropriate coverage of their literature in the information system. Users should also render their opinion on the quality of a book index to the publisher in order to make them aware of the necessity of improving them.

2.5.2 Problems of User Evaluation. But users must also realize that not all present-day requirements could have been foreseen in the past and can also not be foreseen for the future and that they often make unsatisfiable or illusory expectations of computerized information systems (see section 2.5.2.2) and that an information system must display some features, the judgment of which goes beyond the competence of the user, since the user is not an information expert.

Following user demands in the last-mentioned cases may well lead an information system directly into its decline and eventual breakdown in the more or less distant future (see, for example, ISKO/IE, 1992). In the following, some examples of misconceptions in system evaluation are discussed.

2.5.2.1 Precision and Recall. In their system evaluation, users should always either include a well founded judgment on the recall ratio of the system under consideration, in addition to the precision assessment, or be very cautious with any judgment on retrieval quality when they dispense with assessing the recall ratio.

An information system, presently highly praised for its "good" results, may well be emphatically rejected the next day when it reveals to have worked with high proportions of information loss all the time. It may well have driven out another information system which would have produced much more complete responses, even if only at a higher, but still tolerable, expense.

In most contemporary evaluation experiments, any reliable recall check is reported to be omitted (see, for example, Milstead, 1994, p. 581) or replaced by the "relative recall" check (see Harter & Hert, 1997, p. 17), that is, by the comparison of several information systems with respect to their recall ratios. This is done without the attempt to identify the absolute recall values although they should be of primary interest to the user. This omission is due to the high effort which would have to be expended in assessing absolute recall. This omission is also due to the markedly positivistic attitude to disregard what cannot (easily) be observed, as is the case with unretrieved, though relevant, documents. Under these circumstances of superficiality, user satisfaction can easily be attained even with information systems of low recall and high information loss.

2.5.2.2 Relevance versus Pertinence. In assessing retrieval quality, users must distinguish between the relevant responses and the merely pertinent ones. In the framework of our considerations (and, for example, according to Kemp, 1974), relevant responses are those which match the elements of the search request. In contrast, pertinent responses do not (or only partially) match the search request. In spite of that they happen to be of interest to an individual user, but the user failed to define (or was unable to define) their nature beforehand. What is pertinent for an individual user may well not be pertinent for the vast majority of other users, and it may even be pertinent for an individual user only at a particular point in time.

It is the task of retrieval to exclude those responses that are merely pertinent because they have not been requested by the user, however useful they may be for an individual user in his or her specific situation (it does not change the necessity of this distinction if those documents which do not perfectly satisfy the search statements are arranged in levels of decreasing correspondence to the search statements).

A user, often in ignorance of the mechanisms of the delegated search (and any mechanized search is a delegated one), may be inclined to expect that "the computer" will submit all those responses that are pertinent for him or for her (as reported, for example, by Yee, 1991, p. 80). The user is accustomed to encounter pertinent documents during his or her own nondelegated "meandering" search by way of serendipitous browsing. Here, the user has an entirely free hand to gather what happens to be found interesting, irrespective of any predetermined search goal.

But such an expectation is unsatisfiable in a system for the delegated information search. It is (and must be) typically oriented to what had been laid down in advance as the goal of the search. No algorithm is conceivable that might execute a satisfying search for the pertinent documents because, lacking a definable search goal, no instructions could be laid down in advance which an algorithm could follow. This holds true no matter what progress information technology may take.

Nor can the highly idiosyncratic selection, which a user executes in his or her momentary constellation of circumstances and requirements reliably be simulated by a computer, as is sometimes promised by those who are enthusiastic of neural networks. For the "learning" of such a neural network, it would by no means be sufficient merely to utilize experience from earlier pertinence decisions of a user. Documents, new and still unknown to the user, would dramatically change each of these earlier decisions in an unpredictable manner.

Obviously, only what can be defined can satisfactorily be delegated to another person or to a mechanism,[8] and supplying unrequested responses to a questioner as a principle will, during the continual growth of an information system, very probably lead to its decline and even breakdown and to the discontinuation of its service. This is the consequence of a misunderstood type of user friendliness.

Strange to say, this fundamental truth and the important difference between "relevance" and "pertinence" has been widely disregarded in the more recent past, although it has repeatedly been emphasized (see, for example, Soergel, 1985, p. 128).

Here, the information specialist must be strong in contradicting such an unsatisfiable ill-considered expectation on the part of the naïve user. "What cannot be defined, cannot be delegated satisfactorily," and this argument will normally be willingly accepted in a discussion with a disappointed user.

2.5.2.3 Precombinations. Precombinations are terms which comprise the meaning of at least two other terms which are already contained in the vocabulary of the index language or could be entered into it in the future due to their categorical character.[9] For example, if "copper" and "zinc" are vocabulary terms (because they are manifestations of the category "MATTER" in the system [see section 2.3.1.1]), then brass, as an alloy of copper and zinc, is a precombination.

Even if tin is not yet in the vocabulary, bronze (an alloy of copper and tin) is also a precombination, because tin, as a MATTER concept, can also claim to be represented in the vocabulary.

There are many alloys in the metallurgical field for which names have not yet been coined. They can be indexed only through the enumeration of their components. But each name for a precombination contributes to the size of the vocabulary and to the extension and ramification of the relational paths that an indexer and searcher must pursue during the search for the most appropriate terms in the vocabulary. If, for example, an "alloy consisting of 70% copper and the rest zinc" is discussed in a document, the indexer must look for the term in the vocabulary which is the most appropriate one for this alloy, in this case, perhaps "red brass."

Also the searcher will probably choose this term in case of an inquiry, for just this alloy, because it promises to retrieve the desired literature most precisely. Merely "alloy," "copper," and "zinc" would not be sufficient, although they are contained in the vocabulary and may even occur in the text (there are too many irrelevant documents in which, for example, some copper alloy is mentioned, and in another alloy the presence, or even absence, of zinc is stated).

In order to pave the way to the most appropriate descriptors, both copper and zinc should be referenced to brass and red brass and vice versa. Extending from "copper," all references to these related terms will have to be taken into consideration in the search for the most appropriate vocabulary term.

When the information system and its vocabulary have been operational for a few years, from each branching point dozens or even hundreds of references may well have to be pursued by the careful indexer (and questioner). In such a conceptually opaque vocabulary, the most appropriate descriptors will no longer reliably be found by indexer or searcher, although they are offered by the vocabulary. Too much time and attention would have to be used for such a search under the pressure of time in everyday practice. Even the embedding of new precombinations in the existing network of relations may be impeded to impossibility. This is the end of any reliable indexing practice and adequate search.

Many vocabularies have become unmanageable through such a dominance of precombinations and are under redesign (e.g., Sator, 1998, p. 559) or had to be entirely abandoned (which is only rarely reported). Some of the problems with precombinations in the Library of Congress Subject Headings were described by Fugmann (1993, p. 151).

The problem of precombination does not exist in colloquial or expert communication and is entirely unknown there. Hence, users know nothing of precombinations and of the problems they may cause in an index language vocabulary (see also section 2.3.2).

But users are always in favor of precombinations because these promise to increase the specificity of their index language vocabulary. For example, "brass" is more specific than "alloy," "copper," or "zinc." What is overlooked here is that the function of the entire vocabulary may well be jeopardized this way. Here, the information specialist must be strong in contradicting the desire to the unrestricted influx of precombinations in the index language vocabulary.

The "analytico-synthetic" approach (Ranganathan & Gopinath, 1967, p. 109) allows one to avoid precombinations if an effective index language grammar is available. In the first step in this approach, that of analysis, the conceptual (categorical) constituents of a subject are isolated, in the case of "brass," the constituents "copper," "zinc," and perhaps "alloy." But merely enumerating the components is rather unspecific, in particular if several of these analyses have been performed per document. Many wrong combinations can be read out in retrieval from a mere enumeration of the conceptual constituents of different concepts.

Therefore, in the second step, that of (re-)synthesis, the connectivity of the elemental concepts, having previously been isolated through analysis, is represented, for example, through the traditional grammatical-syntactical device of segmentation (Lang, 1973, p. 151; Fugmann, 1993, pp. 162-72; see section 2.3.2.). Segmentation can be defined as the process or the result of joining concepts that are found to be coherent in some sense in a document or inquiry (in this view, Ranganathan's notational facet formulas can be seen as another variation of segmentation).

This step restores the specificity inherent in the precombination and represents concept connections in a predictable manner, which is in sharp contrast to the unpredictability of concept connectivity representation in uncontrolled natural language grammar. In such an approach, no names are needed for indexing alloys—the vocabulary remains small and transparent and is not subject to continual growth.

For the execution of concept analysis and synthesis, one must always answer the question: "What is meant by the expression?" By no means must, for example, the alloy "German silver" merely morphologically be analyzed into "German" and "silver." In other words, the analysis must not proceed on the verbal plane. Instead, the analysis must be executed on the idea plane—i.e., in this case it must yield the conceptual constituents of "copper," "nickel," "zinc," and "alloy."

This analytico-synthetic approach makes possible high specificity without overburdening the vocabulary. It does not gradually lose its manageability as would be the case if the desired specificity had been targeted by precombination. This approach constitutes the solution not only for cataloging but also for large databases. An example is presented in section 4.

In book indexing, the situation is different because the vocabulary is small and not subject to continual growth, and there is no grammar available that will counteract the decrease in representational fidelity during concept analysis and which may provide syntactical search statements for retrieval.

Here, precombinations are an indispensable instrument for precision. They should, however, always be linked to their conceptual constituents through cross references. For example, if there is a subject heading for copper alloys, we need references to all the specific copper alloys such as brass, red brass, German silver, Konstantan, and so on. Similarly, there should also be cross references to the more general concepts—e.g., those from "brass" to "copper alloys" and so on.

The type of grammar which is inherent in the heading/subheading relation is another substitute for index language grammar. In case of a less effective syntax, some specificity will be lost through concept analysis. Here, retaining a moderate degree of precombination may be a good solution.

2.5.3 User Preferences and Satisfaction. Users are not responsible for the survival power of an information system and exclude this criterion from their considerations. Hence, important things such as the maintenance of a sufficient perspicuity and conceptual transparency of the vocabulary during its continuing growth, and the hospitality of the system for new concepts without its ending up in chaos (which would increasingly impede the reliable use of the most appropriate terms from the vocabulary) are normally neglected in user evaluations.

Furthermore, most users are unfamiliar with concept hierarchies (Akeroyd, 1990), and if hierarchies are provided by the system, users only rarely make use of them and their benefits. Thus, they undesirably lose all documents which are more specific than those specified in their search request. Inversely, they also hardly use search statements which are more general than those in their search request. Thus, they lose documents which were indexed with terms that are more general than those in the query (as is normally the case, for example, in book indexing). Hierarchical sub- and superordination is generally alien to most users. Hence, hierarchical information systems do not receive due appreciation by most users.

Users are not normally familiar with Boolean operators (see, for example, Borgman, 1996, p. 498; Larson, 1991a, pp. 136, 138). They prefer known item searches and individual concepts, often as quite imperfect substitutes for general concepts and in case of searches for general topics (Larson, 1991). Users also do not normally undertake efforts in tracing information loss, a most substantial feature of retrieval.

Under these circumstances, users should refrain from making an overall judgment of an information system and should restrict themselves to that on which they can competently render an opinion (although such advice will not meet with much consent among users).

Presently, natural language information systems and keyword searches are preferred by the majority of users because these systems appear user friendly. But is it really user friendly when unmanageable numbers of responses, in which only few relevant ones are buried, are retrieved from the files and when the relevant ones can be found only through hours of text scanning or not at all? Is it user friendly when such a system, having been in operation only a few years, has to be abandoned because of intolerably low ratios of precision and recall and when the users are left without the information system on which they had relied?

It is true, user friendliness is important, but pursuing this goal should not result in methodological primitiveness and ineffectivness. In a more farsighted view, it should also be seen as user friendly if the system provides assured access to all the documents that have been collected and that will be collected in the system.

User friendliness is often deceptively stated for information systems in which, allegedly, merely entering a keyword of interest and pressing the search button is said to be sufficient for retrieving all and only relevant information. Such a statement constitutes a severe misconception of the phenomenon of information retrieval. Often such an approach is sold as one which is superior because it utilizes "advanced modern technology."

2.6 Input Parsimoniousness

It is commonplace that the cheapest approach to solve a problem should not be taken if the envisaged goal cannot be reached this way and if the goal must be reached. The information field does not constitute an exception to this rule. Misplaced parsimoniousness in the input stage is one of the most common reasons for information system failure.

The dilemma of contemporary mechanized information systems is largely caused through such a misconception. The situation is depicted in

Figure 1. Here, three prototypes of information systems A, B, and C are compared with respect to the effort in maintaining and using them on the one hand and to their effectiveness and survival power on the other (see section 2.2.3; Fugmann, 1993, p. 4).

In system C, subjects can be represented at a high degree of representational fidelity in company with an optimum of representational predictability. This makes possible correspondingly highly precise searches in company with a minimum of information loss. Both the precision and recall ratios are (and remain) at a safe distance from the areas of intolerably low ratios of precision and recall (see top and bottom areas of Figure 1) during the continual growth of this information system. This is, along with the employment of adequate technology, the reward of careful and knowledgeable text interpretation (see section 2.1.1).

Expert assistance is needed to exploit the search capabilities of such a system, for example, for handling the concept hierarchies, Boolean logics, the system's grammar (see section 3.3.2), or the execution of weighted searches. Practical examples of type C are presented in section 4.

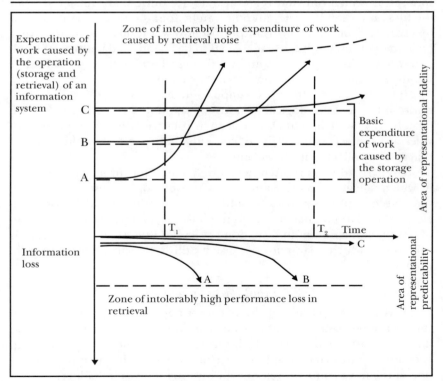

Figure 1. Difference in the survival power of
information systems due to their different bases

The design and the current input of such an approach can cause considerable expenditure. Because of this, it will be difficult to start such a system from scratch. It would take too long a time until the (unmeasurable[10]) benefit begins to balance the extraordinarily high efforts in input. Prospects for starting are better if there has already been negative experience with less advanced information systems, which have already failed or are close to failure and if management is aware of the risk of launching another, seemingly less expensive, but in essence only ephemeral, information system.

A less advanced system of type B in Figure 1 is easier to launch. Here, after careful consideration, some of the devices of the optimal type C have been dispensed with and corresponding savings in input have been gained, deliberately taking the corresponding deficiencies into account.[11]

However, the design of a system of prototype B should be such that it permits an improvement by expansion through the mere inclusion of additional devices, when convincing demand for such an advance emerges in practice. For example, it would be a good strategy to begin with a vocabulary and to add grammar when the necessity has become obvious. The vocabulary could then be kept unchanged to a large extent, and the transition to an information system of type C would be facilitated. Precombinations,[7] resulting from the initial lack of grammar, can then be resolved.

The other extreme is prototype A, easy and fast to implement and to operate, for example, through mere word extraction and keyword searching. But such an information system will consequently suffer from lack of careful and knowledgeable interpretation—i.e., it will suffer from the lack of the indexer's achievements mentioned in the foregoing.

Such a system is restricted to satisfactorily managing those concepts that are lexicalized (and happen to be consistently presented in the lexicalized mode by the authors). Though cheap and fast in its initial stage, such a system may soon cause considerable and incessantly increasing costs (top area of Figure 1) when set to practical use on a large scale, which is characterized through an increase in file size, search frequency, and through increasing demands made on search specificity. It may soon end in the area of intolerably high expenditure through its lack of retrieval precision.

Furthermore, system A is largely memory-based in case of general concepts in the searches. One must remember or guess which modes of expression might have been used by the authors for the topic of interest. The set of search statements will be more and more incomplete, with the result of increasingly incomplete search responses. This system steers the course into the zone of intolerably low recall ratios (bottom area of Figure 1) if anything like complete searches are paramount.

However, information loss from this source largely eludes observation, at least initially. Hence, this deficiency escapes consideration in a purely empirical judgment, and systems of type A have often received an undeserved appreciation and preference.

This happens in particular when system A is tested at the point in time T1. Here, it seems to be superior to systems B and C with respect to its (present and observable) economics in the purely empirical view. Such a system displays low input expenditure and (still) satisfactory performance with respect to the presently prevailing demands concerning precision and recall ratios.

Had the system's evaluation been made at a later point in time, or had the fate of the system been foreseen through mere reasoning, its inferiority would have been obvious. At the point T2, it would hardly be any longer in existence for this reason.

In case of the system's breakdown for all of these reasons, the entire enterprise reveals itself as an enormous waste of time and manpower. Not only is the outcome of all the efforts brought almost to nothing, not only is there no longer secured subject access to the collected documents, but even new enterprises of this type are impeded through the loss of confidence in it on the part of management.

Intellectual subject analysis and indexing have empirically often been found not very effective and not superior to mechanized indexing. Here we often encounter a short-sighted or primitive information system design, one in which the capabilities of the intellectual work have been far from fully exploited. The conceptual and/or technical devices of the indexer may have been inappropriate, too.

It is a common source of information system failure if subject analysis and indexing is naïvely looked upon as a merely clerical process and if too little expenditure and time is allotted for it (reported, for example, by Exner, 1997, p. 24). Not much should be expected of intellectual indexing if a time limit of four minutes per document on the average is felt optimal, as has been the case in the Cranfield experiments (Farrow, 1991).

2.7 The Jurisdictional Claim of Information Technology

Contemporary information scientific research is largely of the technological type. Management has often trusted that artificial intelligence will soon replace the librarian, abstractor, and indexer through machines and programs, at least in the near future. This has often appeared convincing in view of the dramatic advance that computer technology has taken in the past.

We should be skeptical about these predictions. For example, we have in vain been waiting (for more than three decades) for the promised autonomous machine translation (a situation which has been critically stated by Cochrane, 1995, p. 15)—i.e., for a translation which does not require human post-editing.

Some reasoning can help here to draw the line between the achievable on the one hand and mere illusion on the other. To this end we need not study artificial intelligence and not the variety of more or less (un-)realistic mathematical models which have been filling the literature.

We first must realize the line which separates the determinate processes from the indeterminate ones. This distinction has been introduced early in this century, first by Heisenberg in physics. It is inherent in an indeterminate process that the number of possibilities for its progress is infinitely large.

We can watch an indeterminate process, but we cannot make a mechanism correctly execute or simulate the process, for we are unable to phrase completely the set of instructions according to which the mechanism should proceed. It is true, we can phrase instructions for a selection of possibilities and events. But any selection of this type will always represent only a tiny part of the infinity of possibilities and events that would have to be taken into consideration in order to make the process proceed to satisfaction without continuous intervention.

For the mechanization of an indeterminate process, an infinitely large set of instructions would have to be laid down in advance—i.e., without any knowledge of the cases to be processed in their great variety. What can only be achieved here is a set of instructions for situations recurring from the past and for the relatively few foreseeable (and in fact foreseen) future events. Never has an indeterminate process satisfactorily been algorithmically simulated or executed, nor will this ever be the case in the future, except for a (necessarily) limited number of foreseen events.

What would be the result if I decided at the end of a year what to do during the next year and if I strictly clung to these, and exclusively to these, determinations made in advance (just as a computer clings to the determinations laid down in the program)? What if I would have to leave for the holidays, or had fallen ill or a member of my family had, or something in my home needed urgent repair or I might have to look for another job?

After this prolog, we consider the phrasing of natural language text by an author or questioner. It reveals itself as an inherently indeterminate process, too, because the human has at his or her disposal an infinity of possibilities for expressing ideas. This holds true in particular for general concepts or for topics (see section 2.1.1) because it is typical of them that they are encountered in an infinity of possible modes of expression. Logically, any process with an indeterminate point of departure is itself indeterminate, too, because it will necessarily proceed in an unpredictable manner.

Hence, any type of natural language processing is inherently indeterminate—i.e., is a process for which it is impossible to phrase an only approximately complete set of instructions for its simulation or execution, at least for the processing of expressions for general concepts and topics.

Indeterminacy in the information field (and the unpredictability of the modes of expression in uncontrolled natural language) has repeatedly been stated (for example, by Bates, 1986, pp. 360, 361; Blair, 1990, p. 112; 1996, pp. 11, 19; Fugmann, 1985, p. 121; 1993, pp. 62, 213; Wellisch, 1989, pp. 10, 11; 1996, p. 9).

Indexing shares indeterminacy with abstracting and natural language translation and, for example, with medical assistance, child raising, hairdressing, traveling, shopping, home construction, and so on. In all these cases, unexpected events must often be coped with. We will (it is hoped) never have the autonomous automatic physician, lawyer, hairdresser, travel agent, architect, and so on.

Mechanized indexing, abstracting, and translation may be successful for a number of situations, selected from an infinity of recurring or forthcoming ones. Here the program happens to find appropriate instructions for satisfactory processing of a text.

All these examples are dangerously treacherous to the naïve observer (as has been pointed out by Wellisch, 1989, pp. 10-11) because the observer is seduced into generalizing the observations and into believing that the problem is solved through mechanization or will soon be solved—after only a little more research (and only after the consumption of a little more public money).

But inevitably there will be many cases for which the program has no appropriate instructions or even grossly wrong ones. The shooting of a civil aircraft is only one example of the failures when one relies on "the computer" (better to rely on the human programmer) as an assumed infallible authority.

Hence, autonomous translation, abstracting, and indexing (which includes the step of translation) will continue to defy any satisfactory mechanization, and this in spite of the unjustified claims of "indeterminate programming" in all its variations. The reason is the inherent indeterminacy of these processes.

The knowledgeable and carefully working human executes indeterminate processes without difficulty if only assisted by good intellectual and technical tools and if given sufficient time for careful work. Here, one needs not commit oneself to what has been laid down in detail in advance (i.e., a priori, which is impossible). Rather, the human acts facing an encountered situation (i.e., a posteriori, which is easy).

Success of mechanized natural language processing can only be expected for very narrow fields with a highly standardized, completely lexicalized, terminology such as, for example, in weather reports and forecasts. Here, the important concepts are lexicalized and predictable in their modes of expression. Hence, there is only little indeterminacy in the situation of departure.

The problem is not solved if we completely dispense with any instructions in view of the obvious impossibility of the a priori compilation of a complete set of instructions. Such an approach is pursued through the employment of neural networks which are made to "learn" from experience. But any "learning" of this type is necessarily restricted to the store of existing knowledge. However, the task is to satisfactorily process novelties which are incessantly coming up and have to be processed in abstracting, translation, and indexing. For these cases, the network has no precedents from which it could learn.

What could a neural network "learn" from the events of my previous experience in order to autonomously and irrevocably decide (just as the computer would do) what I have to do in my next year, where the future is still in the dark and in the unforeseeable? If we are not able or not willing to decide what a mechanism should do, we must not be surprised when the mechanism does something quite undesirable.

Here, the counter argument is that the neural network will recognize analogical cases from the past and will draw appropriate conclusions even in hitherto unknown cases. However, if we agree on "analogy" to be the coincidence in the essentials, then we again are confronted with an indeterminate situation: What is to be considered "essential" in each individual case and context is subjective. It cannot be stated in advance and not stated validly for every forthcoming, still unknown, situation.

The experiments in artificial intelligence may look promising initially, in particular in the opinion of the experimenters. In view of the progress already achieved, the goal seems attainable (for criticism of this attitude, see Bates, 1998, p. 1186; Fugmann, 1992; Wellisch, 1992, pp. 74, 75). Shpackov (1992) compares some of the research goals of contemporary artificial intelligence with those of the medieval goldmakers. One might add here the illusions of the perpetuum mobilists. In view of the apparent progress that they claim to have already achieved in their research, they all would certainly have vehemently contradicted (if they had been told) the futility of their efforts.

The limited capability of information technology for improving the present situation has been expressly stated by Saracevic (1996) in his acceptance speech for the ASIS Award of Merit. Here he stated "that success of the next generation of information retrieval systems . . . depends on better understanding of human involvement with information and not on more sophisticated technology" (p. 20). Merely relying on technological progress and improving physical access to information has helped us to get to the wrong places more quickly. It is like constructing "faster and faster airplanes without thinking about where we want to go" (Blair, 1990, p. 304).

Autonomous mechanized indexing has prospects of working satisfactorily only if one is content with the processing of individual concepts (because they are lexicalized and thus made well predictable in their modes of expression, this in contrast to general concepts and topics), if one ignores the equivalence of the nonlexical expression for concepts and can afford dispensing with reliable essence recognition, disambiguation, paraphrase lexicalization, establishing concept relationships, ellipses filling, and if the coverage of nontextual information can be dispensed with.

A widespread and technology-biased definition "concept" also contributes to information system failure when "concept" is defined as the meaning of a word (see section 2.1.1 for a better definition). Perhaps perfectly adequate for linguistics, this definition ignores or even pushes out paraphrases as concept representations.

This linguistics-based definition seems to justify the exclusion of paraphrase lexicalization from research and practice. This definition also reflects the lack of distinction between the (observable) "verbal plane" and the (invisible) "idea plane" (Ranganathan & Gopinath, 1967, p. 327).

Unfortunately, information technology has conquered jurisdiction in the information field and has largely expelled information philosophy from the stage. Almost all public funds are devoted to research in artificial intelligence (see Blair, 1996, p. 5). On the other hand, there is neglect of the potential of intellectual indexing and abstracting (critically stated by Milstead, 1994, pp. 577, 579), in particular, in the machine-assisted variations. This neglect constitutes an essential impediment to progress in the field. We will hardly find any mention of the indeterminacy problem in our contemporary, largely empiricistic, information scientific research.

Another obstacle, closely related to the empiricist one, is the prevalence of shortsighted financing models (as reported, for example, by Exner 1997, p. 24). They may be perfectly appropriate for the production of material goods, but they are inadequate for the production of an immaterial entity such as that of order, the "production" of which is the goal in our information systems (Fugmann 1985, p. 120 ["axiom of order"[11]]). This topic is not dealt with in this article. A recommendation is submitted in ISKO/IE (1992a).

Hence, and in conclusion, when we read or listen to a text, we are incessantly, although only latently, executing text interpretation. Any text understanding is preceded by knowledgeable interpretation. Interpretation is incessantly executed by the knowledgeable and carefully working human, and it is interpretation which is contributed by abstractors, translators, and indexers to the texts they are processing.

Interpretation, however, is an inherently indeterminate process—i.e., a process for the execution of which we are unable to phrase rules and instructions which are valid for all forthcoming cases and which an algorithm would badly need for the execution of satisfactory text processing in abstracting, translating, and indexing.

Hence, any fully mechanized information system, in any conceivable state of development, will be devoid of reliable text interpretation—i.e., it will be devoid of what the knowledgeable and carefully working human can contribute with ease during intellectual text processing. The deficiencies of a mode of text processing, which is devoid of interpretation, have been enumerated in the foregoing in this section. In other words, mechanized text processing can never reach the level of perfection which is possible (though, admittedly, not always reached) in intellectual work.

In the view of our considerations, the future of indexing lies in improving the intellectual process of subject analysis and information supply and in more effective machine assistance for its execution.

In particular, for our large and continually growing information systems, we need well designed index languages with both vocabulary and grammar, the former well structured and the latter highly expressive. We also need the careful knowledgeable application of these languages if we wish access to general concepts and topics and if we want to execute more than merely known item searches. Vocabulary categorization is a requirement for the subdivision of the representational work between vocabulary and grammar.

We also need a much more careful information system evaluation with respect to precision (in particular, the clear distinction between relevance and pertinence) and recall (i.e., much more exhaustive recall assessment studies of information loss).

It is true, contemporary intellectual indexing is often of low quality, too. But here we are not confronted with the insurmountable indeterminacy barrier to substantial progress. Rather, through the knowledgeable employment of appropriate intellectual and technical devices, intellectual indexing can be developed to a high quality, as is obvious from operational examples (see section 4).

The illusionary promises of some schools of artificial intelligence have been jeopardizing the existence of what is current human practice without providing a workable alternative. These promises constitute a menace to both indexers and index users (Wellisch, 1989, p.11). These promises appear treacherously achievable, in view of the dramatic advance which mechanization of (always determinate) processes has made in the past. Bad indexes have driven out good ones and "a large number of searches in an automatically indexed database will be of the quick and dirty type, missing all relevant documents whose terms happen to be different from those employed by an end-user" (Wellisch, 1995, p. 49). "Even as access to full text has become available, [intellectual] indexing has remained necessary because the capabilities of retrieval systems to sort out sets on the basis of importance of the items retrieved have been minimal at best" (Milstead, 1994, p. 579).

3. An Insurmountable Obstacle

Variation of word meanings can be another type of obstacle to progress in mechanization that is insurmountable, at least through the efforts of the information specialist. To overcome this obstacle, efforts on the part of the experts in the subject field are necessary.

There are subject fields in which both users and searchers interpret the meaning of a technical term grossly differently. No satisfactory searches can be undertaken with such terms. Very probably, a user will complain on having retrieved "wrong" responses, namely those in which the term of interest appears in a meaning alien to the user. The information specialist or the system (creators) will be blamed for the failures. Such an unfortunate situation prevails, for example, in some fields of the humanities.

Before starting the work of designing an information system in such a field, the information specialist is well advised to check the solidity of its terminology. A list of technical terms should be distributed to future users of the system with the request to submit their definitions for the terms, just as the definitions come to mind. In case of great heterogeneity of the responses, it is foreseeable that the individual user will hardly be satisfied through the searches in such an information system if highly ambiguous terms will be used as search statements. The feasibility of the entire enterprise must be drawn into doubt in these cases.

As has been recommended in section 2.6, skepticism to progress is also apt in the case that management grossly underestimates the size and scientific level of an information project and is not willing to supply the necessary resources, perhaps because of having fallen into the trap of the cheap and fast and allegedly effective fully automatic system. Working under such circumstances may well constitute a waste of time and manpower. Hence, in dependence on the circumstances, the naïvete of management and publishers, as occasionally encountered, may also constitute an insurmountable obstacle to substantial progress.

4. An Example of Advanced Subject Access

A highly effective information system of type C (see Figure 1) can be created if experts in indexing and in the subject field are at work, assisted by advanced intellectual and technical tools, and if ample time is allotted so that they can execute their work with due carefulness. Such a system does not cause steadily increasing expenses and does not suffer from increasing information loss, and it is receptive for new concepts without ending in chaos. It exhibits an optimum of survival power. Since indexing of the quality necessary here cannot be mechanized (see section 2.7), the effort in, and cost of, input is considerable.

An example of this type is the Chemical Abstracts Service (see Weisgerber, 1997) for individual chemical structures. With a limited vocabulary (namely, the approximately 100 chemical elements) and a small set of syntactic devices (namely, only a few types of chemical bonds), it is possible to describe an unlimited number of individual (organic) chemical structures without requiring and using names for them. The structures of many millions of chemical compounds have been stored according to this topological principle, and they can be searched with both 100 percent recall and 100 percent precision in the vast majority of search requests.

Another example is the IDC system (see Fugmann et al., 1974). The analytico-synthetic approach of the Indian School (Ranganathan & Gopinath, 1967) is consistently pursued here. For generalized chemical structures, the similarly concise vocabulary of GREMAS is used, in company with a similarly powerful grammar. Another grammar is employed to display the connectivity of non-structural chemical concepts (Fugmann, 1993, pp. 170-72).

Professional assistance to the searcher is necessary, at least for the use of the system's grammar. The unequaled effectiveness of this system has been proved in comparison with competing commercially available systems (Franzreb et al., 1990). This has justified the considerable effort in the input stage, which is three patents per day per indexer on the average.

5. Conclusion

Contemporary information scientific research concentrates on information technology and is—even if only latently—dominated by a basically inadequate and obsolete philosophy, positivistic empiricism. Having been overcome in the natural sciences for its obvious inadequacy, the widespread clinging to this philosophy constitutes a fundamental obstacle to substantial progress in library and information science.

For example, text interpretation (see sections 2.1.1 and 2.7) has almost completely been disregarded in "modern" information scientific research when it concentrates on the processing of noninterpreted natural language text or on its (necessarily and inherently inadequate) mechanical interpretation.[12] Here, the task of providing effective information supply is grossly misunderstood as one of mere textword processing, to be executed fast and cheap by computer. In doing so, we restrict ourselves to the visible, namely the verbal, plane and omit the necessary transition to the (invisible) idea plane (in the terminology of Ranganathan & Gopinath, 1967). But interpretation is a requisite for any text understanding and, hence, for any sensible text processing. The consequences of this stance are obvious from the miserable effectiveness of those information systems which are based in such a superficial approach.

A most prominent example of such an attitude of empiricistic instrumentalism is the misplaced use of statistics. In the social sciences, for example, the most frequently cited authors are Marx and Engels, the founders of communism (Piternick, 1992). But which conclusions can be drawn from their top position in citation frequencies?

Another example is so-called "information theory," which has for decades dominated the field of library and information science and is still persistent in some circles. It deliberately ignores dealing with the (invisible) meaning of a message and concentrates on the (visible and measurable) frequency with which the wording of a message recurs. But, in library and information science, we are primarily interested in what is meant through a message. Shannon and Weaver's theory was intended for a field quite different from information storage and retrieval, namely for the economics of signal transmission. The result of such a misplaced application of theory is a tremendous amount of futile research work and a waste of time and manpower.

At least, in addition to information technology, more attention should be paid to research and development in what may be called an information philosophy. In particular, we must undertake a re-assessment of the presently dominant thinking in the profession and acknowledge the inherently indeterministic nature of human behavior, including authors and information searchers.

To achieve substantial progress, we must cast off positivism and empiricism in all their obvious and latent variations and adopt another more adequate epistemological foundation for library and information science. Budd's (1995) "hermeneutic phenomenology" (pp. 304-15) presently seems to constitute the best possible foundation for the tremendous task still to be solved in libraries and for database design. It comprises provision for:

- the knowledgeable interpretation of observed reality;
- an adequate employment of human resources where they are indispensible for adequate results;
- the phrasing of meaningful questions in research;
- the design of correspondingly meaningful experiments; and
- the design of genuinely effective libraries and information systems.

This philosophy could have warned against "the mechanical and uncritical application of habits of thought to fields different from those in which they have been formed" (cited by Budd, 1995, p. 303), for example, against the uncritical adoption of "information theory."

The recognition of such a philosophy has in its wake an increased expenditure in the input stage. But many information systems that are (often only treacherously) cheaper in their initial stage of development have eventually proven extremely expensive when they had to be abandoned because of their steady decrease in effectiveness.

Should an inadequate philosophy be counted among the insurmountable obstacles, especially where this philosophy has been deeply rooted for a long time? How many decades or even centuries does it take for a community to change an accepted philosophy or scientific paradigm? Can pressure from practice change the minds of the majority of researchers who have based all their work on such a philosophy?[13] We are reminded of a saying of the German physicist and Nobel Prize winner Max Planck: "A new theory can spread only to the extent to which the proponents of the old theories die out." Is this skepticism, and the one articulated by Wellisch,[14] justified in the field of library and information science, too?

Accepting a more adequate philosophy and bringing it into effect in practice in the profession would activate a large and hitherto widely unused potential for advancement. It would lead to libraries and information systems with substantially improved effectiveness and survival power.

Notes

[1] Belkin pointed out that typical information retrieval system performance rates average only 60% recall and 40% precision and are nowhere close to an ideal of 100% recall and 100% precision (cited from Schamber, Eisenberg Nilan in *Information Processing and Management, 26* [1990], 758). Beyond this, unrealistically high recall ratios are reported in the literature. The reason is that completely assessing information loss is time consuming and expensive (Blair, 1996, p. 14).

[2] Svenonius's criticism is obvious from her example which reflects a typically positivistic attitude: For the logical positivist a sort of proposition, for instance: "It is good to love your neighbor" were deemed metaphysical and meaningless (Svenonius, 1992, p. 6, bottom). Only scientific propositions are meaningful to the positivist and worth being considered, because it is only propositions of this sort that could be verified empirically.

[3] "It may be unwise to accept the results of an experimental study in this area before the study design has been scrutinized to ensure that all the effects and interconnections discussed here have been considered and that all the pitfalls have been avoided" (Soergel, 1994, p. 598).

[4] Here, Dahlberg refers to the philosophers Immanuel Kant and Gottlob Frege.

[5] Axiom of predictability: "The accuracy of any directed search for relevant responses (and especially the recall ratio) depends on the predictability of the modes of expression for concepts and concept relations in the search file" (Fugmann, 1993, p. 62; 1985, p. 121).

[6] Lichtenberg: "He who does not know the goal will not find the way."

[7] Precombination prevails if a vocabulary term comprises the meaning of at least two terms which are already contained in the vocabulary or which, through their categorial nature, may well be entered into the vocabulary.

[8] Axiom of definability: "The compilation of information relevant to a topic can be delegated only to the extent to which an inquirer can define the topic in terms of concepts and concept relations" (Fugmann, 1985, p. 118; 1993, 41, 45).

[9] This definiton is based on vocabulary categorization (cf. section 2.3.1.1) and is necessarily different from other definitions which make no use of semantic categories.

[10] That the true benefit of an effective information system cannot be calculated in money has often been convincingly stated in the literature.

[11] Axiom of order: "Any compilation of information relevant to a topic is an order-creating process," and "order" is the "meaningful proximity of the parts of a whole at a foreseeable place" (Fugmann, 1985, p. 127).

[12] Text interpretation is an inherently indeterminate process, i.e., a process which defies any satisfactory mechanization (see section 2.7).

[13] The ancient geocentric world view, obsolete since the times of Galileo, has persisted until 1993 in some circles.

[14] "Maybe we still need to wander another forty years in the desert of inadequate methods and faulty systems before we are allowed to even see the Promised Land of indexing from afar" (Wellisch, 1989, p. 12).

References

Aitchison, J., & Gilchrist, A. (1987). *Thesaurus construction—A practical manual* (2d ed.). London: ASLIB.

Akeroyd, J. (1990). Information seeking in online catalogues. *Journal of Documentation, 46*(1), 33-52.

Anderson, J. D. (1997). *Guidelines for indexes and related information retrieval devices: A technical report*. Bethesda, MD: NISO Press.

Austin, D., & Dykstra, M. (1984). *PRECIS: A manual of concept analysis and subject indexing* (2d ed.). London: British Library.

Bates, M. J. (1986). Subject access in online catalogs: A design model. *Journal of the American Society for Information Science, 37*(6), 357-376.

Bates, M. J. (1998). Indexing and access for digital libraries and the Internet: Human, database, and domain factors. *Journal of the American Society for Information Science, 49*(13), 1185-1202.

Bhattacharyya, G. (1982). Classaurus: Its fundamentals, design, and use. In I. Dahlberg (Ed.), *Universal classification I: Subject analysis and ordering systems* (Proceedings of the 4th International Study Conference on Classification Research, June 28-July 2, 1982, Augsburg, Germany) (pp. 139-148). Frankfurt: Indeks Verlag and Wuerzburg: Ergon Verlag.

Blair, D. C. (1990). *Language and representation in information retrieval*. New York: Elsevier.

Blair, D. C. (1996). STAIRS redux: Thoughts on the STAIRS evaluation ten years after. *Journal of the American Society for Information Science, 47*(1), 4-22.

Borgman, C. L. (1996). Why are online catalogs still hard to use? *Journal of the American Society for Information Science, 47*(7), 493-503.

Boulding, K. E. (1956). *The image*. Ann Arbor: University of Michigan Press.

Boyce, B. R., & McLain, J. P. (1989). Entry point depth and online search using a controlled vocabulary. *Journal of the American Society for Information Science, 40*(4), 273-276.

Budd, J. M. (1995). An epistemological foundation for library and information science. *Library Quarterly, 65*(3), 295-318.

Cleverdon, C. W. (1967). The Cranfield Tests of index language devices. *ASLIB Proceedings, 19*(6), 173-194.

Cochrane, P. A. (1982). Classification as a user's tool in public access catalogs. In I. Dahlberg (Ed.), *Universal classification I: Subject analysis and ordering systems* (Proceedings of the 4th International Study Conference on Classification Research, June 28- July 2, 1982, Augsburg, Germany) (pp. 260-268). Frankfurt: Indeks Verlag and Wuerzburg: Ergon Verlag.

Cochrane, P. A. (1995). Dr. Adkinson and NSF/OSIS leadership. *Bulletin of the American Society for Information Science, 22*(1), 14-15.

Cooper, W. S. (1969). Is interindexer consistency a hobgoblin? *American Documentation, 20*(3), 268-278.

Dahlberg, I. (1976). Über Gegenstände, Begriffe, Definitionen und Benennungen (On referents, concepts, definitions and denominations). *Muttersprache, 86*(2), 81-117.

Dahlberg, I. (1994). Environment-related conceptual systematization. In P. Stancikova & I. Dahlberg (Eds.), *Environmental knowledge organization and information management* (Proceedings of the First European ISKO Conference, September 14-16, Bratislava, Slovakia) (pp. 84-94). Frankfurt/Main: Indeks Verlag and Wuerzburg: Ergon Verlag.

Desai, B. C. (1997). Supporting discovery in virtual libraries. *Journal of the American Society for Information Science, 48*(3), 190-204.

Drabenstott, K. M. (1996). Classification to the rescue: Handling the problems of too many and too few retrievals. In R. Green (Ed.), *Knowledge organization and change* (Proceedings of the Fourth International ISKO Conference, July 15-18, 1996, Washington, DC) (pp. 107-118). Frankfurt/Main: Indeks Verlag and Wuerzburg: Ergon Verlag.

Ellis, D. (1996). The dilemma of measurement in information retrieval research. *Journal of the American Society for Information Science, 47*(1), 23-36.

Exner, F. (1997). Indexing integrated manual sets at Northern Telecom. *Bulletin of the American Society for Information Science, 23*(4), 20-24.

Farrow, J. F. (1991). A cognitive process model of document indexing. *Journal of Documentation, 47*(2), 149-166.

Franzreb, K. H.; Hornbach, P.; Pahde, C.; Ploss, G.; & Sander, J. (1991). Structure searches in patent literature: A comparison study between IDC GREMAS and Derwent chemical code. *Journal of Chemical Information and Computer Sciences, 31*(2), 284-289.

Fugmann, R.; Dombois, C.; Fricke, C.; Isenberg, M.; Kusemann, G.; & Ploss, G. (1974). The IDC system. In J. E. Ash & E. Hyde (Eds.), *Chemical information systems* (pp. 195-226). Chichester, England: Ellis Horwood Limited.

Fugmann, R. (1985). The five-axiom-theory of indexing and information supply. *Journal of the American Society for Information Science, 36*(2), 116-129.

Fugmann, R. (1984). Das "bessere" Informations system. *Mitteilungsblatt (Gesellschaft Deutscher Chemiker. Fachgruppe Chemie-Information), 6* (English translation available from the author).

Fugmann, R. (1992). Illusory goals in information science research. In N. J. Williamson & M. Hudon (Eds.), *Classification research for knowledge representation and organization* (Proceedings of the 5th International Study Conference on Classification Research, Toronto, Canada, June 24-28, 1991) (pp. 61-68). New York: Elsevier.

Fugmann, R. (1992a). [Review of the Book *Indexing and Abstracting in Theory and Practice*]. *International Classification, 19*(4), 227-228.

Fugmann, R. (1993). *Subject analysis and indexing: Theoretical foundation and practical advice* (Lectures held at the School of Library and Information Science at Indiana University, Bloomington, IN, 1993). Frankfurt: Indeks Verlag and Wuerzburg: Ergon Verlag.

Fugmann, R. (1994). Galileo and the inverse precision-recall relationship: Medieval attitudes in modern information science. *Knowledge Organization, 21*(3), 153-154.

Fugmann, R. (1997). Bridging the gap between database indexing and book indexing. *Knowledge Organization, 24*(4), 205-212.

Gey, F. C., & Dabney, D. P. (1990). [Letter to the editor]. *Journal of the American Society for Information Science, 41*(8), 613.

Green, R. (1992). The expression of syntagmatic relationships in indexing: Are frame-based index languages the answer? In N. J. Williamson & M. Hudon (Eds.), *Classification research for knowledge representation and organization* (Proceedings of the 5th International Study Conference on Classification Research, Toronto, Canada, June 24-28, 1991) (pp. 79-88). New York: Elsevier.

Harmon, G. (1970). *Information need transformation during inquiry: A reinterpretation of user relevance* (Proceedings of the ASIS Annual Meeting) (vol. 7, pp. 41-43). Westport, CT: Greenwood Publishing Corporation.

Harter, S. P. (1990). Search term combinations and retrieval overlap: A proposed methodology and case study. *Journal of the American Society for Information Science, 41*(2), 132-146.

Harter, S. P. (1996). Variations in relevance assessments and the measure of retrieval effectiveness. *Journal of the American Society for Information Science, 47*(1), 37-49.

Harter, S. P., & Hert, C. A. (1997). Evaluation of information retrieval systems: Approaches, issues, and methods. *Annual Review of Information Science and Technology, 32*, 3-94.

Heine, M. H., & Tague, J. M. (1991). An investigation of the optimization of search logic for the MEDLINE database. *Journal of the American Society for Information Science, 42*(4), 267-278.

Hjorland, B. (1997). *Information seeking and subject representation: An activity-theoretical approach to information science.* Westport, CT: Greenwood Press.

ISKO/IE. (1992). Recommendation No. 1: User evaluation of information systems. *International Classification, 19*(3), 151-153.

ISKO/IE. (1992a). Recommendation No. 2: On the financing of information services. *International Classification, 19*(3), 154-156.

Jordan, J. S. (1989). Letter to the editor. *Journal of the American Society for Information Science, 40*(5), 362-363.

Kemp, D. B. (1974). Relevance, pertinence, and information system development. *Information Storage and Retrieval, 10*(2), 37-47.

Kiel, E. (1994). Knowledge organization needs epistemological openness. *Knowledge Organization, 21*(3), 148-152.

Knorz, G. (1998). Testverfahren fuer Intelligente Indexierungs–und Retrieval Systeme anhand deutschsprachiger sozialwissenschaftlicher Fachinformation. *Nachrichten fuer Dokumentation, 49*, 111-116.

Lancaster F. W. (1991). *Indexing and abstracting in theory and practice.* Urbana-Champaign: University of Illinois, Graduate School of Library and Information Science.

Lancaster. F. W. (1992). [Letter to the editor]. *Information Technology and Libraries, 11*(2), 198.

Lang, F. (1973). Die inhaltliche Erschliessung von Dokumenten: Die Dokumentationssprache. In F. Lang & F. Bock (Eds.), *Wiener Beiträge zur elektronischen Erschliessung der Information im Recht* (pp. 123-157). Wien: IBM Österreich.

Larson, R. R. (1991). The decline of subject searching: Long-term trends and patterns of index use in an online catalog. *Journal of the American Society for Information Science, 42*(3), 197-215.

Larson R. R. (1991a). Classification clustering, probabilistic information retrieval, and the online catalog. *Library Quarterly, 61*(2), 133-173.

McIlwaine, I. C. (1997). Preface. In *Knowledge organization for information retrieval* (Proceedings of the Sixth International Study Conference on Classification Research held at University College London, 16-18 June 1997) (p. v). The Hague, Netherlands: International Federation for Information Documentation.

Meincke, P. P. M., & Atherton, P. (1976). Knowledge space: A conceptual basis for the organization of knowledge. *Journal of the American Society for Information Science, 27*(1), 18-24.

Milstead, J. (1994). Needs for research in indexing. *Journal of the American Society for Information Science, 45*(8), 577-582.

Neill, S. D. (1992). *Dilemmas in the study of information: Exploring the boundaries of information science.* New York: Greenwood Press.

Piternick, A. (1992). Name of an author. *The Indexer, 18*, 95-100.

Ranganathan, S. R. (1962). *Elements of library classification* (3d ed.). London: Asia Publishing House.

Ranganathan, S. R., & Gopinath, M. A. (1967). *Prolegomena to library classification* (3d ed.). London: Asia Publishing House.

Riggs, F. (1996). Onomantics and terminology Pt. I: Their contributions to knowledge organization. *Knowledge Organization, 23*(1), 25-33.

Saracevic, T. (1989). Indexing, searching, and relevance. In B. H. Weinberg (Ed.), *Indexing: The state of our knowledge and the state of our ignorance* (Proceedings of the 20th Annual Meeting of the American Society of Indexers, New York, May 13, 1988). Medford, NJ: Learned Information, Inc.

Saracevic, T. (1996). ASIS Award of Merit: Saracevic accepts ASIS' highest honor [Acceptance Speech]. *Bulletin of the American Society for Information Science, 22*(3), 19-21.

Sator, K. (1998). Die Pressedokumentation beim deutschen Bundestag: Probleme der Einfuehrung eines Thesaurus (Documentation of the press for the German parliament: Problems with the introduction of a thesaurus). *Nachrichteu fuer Dokumentation (NFD): InformationWissenschaft und Praxis, 49*(6), 353-360.

Schwarz, C. (1990). Automatic syntactic analysis of free text. *Journal of the American Society for Information Science, 41*(6), 408-417.

Shpackov, A. A. (1992). The nature and the boundaries of information science(s). *Journal of the American Society for Information Science, 43*(10), 678-681.

Soergel, D. (1985). *Organizing information: Principles of data base and retrieval systems.* Orlando, FL: Academic Press, Inc.

Soergel, D. (1994). Indexing and retrieval performance: The logical evidence. *Journal of the American Society for Information Science, 45*(8), 589-599.

Spang-Hansen, H. (1976). Roles and links compared with grammatical relations in natural languages. *Dansk Teknisk Litteraturselskab skriftserie,* nr. 40. Lyngby; ISBN 87-7426-013-8.

Svenonius, E. (1981). Directions for research in indexing. *Library Resources & Technical Services, 25*(1), 88-103.

Svenonius, E. (1992). Classification: Prospects, problems and possibilities. In N. J. Williamson & M. Hudon (Eds.), *Classification research for knowledge representation and organization* (Proceedings of the 5th International Study Conference on Classification Research, Toronto, Canada, June 24-28, 1991). New York: Elsevier.

Svenonius, E. (1995). Precoordination or not? In R. P. Holley, D. McGarry, D. Duncan, & E. Svenonius (Eds.), *Subject indexing: Principles and practices in the 90's* (Proceedings of the IFLA Satellite Meeting, Lisbon, Portugal, 17-18 August 1993) (pp. 231-255). London: K. G. Saur.

Van Rijsbergen, C. J., & Sembok, T. M. T. (1990). SILOL: A simple logical-linguistic document retrieval system. *Information Processing and Management, 26*(1), 111-134.

Wellisch, H. H. (1989). The literature of indexing. In B. H. Weinberg (Ed.), *Indexing: The state of our knowledge and the state of our ignorance* (Proceedings of the 20th Annual Meeting of the American Society of Indexers, New York, New York, May 13, 1988) (pp. 1-14). Medford, NJ: Learned Information, Inc.

Wellisch, H. H. (1992). The art of indexing and some fallacies of its automation. *Logos, 3*(2), 69-76.

Wellisch, H. H. (1996). Aboutness and the selection of topics. *Keywords,* (March/April), 7-9.

Wellisch, H. H. (1995). *Indexing from A to Z* (2d ed.). New York: H. W. Wilson.

Weisgerber, D. W. (1997). Chemical abstracts service chemical registry system: History, scope, and impacts. *Journal of the American Society for Information Science, 48*(4), 349-360.

Yee, M. M. (1991). System design and cataloging meet the user: User interfaces to online public access catalogs. *Journal of the American Society for Information Science, 42*(2), 78-98.

On MARC and Natural Text Searching: A Review of Pauline Cochrane's Inspirational Thinking Grafted onto a Swedish Spy on Library Matters

✦ Bjorn Tell ✦

Introduction

The following discussion is in appreciation of the invaluable inspirations Pauline Cochrane, by her acumen and perspicacity, has implanted into my thinking regarding various applications of library and information science, especially those involving machine-readable records and subject categorization. It is indeed an honor for me at my age to be offered to contribute to Pauline's Festschrift when instead I should be concerned about my forthcoming obituary. In the following, I must give some background to what formed my thinking before my involvement in the field and thus before I encountered Pauline.

Meteorologist versus Librarian

I started my career in international bookstores in Stockholm and Paris. In hindsight, I have always been amazed how one in the bookselling profession could retrieve and deliver requested books without access to a more elaborate bibliographic apparatus than the national bibliography and sales catalogs.

Another point for astonishment stemmed from my experiences as a meteorologist in the Air Force. It should be mentioned that such a position I held, together with a classification pioneer and friend, Malcolm Rigby. Weather is a complicated mechanism that is crudely described by means of a number of parameters expressed by the international weather code. During World War II, Germany and Russia scrambled that code to make it unintelligible to the enemy and even to us as a neutral state and a state which depended for our operations on weather development in occupied countries such as Norway and Poland.

But that code could not be too complicated as it had to be decoded rapidly before the weather changed so much as to endanger flight operations. To crack the code promptly was a must, and usually we succeeded. Then, the weather unit in our division had to produce a weather map from many hundreds of observations. That experience has made me compare the intricacies of describing a weather situation to a book or a document. A librarian is, thus, commonly regarded as efficient if he or she is able to catalog ten to twelve books a day with MARC. I have been asking myself why the latter should be such a complicated and time consuming task or, as Francis Miksa (personal communication, 23-25 October, 1994) addressed this at the Allerton Institute in 1994, "MARC was a great invention, but awfully redundant!"

Another similarity is that the weather record had to be translated into a standardized station model which gave the analyst an overview so he could make a forecast. That earlier manual drafting work has become automated, but the station model looks the same. Since medieval times, the bibliographic record has been presented in the form of book catalogs. Since more than a century, however, libraries have used 3x5 catalog cards with their limited format. With automation, most libraries still stick to that format when it is presented on the screen.

Only a few librarians have taken the opportunity to present an output format that is more like an entry in a printed book catalog. So, for example, the Royal Library in Sweden, responsible for the national bibliography, resisted for years making a more user-friendly screen layout in the national system, LIBRIS, available over the net. Instead, another Swedish library made a presentation format which was later adopted by the Royal Library. Recently, I have noticed that now even libraries in developing countries have found such a procedure useful for users. Thus, the Historic Institute of the Central American University of Nicaragua has shown the good taste to present a user-friendly screen but, to satisfy the traditional catalogers, it also presents two alternative output formats with all the indicators and identifiers in a card format. It is up to the user to make the choice.

From Punched Cards to MARC

In the late 1940s and early 1950s, I worked on Hollerith punched card machines. It was necessary to code the elements of a bibliographic record rather carefully to be able to print out ordered lists, and there were no screens to scan at that time. It seems to me that MARC must have been born and delivered by people who had the same experience.

Soon, with the advent of more powerful computers, the scene changed. As librarian at the Swedish Nuclear Establishment, I was lucky to have at my disposal a powerful computer. A first trial in 1961 with punched tape resulted in a printed union catalog of periodicals which, internationally, was a very early one in the field. The establishment was the national depository for technical reports which usually the academic librarians were not well-disposed to handle in a way that was useful to the readers, or as Claire K. Schultz (personal communication, 12-23 July, 1965) has remarked: "Intellectually this material strains the classification systems . . . of which the inventors of classification systems, such as Melville Dewey, never dreamed." Thus ways had to be found to retrieve and present this material so that the information needs of the researchers could be met.

KWIC and Its Poor Typography

The same year, 1961, I was invited to the first Gordon Research Conference on Scientific Information in the United States. That conference set the stage for more computer usage in scientific information work. I keep in fresh memory the discussions I had with Peter H. Luhn about his KWIC-index. Being an "amateur des livres d'art," I commented upon the poor typography and Peter was upset, saying that I didn't appreciate the beauty of his invention, which I definitely did. It also gave me the opportunity to meet with Claire Schultz and also with Jessica Melton and Robert Fairthorne at Western Reserve University and to discuss the use of computers in information work.

First Meeting with Pauline

Thus, I had good knowledge of a computer's potential when I first met Pauline at the FID-conference in Stockholm in 1963. She was then with the American Institute of Physics. Classification matters were at the forefront of discussions at that meeting. After the meeting, Pauline (Atherton, 1963) sent me her classic chapter "File Organization. Principles and Practices for Processing and Maintaining the Collection" in the book *Information Handling: First Principles* (Washington, 1963). We collaborated more closely also during and after the Elsinore Conference on "Classification Research" in 1965, where Pauline was on the organizing committee and later editor of the proceedings (Atherton, 1965). The work by Peter Luhn and his KWIC-index, which made use of machine reprocessing of bibliographic material and natural text in order to help users, was under discussion.

ABACUS—Something to Count On

When coming home, I drew up an automated acquisitions list. Instead of a KWIC-index, it was supplied by a KWOT-index using upper- and lowercase lettering just to show that a better typography and legibility could be achieved by computers at that time. That exercise made me realize the potential that natural text in a bibliographic description offers in specific fields, and that it can be used for machine retrieval of documents. That came easily when we, in 1967, started an SDI service with the program ABACUS. The acronym, ABACUS, for AB Atomenergi Computer User-Oriented System, was a contribution by Pauline, at that time a professor at Syracuse University, who happened to be in Sweden when the system was presented and we had to find a name for it. Thus we said that ABACUS was becoming something to count on in bibliographic work.

For its time, ABACUS had a sophisticated batch processing search engine which combined fast algorithms by using hash coding and tree structures, allowing searches for words within words and both left- and righthand truncations. It used a standard record format, divided into eleven variable data fields for storing bibliographic records. Most programs at that time used fixed length fields, but our approach was different. A directory told about the field tags and the starting position of each data field, its length, and so on. So, the stage was set for exploring what could be left to the computer to do and what had to be done by us humans.

Our format was used for storing and searching for Selective Dissemination of Information—SDI—for the various magnetic tape services which were coming on the market at that time. We subscribed to a couple of them such as CAC, Inspec, and ISI. These services all had different formats, so we realized that we had to write a reformatting program for each original database to fit their records into the ABACUS format. Then search processing could take place and results sent in a uniform output format to the customers regardless of which service a record stemmed.

Tape Services and SDI Profiles

Users' queries were formulated in an SDI profile. In order to create such a profile, we found it necessary to know about the vocabularies of the various databases. Word frequency lists taken from the titles were most helpful. When constructing a profile, we were cautious about high frequency words.

That exercise strengthened my attitude toward free-text searching that already had been awakened by the KWOT index. However, the various tape formats caused frustration and annoyance in international quarters. The O.E.C.D. in Paris started a System Interconnection Panel as it feared that the whole field would fragment if no mechanisms for interconnection could be found. Even Unesco, preparing its UNISIST program, became interested in drawing up guidelines for a standard format for scientific and technical documentation. Almost simultaneously, the MARC II format was presented in wider circles at the MARC II seminar in San Francisco in September 1969. At that event, I met Henriette Avram, and we compared our format design with MARC, and that started a lengthy dialog for establishing an international standard.

Pauline and I had, over the years, discussed the analytical subdivision of the bibliographic record into elements in MARC. I questioned the minute detail. From my ABACUS background, I was accustomed to larger chunks when reformatting the descriptive records of various tape services without losing the opportunity to present adequate outputs. Pauline argued that it was necessary to go into the smallest detail in the analysis in order to later, perhaps, be able to recombine the elements into bigger ones. It seems to me that after all these years this idea has not yet occurred to most catalogers worldwide.

Why Buy First-Class Tickets?

From an administrator's viewpoint, MARC is a question of economy that everyone becomes conscious of when trying to catalog according to MARC. A mini MARC would rapidly lower cataloging costs. Somebody has said that there is no reason to pay for a first-class ticket when economy class ends up at the same airport. Why so many libraries buy first-class tickets was a matter that worried me for many years.

As MARC now was on the table internationally, we in the Swedish Standardization Organization wanted to know more about its record layout and have it tested in order to understand its structure. At a Nordic meeting in Copenhagen in 1970, it was suggested that a Nordic group should study a proposal for an international ISO-format. As a result, we proposed to Unesco/UNISIST to have Unesco establish a Working Group on Bibliographic Description. As a first step, it should try to get a consensus on a sort of container, a content-empty structure. Later it could try to agree upon "flagging and tagging." The content elements in that structure would be discussed, at this stage avoiding a stand on any of the MARC, Inspec, or INIS formats. We were, so to speak, looking for an empty versatile container which later could be filled with various properly tagged things.

The European community now started to realize the importance of records such as MARC. Germany, in 1971, arranged an international seminar on the MARC II format and the exchange of bibliographic records in machine readable form. It was recommended that national libraries should adopt an international standard for cataloging. There should be a file structure similar to MARC so that libraries and MARC could be compatible. A librarian from Bath in Great Britain remarked that MARC had been designed "bottom-up in a nitty-gritty fashion," and that definitely it was overshooting its target to make a machine version of a bibliographic record.

Other international activities during these years concentrated on thesaurus building—e.g., in Council of Europe, IAEA, Euratom, ISO, and FAO. I maintained that you cannot build a thesaurus without knowing which words in fact are used in the majority of document titles or abstracts in a field. To prove that, we ran word frequency lists from thousands of titles both for the Council of Europe and for ISO. The Council of Europe was somewhat irritated by our disrespect for the thesaurus construction they had invested in, but ISO took our efforts more seriously and dropped its thesaurus panel as our list showed that, with regard to documents about standards, the natural text search from titles was quite sufficient for retrieval. We even proved that we could make better searches from the ERIC tapes by natural text versus its thesaurus terms. Our efforts may have caused a new edition of the thesaurus.

Natural Text Searching

I thought that using natural text in titles or abstracts had given evidence enough that the computer could do the subject categorization in specific fields and do it cheap. The idea struck me that if you were within a defined subject field—e.g., physics, nuclear physics, biophysics, and so on—you could with confidence use natural text searching and receive a high degree of recall or precision. As I was closely involved with Unesco, I proposed that Unesco should arrive at an international consensus of about 300 to 400 defined and enumerated science fields on the same level without hierarchies. That would definitely help various search engines using free text. Unesco adopted the idea and commissioned the International Federation of Documentation—FID—to come forward with such a subject list. However, the result was a complete revision of the UDC and brought forward a list of 4,000 subject fields in hierarchies, which was considered a failure.

UDC and Pauline

I knew about the appreciation the library community in the United States attached to the work of Pauline and Robert R. Freeman on the use of UDC as an indexing language. We had used UDC for decades in Europe and believed it could be used for machine retrieval, especially since it already included figures that computers loved to process. The question was more how deep one should go down in UDC hierarchies when retrieving documents? Nuclear technology, for example, started on the sixth digit, so you actually had to go very deep in indexing, and still this might not give the results a researcher wanted. Additional subject indicators had to be found, so why not combine indexing with natural text since authors know pretty well what they are writing about?

Henriette Avram and I shared the task of bringing an interchange format up to an internationally acknowledged standard during this time, but it took until 1981 before it became the ISO 2709 standard for bibliographic information interchange on magnetic tape. However, during the five years of probation as a draft, it had not received any serious objections.

However, there had been many stumbling blocks to circumvent. Foremost, the standardization people in Germany could not understand the beauty of variable fields. Instead, they wanted only fixed fields, accustomed as they were to the fixed fields of the Siemens system utilized at the Munich Olympics. I understood that the realization of a standard for an empty container with ample information about how to handle the various empty boxes which could contain information was a problem because many librarians at that time were unfamiliar with computer records.

However, after confronting my colleagues about the possibilities of agreeing on a tagging scheme and a standard for the information content, their many views upon the matter seemed to me to create such an overwhelming task for arriving at further standards that I reluctantly left that to Henriette Avram.

ICSU and UNISIST

As the United States under Reagan stepped out of Unesco, many Americans may not be familiar with the developments within information systems and services developed by Unesco under the UNISIST umbrella. UNISIST was the result of a close cooperation between Unesco and the International Council of Scientific Unions (ICSU). Eventually that ended in a feasibility study on a World Science Information System—the UNISIST. A number of recommendations to the Member States were made and adopted. The ICSU especially stressed the need to formulate an information policy, to set up national scientific information agencies, and to commit public resources. The O.E.C.D. had already, for a couple of years, been active and effective in this area for its member countries, and now it was time for the developing countries.

On a global scale, Unesco and ICSU were concerned that the UNISIST program should make provision for redressing the imbalance between providing information services in developing countries and the developed ones. Therefore, two recommendations were especially directed to developing countries in order to build their infrastructure and the linkage to UNISIST. Special priority was given to the need to develop tools for systems intercommunication. It was found useful to bring together in a simple and concise fashion the concepts and prevailing practices concerning the planning and functioning of information systems and services. The preparation of a handbook was recommended, and the work was entrusted to Professor Pauline Atherton of the School of Information Studies at Syracuse University in New York.

A Handbook for the Developing World

The resulting *Handbook for Information Systems and Services* was published by Unesco in 1977. As I have been instrumental for spreading the UNISIST program and establishing national information policies over the years in many developing countries, the handbook has been invaluable. If you go to developing countries, you will find such a trust in Unesco and in what it does in libraries, and Pauline's handbook has been of utmost importance for making the field more unified.

Pauline refers to another handbook which also was a result of the UNISIST efforts, namely, the *Reference Manual for Machine Readable Bibliographic Descriptions* written by D. Martin (1974). She pointed out that the manual "would be most helpful" if the ISBD(M) description on a catalog card was put into machine readable form (Atherton, 1977, p. 134). She says explicitly: "In it an essential minimum set of data or data elements are defined which may be regarded as constituting an adequate bibliographic citation" (p. 173). That was the same as saying that there are essential elements in a bibliographic record that should be taken care of. Why bother about ephemerals?

She also says that "the rule for choice and form of entry is a fundamental problem in library cooperation" referring to the difficulties of exchanging catalog information on an international level. I have never been able to discern why there has been so much fuss about the so called "main entry" (Gorman & Winkler, 1978, chap. 21). In a machine readable catalog, anything could be a "main entry" and stand out as an access point. Another of my points has been to avoid hierarchies in a record and instead try to keep all elements on practically the same level in order to facilitate processing for searches and printouts. David Martin (1974) and I discussed that matter in the UNISIST task group and, when he wrote the *UNISIST Reference Manual,* he tried to keep that in mind.

For me as an international expert to some countries in South East Asia, I have noticed many backlogs in cataloging departments because of the adherence to MARC. I tried to convey that to Dorothy Anderson, the Unesco protagonist for Universal Bibliographic Control, suggesting a minimum standard of essential elements. The answer was that anyone was free to use a reduced record.

That was not very helpful for those relying on the Unesco authority. If developing countries should adhere to such a reduced standard record, first it had to be endorsed just by a body such as Unesco, otherwise they felt forced to adhere to the full MARC record. That idea never seems to have occurred to Dorothy Anderson and her acolytes.

Books are for Use—The SAP Project, Another Fruitful Idea

Returning to most librarians' devotion to the AACR2 and the card format, I would like to acknowledge one of Pauline's greatest contributions to the field—namely, her SAP project. When in 1978, as her "Swedish Spy," I got her *Books Are For Use*, I immediately grasped its potential for better subject access using natural language searches. Here she included text from the contents list or the index according to simple, almost clerical, rules. The card format was definitely out, because now the records increased on the average from 400 to 4,000 characters. At that time, devices for storing a full-text document for searching had not yet come to light.

For years I had been amazed by how easily it was to search services such as Chemical Abstracts, Inspec, or ISI for a single author name among a collective of authors. A good example was the experimental proof of the last elementary particle omega minus. The article contained just two pages, and the first page was filled with thirty-two author names, each retrievable in Inspec or ISI. Comparing that with the cataloging rule to put in just two of them and then "et al." has drastically restricted retrieval of author names in many OPACs. More and more books are written by a team of authors, and libraries which stick to the rules are deliberately suppressing or censoring many authors, especially since a machine record could store any number of names. Pauline has, for some years, pointed out this lack of completeness in cataloging.

The SAP methodology improved subject access in a similar fashion. Take, for example, the Swedish legislative system which is based on committees which the government put up for various issues. The result of a committee is a report to the government including a proposal for new legislation. These reports contain a wealth of information including graphs, tables, and statistics. Ten years of reports—i.e., over a thousand records—were cataloged according to the SAP rules. We didn't bother about the bibliographic description which had been done by the Royal Library for the national bibliography. These records of about 300 characters were just taken over in machine readable form. The effort was then a simple clerical routine, namely to create a deep analysis database to moderate costs. Besides selecting terms out of the contents list as was done in the American SAP, we made a further improvement by including the captions to tables and graphs. Such captions are more reliable text strings than titles, for example, because there is an awareness of the fact that figures and tables should be logically complete units, independent of the main text.

That meant that from captions it was possible to retrieve numerical data. The length of the records was augmented by 4,000 characters on the average. At that time, in the national bibliography and its computerized equivalent LIBRIS, the only search entries were the serial number of the report, the ISBN, the ministry under which the committee worked, and no further classification. That was unsatisfactory since the information in the reports met certain standards for accuracy and dependability. It was so obvious that this information could be used more widely if more access points were available.

Even today, this database continues and is publicly available. During the exercise, I became tutor for a collaborator in this work, Irene Wormell (1985), and it can be seen as a by-product of our SAP efforts that in 1985 she wrote a thesis at Lund University entitled: *SAP: Improved Subject Retrieval for Monographic Publication.* Nicholas Belkin and Will Lancaster were among the examiners at the dissertation occasion. The same afternoon, the Danish Queen Margareth nominated Wormell to be a professor in the Library School in Copenhagen.

No One is Prophet in His Own Country

Since many of my efforts were not traditional, it was hard to get acknowledgment for them in my country. Many have asked me if I wasn't frustrated when my advice about bibliographic descriptions in machine language was not followed. Of course I was upset by all those newborn "specialists" on computer records who did not understand what can be done with a computer. Instead of dealing with all the redundancies in a MARC record and letting the computer lift off much of their burden to identify, flag, and tag bibliographic elements, they seemed amazed to do the nitty-gritty work themselves, especially not taking into account the costs for the MARC records. In vain I waited for the time foreseen by Pauline when the minute elements in MARC would be compounded into bigger chunks.

The first sign of this was in 1994 in the article by Willy Cromwell: "The Core Record: A New Bibliographic Standard." It was comforting to read, since it came very close to what I had proposed to the National Library of Nicaragua in 1988.

Thank God for Other Playgrounds

Although frustrated by my efforts, there was always another playground to go to. As an international expert for Unesco working in many countries in Europe, Asia, and in Latin America, I often was confronted with the enormous backlogs of the national bibliographies even if automation had been introduced. The reason for that was that catalogers were following AACR2 and MARC in minor details. As has been well noted by R. Fidel and M. Crandell in their 1988 article in *Library Quarterly*, the arrangement in AACR2 "is incompatible with the principles of database design" (p. 133). I have always thought a better approach could be found.

Twelve Fields Make It

During a Unesco project to the National Library of Nicaragua in the late 1980s I discovered their backlog, and my choice was to propose a record similar to what we had utilized in the nuclear establishment in the 1960s making use of the eleven fields. After much discussion, however, we ended up with twelve fields, approved by the national librarian. I could certainly live with that in order to make an "adequate bibliographic citation." That was not so very different from the core record mentioned above.

The updating of the national bibliography started by using the Unesco CDS/ISIS system for data entry and a tagging scheme borrowed from IBERMARC. This is a system which might not be widely used in the United States but, in Latin America, more than 6,000 systems are in operation for building databases, and it is kept up-to-date by an international body like Unesco. So, using the essential elements, the input went on and, by the end of 1991, *Bibliografia Nacional de Nicaragua, 1979-1989* (Arellano, 1991) could be published in a printed volume from floppy discs which were sent to a printshop. The enumerated catalog contained three indexes: author, corporate author, and title. A continuous updating has consistently taken place to keep the bibliography up-to-date.

The backlogs in the national bibliographies of other Central American countries were almost as bad as it had been in Nicaragua. The national librarians therefore convened in Managua, and it was decided that the same procedure should be followed in all the national libraries. Of course, it was not easy to convince the catalogers in these libraries that they might benefit from a common standard of essential elements. The participants put forward their formats for discussion. For instance, Panama used forty-one fields and Guatemala forty-four. It was agreed that the essential elements for a union catalog could be accommodated in the proposed standard format. However, each library could add any field they thought useful in addition to the prescribed fields. The standard was followed by some of the countries without any additions. Also, they agreed to use the Dewey classification system (but only the first three figures). A thesaurus by C. Rovira and J. Aguayo (1969), *Lista de Encabezamientos de Materia*, was used for subject headings.

As ISIS has the feature to create an export format according to the above ISO standard, it was suggested that the national libraries in the area should exchange floppy discs in order to produce a future Central American Bibliography. Lately, I have introduced CDS/ISIS also at the library of Universidad Nacional Autonoma de Nicaragua de León. They are now building up databases of local material, articles in newspapers and periodicals, and a base of their masters theses. The ISIS search engine is used for searching both keywords and natural text. You can also get a frequency listing, for example, of the words in titles.

My interest when confronted with policy makers in developing countries has, for the last two decades, concentrated on what is called "social intelligence," and I have shared its development with colleagues such as Stevan Dedijer, William E. Colby, Blaise Cronin, and others. William E. Colby, referring to the future dimension of intelligence, said: "It must become an international resource to help humanity identify and resolve its problems through negotiation and cooperation rather than continue to suffer or fight over them" (personal communication, October 1992). I have maintained that libraries and information services might play an important part in maintaining a common understanding of the facts and factors involved rather than believing they can profit from private and secret knowledge withheld from each other.

Life Begins at Seventy

Lately, the UN/CEPAL in Santiago de Chile put my lecture at the National Library of Venezuela entitled: "La Biblioteca Capacitadora" (The Tutorial Library) (http://www.tips.org/tips/forum/ibict/noti047.htm) on the Web. Now in my eighties, I might even go for another time to Latin America to follow up on my heretical views about MARC and subject classifications when building databases. That has kept me alive since I took my retirement, and much about what I have written above has been to show that it is what I really have wanted to do during my life and am still doing. So, my wish to Pauline is that she also finds that formal retirement does not mean that the brainwork is over. Now you are free to do what you want to do, so do not just let the weaving soothe your mind!

References

Arellano, J. E. (Ed.). (1991). *Bibliografia nacional de Nicaragua, 1979-1989*. Managua, Nicarague: Instituto Nicaragüense de Cultura.

Atherton, P. (1963). File organization: Principles and practices for processing and maintaining the collection. In P. W. Howerton (Ed.), *Information handling: First principles*. Washington, DC: Spartan Books.

Atherton, P. (Ed.). (1965). *Classification research* (Proceedings of the Second International Study Conference held at Hotel Prins Hamlet, Elsinore, Denmark, 14th-18th September, 1964). Copenhagen, Denmark: International Federation for Documentation.

Atherton, P. (1977). *Handbook for information systems and services*. Paris: Unesco.

Atherton, P. (1978). *Books are for use: Final report of the subject access project to the Council on Library Resources.* Syracuse, NY: School of Information, Syracuse University.

Cromwell, W. (1994). The core record: A new bibliographic standard. *Library Resources & Technical Services, 38*(4), 415-424.

Fidel, R., & Crandell, M. (1988). The AACR2 as a design schema for bibliographic databases. *Library Quarterly, 58*(2), 123-142.

Gorman, M., & Winkler, P. (Eds.). (1978). *Anglo-American cataloguing rules* (2d ed.). Chicago: American Library Association.

Martin, M. D. (1974). *Reference manual for machine-readable bibliographic descriptions.* Paris: Unesco.

Rovira, C., & Aguayo, J. (1967). *Lista de encabezamientos de materia para bibliotecas.* Washington, DC: Unión Panamericana.

Wormell, I. (1985). *SAP: Improved subject retrieval for monographic publications.* Unpublished doctoral dissertation, Lund University, Sweden.

Blazing New Trails:
In Celebration of an Audacious
Career

✦ Donald W. King ✦

Prologue

I had the distinct pleasure of working with Pauline Atherton (Cochrane) during the 1960s, a period that can be considered the heyday of automated information system design and evaluation in the United States. I first met Pauline at the 1962 American Documentation Institute annual meeting in North Hollywood, Florida. My company, Westat Research Analysts, had recently been awarded a contract by the U.S. Patent Office to provide statistical support for the design of experiments with automated information retrieval systems. I was asked to attend the meeting to learn more about information retrieval systems and to begin informing others of U.S. Patent Office activities in this area. At one session, Pauline and I questioned a speaker about the research that he presented. Pauline's questions concerned the logic of their approach and mine, the statistical aspects. After the session, she came over to talk to me and we began a professional and personal friendship that continues to this day.

During the 1960s, Pauline was involved in several important information-retrieval projects including a series of studies for the American Institute of Physics, a dissertation examining the relevance of retrieved documents, and development and evaluation of an online information-retrieval system. I had the opportunity to work with Pauline and her colleagues on four of those projects and will briefly describe her work in the 1960s.

One aspect of Pauline's research that I found both interesting and very useful to the research community was her innovative approach to this research. This was a lesson I learned from her that I applied through the remainder of my career. In order to place Pauline's contributions in perspective, I will provide a brief history of information retrieval evaluation measures during that time, illustrate her contribution to measurement, and describe how she involved users in the design of index structure and content and in search system design.

American Institute of Physics Studies

During the early 1960s, Pauline and several colleagues at the American Institute of Physics (AIP) conducted a series of pioneering studies on various aspects of information retrieval systems. One of these studies involved analysis of search needs and formulation of search queries. Most evaluations of information retrieval at the time were performed with existing systems, all of which had constraints resulting from their novelty. As a result of these constraints, search requests were dictated to some degree by limited system capabilities and user expectations of these capabilities. While these studies contributed valuable knowledge to the field, it was helpful to have another approach unencumbered by system flaws, that examined searches as though an "ideal information retrieval system" was in place. This is the very different, but revealing, approach taken by Pauline as part of the "Documentation Research Project" performed for AIP.

Yet another important aspect of this research is that Pauline demonstrated that scientists—in this case, research physicists—would be willing to participate in such studies. A questionnaire was mailed to 2,000 U.S. research physicists and approximately 50 percent of them responded. The physicists were asked to formulate search requests to a hypothesized "ideal information reference retrieval system" for lists of current and past literature that related to their work. The respondents provided an average of five search requests per physicist yielding a total of about 5,000 active requests. Analyses of this rich collection of actual search requests helped develop design criteria for an ideal information retrieval system. In particular, results revealed the relative frequency of current searches, requirements for retrospective searches (and, thereby, the need for retrospective requirements to be incorporated into automated systems), and the nature of search requests such as the relative frequency with which experimental, theoretical, or combined information was sought. It also served to establish indexing parameters, for example, to index properties, objects, and methods.

Results indicated that three-fourths of the requests involved references to current literature (at three to four month intervals), and less than 40 percent of the retrospective search requests asked for any literature published prior to 1940 (twenty to twenty-five years old). It was found that categories such as "property," "object," and "method" served as a useful way to organize index terms.

Largely as a result of this research, Pauline helped develop a comprehensive approach to indexing AIP journals and other literature, including vocabulary development and standardization, centralization of indexing of AIP journals, and standardization of index entry format. She also facilitated author participation through "Aid-to-Indexing" forms they were asked to complete at the time a paper was accepted for publication. This information enhanced indexers' ability to perform their work faster and more effectively. Later, Pauline and Vance Weaver devised a clever method for preparing both author and subject indexes. This involved a single card prepared with the full citation of an article to be indexed. The card was then photocopied onto cards for each co-author and for each subject heading. One deck of cards was prepared and sorted in alphabetical sequence by author. A second deck was sorted by an appropriate sequence of subject headings (either alphabetized or in hierarchical order). From these two decks, images were produced as offset plates for printing. This scheme was devised before computer-based publishing and information retrieval systems.

The 5,000 requests from the AIP/DRP Study of User Requirements also served as a testbed for performing factor analyses: an approach to clustering being actively promoted by System Development Corporation at that time. The analyses, performed by Hal Borko and Pauline, involved search requests and work descriptions under unusually stringent "blind" conditions. Also using word frequency data within a document (or document collection) as an indicator of relevance, it was found that there was about a 50 percent correlation of such clusters of documents with corresponding classes that had been pre-established by human judges.

Pauline and Stella Keenan also performed a detailed study of more than 20,000 abstracts from one year of *Physics Abstracts*. The analysis ranked journals according to the number of articles abstracted. Results showed a highly skewed distribution, with 25 percent of the articles in the top six journals in every subfield of physics, 25 percent in the next 13, 25 percent in another 29, and the low quartile involving 357 journals (of which 197 had fewer than six articles). Finally, Pauline's methodical and comprehensive approaches to these studies were highly respected in the field. In fact, Charles Bourne (1966) suggested that researchers would help their readers and reviewers if they would report "all of the data suggested previously by Atherton as a standard for reporting index test data." During this early era, Pauline contributed to the field in many ways.

References to the AIP Projects

Atherton, P., & Weaver, V. (1963). *A suggested method for producing journal indexes: Report* (Documentation Research Project). New York: American Institute of Physics (AIP/DRP 63-3 or PB 164 180).

Keenan, S., & Atherton, P. (1964). A comprehensive study based on *Physics Abstracts: 1961 Issues. Journal Literature of Physics* (AIP/DRP PAI).

Atherton, P., & Borko, H. (1965). *A test of the factor-analytically derived automated classification method applied to descriptions of work and search requests of nuclear physicists: Report.* New York: American Institute of Physics (AIP/DRP 65-1).

Atherton, P. (1965). *American Institute of Physics Documentation Research Project: A review of work completed and in progress, 1961-65.* New York: American Institute of Physics (AIP/DRP 65-3).

Atherton, P. (1965). Is compatibility of authority files practicable? In S. M. Newman (Ed.), *Information systems compatibility.* Washington, DC: Spartan Books.

Atherton, P. (1965). Ranganathan's classification ideas: An analytico-synthetic discussion. *Library Resources & Technical Services, 9*(Fall), 463-473.

Atherton, P. (1965). *A proposed standard description for evaluation tests of retrieval systems* (Documentation Research Project). New York: American Institute of Physics.

Atherton, P. (1966). An action plan for indexing. *Physics Today,* (January), 58-60.

Bourne, C. P. (1966). Evaluation of indexing systems. In C. A. Cuadra (Ed.), *Annual review of information science and technology* (vol. 1, pp. 171-190). New York: John Wiley & Sons.

Evaluation of the Universal Decimal Classification and Development of "Audacious," an Interactive Search System

The Universal Decimal Classification (UDC) was a well-known classification system in European libraries and documentation centers and, in some scientific fields in the United States, was an applied classification scheme for abstracting and indexing services. Pauline and colleagues performed a series of innovative and revealing studies concerning automation of the UDC in the fields of oceanography and nuclear science. Initially, the studies addressed the application of UDC in an automated batch processing mode. Since, at that time, interactive systems were beginning to be examined, they developed an interactive system (Audacious) to determine its applicability to the UDC and to compare the UDC input to an index file. Pauline and Robert Freeman first evaluated the UDC input using a collection of 250 documents in oceanography followed by research on a UDC file of 2,800 nuclear science documents. These studies were characterized by the detailed attention given to the range of variables involved and the conditions impinging on the studies. This care made their analyses and results far more useful to the information community than many other studies performed at that time. Another useful aspect of this work was the characterization of information-retrieval systems consisting of five principal functions: analysis and control, surrogation, physical transformation, file processing, and display.

The Universal Decimal Classification batch processing retrieval system used software developed at IBM (i.e., the IBM Combined File Search System). This system provided both a linear (or serial) document file and an inverted descriptor file. Boolean queries were able to be read into the computer in batches. The online system used was operated by Xerox in Rochester, New York, and was called Datatrol.

These studies showed that the hierarchical and multifaceted Universal Decimal Classification could be adapted to an automated information retrieval system that operates in a batch processing mode. They spelled out the conditions under which automated UDC retrieval systems can work. They felt that the UDC could operate successfully in either a batch processing or interactive mode. However, they did also conclude that the UDC is not as efficient as using an indexing language that is specifically designed for automated searching. To examine the interactive mode more closely, they adopted an existing system as a model of an updated interactive retrieval system in which users could interact with the computer at various stages in the process. At this time (1965), such a system was considered quite innovative.

Pauline and Robert Freeman developed an interactive information retrieval system they dubbed AUDACIOUS, based on the two earlier Universal Decimal Classification databases. Later, using AUDACIOUS and another database of 2,800 items from nuclear science, they teamed with me to evaluate and compare the UDC input with an index input from *Nuclear Science Abstracts* which used an alphabetic controlled vocabulary. This research produced some interesting and useful results. First, while both the UDC and alphabetic index input were satisfactory, it was found that the two content coding schemes used together provided a much more powerful search tool. In other words, the UDC codes were used to "surround" relevant documents within broad categories, and the index terms were used to search in-depth within the broad categories. The search strategies were to search up or down the UDC classification structure with index terms held relatively constant (the same result was found also for patent classification used in conjunction with index search terms).

Second, the evaluation involved a diagnostic failure analysis of ten carefully defined reasons for retrieval failure (e.g., missed relevant documents and retrieval of nonrelevant ones). Each failure was carefully analyzed, and the frequency of failure assigned to each of the ten reasons was established. As it turned out, query formulation was the biggest source of failure and was particularly pronounced for differences between search analysts. The second largest source of failure concerned the inability to properly index topics specifically mentioned in titles or in abstracts.

Finally, a novel method was designed to measure recall—that is, the proportion of relevant documents that are retrieved. Measuring recall was always a highly contentious aspect of evaluation because no one could be certain that every relevant document in the file (retrieved or not) had been identified and counted in the denominator of the proportion of relevant documents retrieved except in very small test collections—e.g., the Cranfield collections. Usually, evaluators relied on an exhaustive search, sometimes performed after the fact, to identify the entire set of relevant documents for each search request. In this research, a random sample of documents was added to the retrieval set and used as a base for assessing relevance of nonretrieved documents and a statistical estimate for missed relevant documents. The sample size was determined statistically to establish a predetermined probability that no relevant documents were missed (or that additional relevant documents were missed if one or more had been found in the sample). Later, users were asked to list documents known to be relevant at the time the search request was made. These items are used to estimate the recall ratio. It was shown that, if one can assume that the known relevant documents are as likely to be retrieved by the system as any other relevant documents, then the statistical maximum likelihood estimate of the recall ratio is the fraction of known relevant documents retrieved. The list of relevant documents also provided a means of continued searching until all known relevant documents were retrieved thus providing a "cost" required to achieve various levels of recall. In a sense, this was a precursor to relevance feedback.

References to the Universal Decimal Classification Research

Freeman, R. R., & Atherton, P. (1967). *File organization and search strategy using the Universal Decimal Classification in mechanized reference retrieval systems.* New York: American Institute of Physics, UDC Project (AIP/UDC-5).

Freeman, R. R., & Atherton, P. (1968). *AUDACIOUS—An experiment with online, interactive reference retrieval system using the Universal Decimal Classification as the index language in the field of nuclear science.* New York: American Institute of Physics, UDC Project (AIP/UDC-7).

Atherton, P.; King, D. W.; & Freeman, R. R. (1968). *Evaluation of the retrieval of nuclear science documents references using the Universal Decimal*

Classification as the indexing language for a computer-based system. New York: American Institute of Physics, UDC Project (AIP/UDC-8).

Pauline's Dissertation

In the mid-1960s, Pauline conducted a series of experiments which determined the accuracy of intermediaries in screening search output on behalf of users. A series of searches were made by two proxy users, and twenty-five documents were reviewed by them to determine their relevance to the search queries. The testbed of twenty-five documents had five types of "document representations" which intermediaries could use to establish the relevance of the items retrieved, including titles, titles and abstracts, and index terms from three sources. The "search outputs" were screened by four intermediaries. Thus, the experiment provided evidence of the general accuracy of screening, the effectiveness of five document representations, and accuracy of intermediary selection. Most of all, the experiments provided a statistically valid experiment[1] that could be replicated by others and used to evaluate screening (e.g., as a means of implementing quality control of screening). The principal measures were the proportion of relevant documents chosen by the screeners and the proportion of documents chosen as being relevant that were not. Results showed that title and abstract was by far the best document representation, intermediaries varied substantially in their ability to screen, and there was a difference in results between the two users (suggesting a problem in interpreting their queries and/or their uncertainty as to what they sought). However, the results also suggested that the intermediaries generally tended to screen too tightly resulting in a very small proportion of nonrelevant items being chosen by the intermediaries but, as a result, many relevant items were overlooked.

SUPARS Development and Evaluation at Syracuse University

Pauline and colleagues at Syracuse University's School of Library Science (now School of Information Studies) constructed, operated, and evaluated an innovative online reference retrieval system involving 35,000 abstract entries (two years) from the American Psychological Association's *Psychological Abstracts.* The system, called SUPARS (Syracuse University Psychological Abstract Retrieval Service), was novel in several respects. Input and retrieval were free of controlled vocabulary index terms and relied exclusively on free-text searching of the titles and abstracts. A second novel aspect of the research was the way in which real users (i.e., end-users) could use the system through terminals located throughout the campus. Finally, the user assistance, participation, and assessment were exemplary for systems at this time. A clear theme emerges again for a project involving Pauline as expressed by Lin and Garvey: "[T]he project demonstrates that much can be gained from technical innovations when the user component is given consideration in the innovation design and when studies of user feedback are an integrated part of an innovation."

The project involved Pauline, Jeffrey Katzer, Kenneth Cook, Eleanor Frierson, and Lynn Trump and was funded by the Air Force, Rome Air Development Center. The retrieval system, DPS, developed by IBM for the Biomedical Communication Network, was borrowed from the SUNY Upstate Medical Center, just across the street from Syracuse University. The online communication allowed simultaneous use on seventy-five IBM telecommunication terminals located throughout the campus. The overall research involved a pilot study and a two and a half month operational phase following an extensive publicity and training campaign, which continued throughout operations. Part of the operations involved a help line (Telephone Aid Access) that was on-call for answering questions. The users were given a pocket reminder card which encouraged them to seek help when necessary. While the service was available to students, faculty, and staff, most of the 349 persons who registered for the program were graduate students from the fields of psychology, education, and library science. During the brief operational phase, there were 4,388 searches made, and the Telephone Aid Access service received a total of 551 inquiries. Users were asked to indicate why they used the retrieval system (e.g., 59 percent said they wanted to review an area exhaustively). As a historical note, most of the participants (66 percent) had no experience with computer terminals or with computer-based information retrieval systems (75 percent). In-depth interviews with ten psychologists and ten others, showed that about one-half of them said they successfully retrieved what they had wanted (recognizing that the file was limited to *Psychological Abstracts* and was only two years old). To appreciate its novelty, one should recognize that this work was done shortly after DIALOG and SDC's ORBIT started their retrieval services.

References Concerning Supars

Cook, K. H.; Trump, L. H.; Atherton, P.; & Katzer, J. (Eds.). (1971). *Supars: Syracuse University* Psychological Abstracts *Retrieval Service. Large scale information processing systems. Final report* (six sections). Syracuse, NY: Syracuse University, School of Library Science.

Atherton, P. (1971). Section IV-B. The user component of the system. In K. H. Cook, L. H. Trump, P. Atherton, & J. Katzer (Eds.), *Supars: Syracuse University* Psychological Abstracts *Retrieval Service. Large scale information processing systems. Final report*. Syracuse, NY: Syracuse University, School of Library Science.

Frierson, E., & Atherton, P. (1971). Survey of attitudes towards SUPARS. In *American Society for Information Science 34th Annual Meeting Proceedings, vol. 8. Communication for Decision Makers*. Westport, CT: Greenwood Publishing.

Lin, N., & Garvey, W. D. (1972). Information Needs and Uses. In C. A. Cuadra (Ed.), *Annual review of information science and technology* (vol. 17, pp. 5-37). Washington, DC: American Society for Information Science.

Lessons Learned in Working with Pauline Atherton

During the early 1960s, there was a tremendous interest in the design and evaluation of information retrieval systems with substantial research and development funded by the U.S. government and industry.[2]

Major automated systems were being developed at the National Library of Medicine (MEDLARS), NASA (RECON), by the intelligence community, and elsewhere. Versions of these systems were eventually commercialized by Lockheed (DIALOG), Systems Development Corporation (ORBIT), and Battelle (BASIS). The National Science Foundation (NSF) Office of Scientific Research, the U.S. Patent Office, the National Library of Medicine, the Atomic Energy Commission, the Department of Defense, the Air Force Office of Scientific Research and Rome Air Development Center, and other agencies engaged in, or supported, research in information retrieval as did many companies such as DuPont, IBM, AT&T Bell Labs, and others. The research took several distinct approaches including development of information retrieval testbeds (Cranfield collections developed by Cleverdon in England, SMART system developed by Salton at Harvard and later Cornell, and the intelligence community), evaluation of operating systems and evaluation of simulated or partial systems (including several promising associative retrieval systems).

As with many scientific disciplines, there was a great deal of competition among systems development approaches, evaluation methods and, particularly, evaluation measures. One could not attend any conference without hearing heated arguments and debates about what "relevance" was and how to measure it. Pauline was in the middle of many of these debates because much of her research revolved around this issue. As statisticians, Edward Bryant and I were asked to advise researchers at the U.S. Patent Office in the area of design of statistical experiments relating to indexing and retrieval of patents. It quickly became clear that the big issue was not so much "how" to measure but rather "what" to measure. At that time, there were two principal information retrieval performance measures (promoted primarily by Cyril Cleverdon at Cranfield): (1) the proportion of items retrieved that are relevant (i.e., precision), and (2) the proportion of relevant items in a database that are retrieved (i.e., recall).

However, if you asked ten researchers what "relevance" was, you would likely get ten distinct answers. For much of the early 1960s, this issue dominated many conference sessions and publications.[3]

It was important in a sense because the perceived "success" of competing systems depended on evaluations of their performance using these measures and because evaluators themselves had a stake in the acceptance of their measures. In many ways the discussions were intellectually stimulating, but probably, in retrospect, they occupied a disproportionate amount of time and energy.

Although involved with the Patent Office experiments and some of Pauline's research, I was more of an observer than a participant in the "relevance" controversy. In lengthy discussions with Pauline and her colleagues and through preparation of a chapter for the *Annual Review of Information Science and Technology*, it became clear that the different perspectives on the issue of "relevance" and its application in various measures all had merit (including Pauline's unique approach). There were basically two ways that relevance was defined as exemplified by Rees and Schultz at Case Western Reserve and by Cuadra and Katter at Systems Development Corporation (SDC). Rees and Schultz defined relevance as a relationship between system responses and an expression of the user's request—that is, the system responds to a question based on index terms (or other surrogate descriptions of the documents' information content) which is the system's assessment of relevance. Each document in the file is, in effect, assessed as to its relevance to the question posed. In some systems, the assessment is yes (1) or no (0), and in others the relevance values can be continuous (say, 1 to 100) or multivalued (say, 1, 2, 3, 4, 5, 6, 7, 8). This relevance might be termed a "system relevance response."

The Systems Development Corporation research defined relevance as a relationship between a document and a user's "information requirement statement" (i.e., a search question). Here an assessment of relevance of documents to search questions is made by users—that is, each document in a file (or sample) is assessed by users as to its relevance to their search questions. Again, the assessment can be given a binary value, multivalues, or continuous values. In fact, some of SDC's research dealt with determination of optimum relevance values. They also did some factor analysis on the relevance values. This type of assessment might be termed "user relevance judgment."

As mentioned, the system's relevance response is usually a quantile binary or dichotomous measure—that is, relevant or not (1 or 0). Which means it is retrieved or not. However, the response could be continuous, say from 0 to 1, as was true with some associative retrieval systems which based responses on mathematical or other ways of weighting terms and their relationship within documents and/or citation relationships among documents. Similarly, users could assess the relevance of documents to their search request as yes or no, as multivalued ratings, or as continuous values. Thus the system performance could be measured by the relationship of system relevance response and user relevance judgments as shown in Figure 1 (continuous values), Figure 2 (multivalues such as Likert rating scales), or Figure 3 (simple yes or no). All these relationships might be called the accuracy of the system. Some of the controversy during that time revolved around which level of measure was best when, actually, they are not all that different since the relationships contribute to valid measures of "accuracy."

In Figure 1, search systems establish a level at which document representations (i.e., titles, abstracts, etc.) are printed out. In the figure, an amount is shown by D_s, above which documents are retrieved. Similarly, users might consider all documents to the right of D_u as being relevant to the search question. The number of items in each quadrant could be counted and displayed as in Figure 3. Referring to Cleverdon's measures of recall and precision, recall would be 0.75 (i.e., 50/67) and precision would be 0.40 (i.e., 50/125). By raising and lowering the system "decision" criterion D_s, the relationship tends to vary in an inverse way (i.e., as

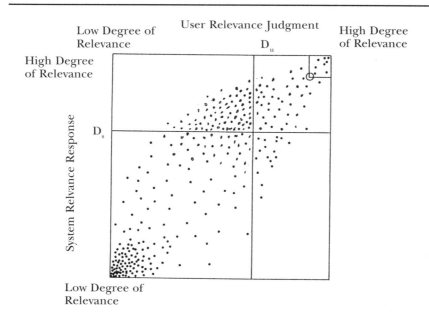

Figure 1. User relevance judgment plotted against system relevance response for individual documents and a given search question

	User Relevance Judgment		
	Low Degree of Relevance	D_u	High Degree of Relevance
High Degree of Relevance	12 · · · · ·· ·· · · · ·		8 · · · · · ···
	20 ····· · · · ·· · · ·········		5 ·· · · ·
	31 ··· ····· ····· ···· · · · ·		4 · ·· ·
D_s	42 ···········-·····-···· ····· ··· ···· ··		3 · · ·
	58 ·····-···-······· ·· ·· · ····· ····· ···· ·		2 · ·
	74 ·····-·········· · · ··· · · ···· ·		1 ·
	98 ··-··········· · ·· · ··· · ··		2 ··
Low Degree of Relevance	640 ·······		0

Figure 2. User relevance judgment plotted against
multi-values of system relevance response

recall increases, precision decreases) as shown in Figure 4. Although this inverse relationship is not as inevitable as Cleverdon proclaimed.

There were several other combinations of relevance measures proposed by researchers at the time. For example, some proposed comparing recall and fallout, where fallout is the proportion of nonrelevant documents that are retrieved as shown in Figure 5. The calculation of fallout from the figure would be 0.08 (i.e., 75/933). As one lowers the system decision criterion (D_s), the recall increases and the fallout also increases. In Figure 6, the continuous values are calculated in a way similar to statistical Type I and Type II errors—that is, accepting a false hypothesis (or retrieving a "false drop" or nonrelevant document) and rejecting a true hypothesis (or not retrieving a relevant document). Another proposal was to combine all four measures as shown in Figure 7. Here the ratios are depicted by the letters shown in Figure 3. Other measures included recall and the proportion of documents retrieved (that is, 0.125 or 125/1,000) as shown in Figure 8 and, finally, recall and the total number of documents retrieved (Figure 9). The point is that there are many measures, each conveying a different meaning or way of assessing the "accuracy" of retrieval systems.

A more serious question became evident, which was why some user-assessed "relevant" documents were not retrieved and why some user-assessed "nonrelevant" documents were. In fact, there are several activities (and related decisions) in which errors can occur. For example, if an intermediary (e.g., search expert or reference librarian) conducts the search,

User Relevance Judgment

		Not Relevant Dv	Relevant	Total
System		a (75)	b (50)	a + b (125)
Relevance	Ds			
Response		c (858)	d (17)	c + d (875)
Total		a + c (933)	b + d (67)	a + b + c + d (1,000)

Figure 3. Retrieval categorization with dichotomous values
of user relevance judgments and system relevance response

there can be a problem of properly communicating or expressing the search question to the intermediary, the intermediary can choose the wrong search terms, an indexer could have made an indexing error and, if an intermediary (or user) screens the output using the document titles, abstract, and other errors can occur. One can measure the "accuracy" of each activity based on pairs of relevance assessments made, as shown in Figure 10. In this schema, there are five relevance assessments.

1. *User relevance judgment,* which is the user's assessment of the documents' relevance to the user's question.
2. *Intermediary relevance judgment,* which is the intermediary's assessment of relevance of documents to the user's question.
3. *Interpretation accuracy* is the relationship of the two above judgments, which ideally would be exactly the same if intermediaries interpreted the questions perfectly.

4. *Query relevance* is an assessment of the relevance of query concepts (or language) to the information content of the document.
5. *Query accuracy* is the relationship between the intermediary's relevance judgment (or user's if there is no intermediary) and query relevance.
6. *System relevance response* is an assessment by the system of the relevance of documents to the query posed, where errors enter due to indexing mistakes (i.e., the query concepts match information in the document, but the concepts were not coded or invalid concepts were coded).
7. *Input accuracy* compares query relevance and the actual system relevance response based on index terms used. Finally, if the system output is screened, there is a *screened system relevance response*, which is an assessment by an intermediary (or user) as to the relevance of document descriptions (i.e., title, abstract, etc.) and the user's question.
8. *Screening accuracy* is the relationship between the system relevance response and screened response. In this case, system accuracy is the relationship between the screened relevance response (i.e., items presented by an intermediary or examined by a user) and the user relevance judgment.

While the schema shows continuous measures of accuracy, most observations were dichotomous (i.e., 1 or 0). The dichotomous values could then be derived as conditional probabilities. For example, input accuracy could be expressed as the probability that a coder's terms were chosen given that the document is relevant and the probability that a coder's terms are chosen given that the document is not relevant. These conditional probabilities were combined and described as a finite Markov chain with absorbing states (see King & Bryant, 1971). This permits one to determine the relative contribution each activity makes to missing relevant documents and retrieving nonrelevant documents and to compare alternative approaches to the activities (e.g., using scientists as intermediaries and indexers) in terms of system accuracy. Combined with costs and other system attributes—such as response time, availability, and accessibility—the model provided a useful evaluation tool, and it was also computerized at one university and used in a system design course to illustrate the cost and effectiveness tradeoff of various design options.

Pauline's research contributed to this model in three important ways. First, her research into relevance produced the only data available at that time concerning screening accuracy, and her data (i.e., two conditional probabilities) concerning screening options were incorporated into the model. Second, her research into user relevance judgments and input accuracy were also incorporated into the model. Finally, her insights and valuable discussions helped immensely in conceptualizing the model.

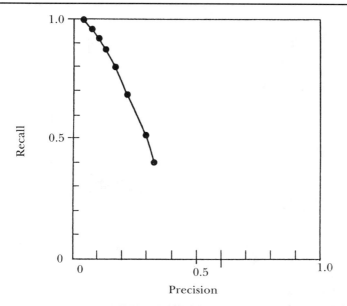

Figure 4. Recall versus precision

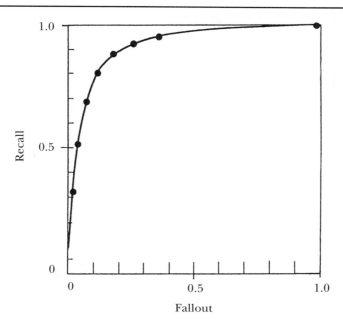

Figure 5. Recall versus fallout

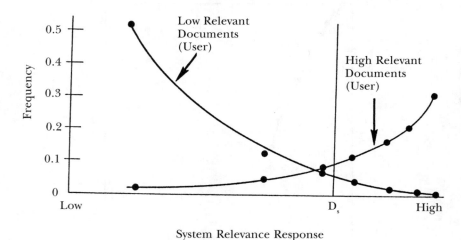

Figure 6. Frequency of system relevance response for
documents judged of high and low relevance by users

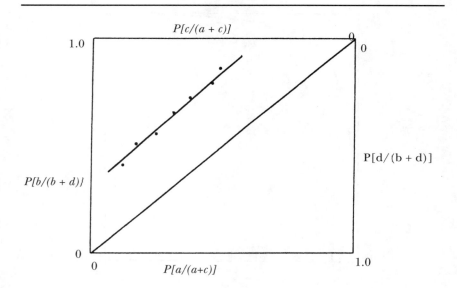

Figure 7. Frequency plots of system relevance scores for
documents judged relevant or nonrelevant by users

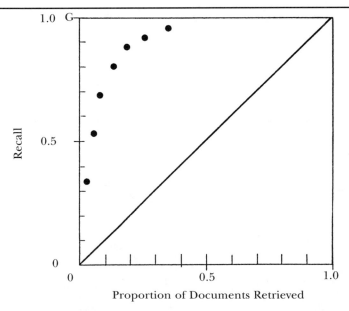

Figure 8. Recall versus proportion of documents retrieved

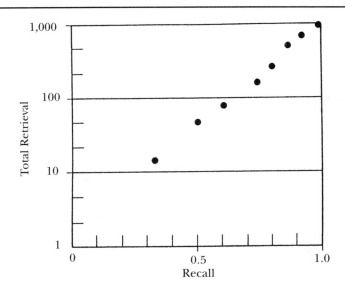

Figure 9. Recall versus total retrieval

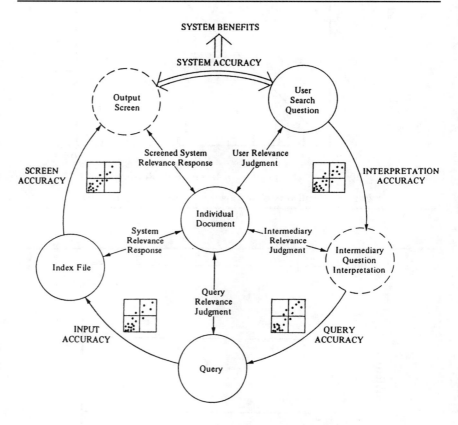

Figure 10. Schema presenting system accuracy
and relationships that contribute to it

Epilogue

Following the evaluation of AUDACIOUS and SUPARS and a few other online systems, there were few in-depth studies performed. For a time, interest in advanced systems, such as associative retrieval systems, waned in the United States, but these were carried on in the United Kingdom and other countries. Part of the reason for this development in the United States was a shift in the 1970s in the direction of research funded by NSF to electronic publishing and other science communication, and by a reduction of research by other agencies and companies. NSF funding for scientific communication essentially dried up in the early 1980s. Recently, however, Internet and the digital libraries initiatives funded by NSF and others have renewed an interest in information retrieval, electronic publishing, and other aspects of communication. However, it is clear that there has been a disconnect between systems research and development, evaluation, and economic research performed in the 1960s and 1970s and current activity. Unfortunately, a great deal that was learned in those years is being relearned and reinvented rather than building on an enormous base of knowledge. There are, of course, many reasons for this. One reason is that much of the research funded at that time was reported exclusively in the technical report literature (e.g., through NTIS, AIP, etc.) which was, at that time, considered highly relevant and comprehensive research. Searchers tend to screen this literature out or, when it is not, it is hard to locate and retrieve, although most academic libraries have it at least in microform. A second reason seems to be a lack of appreciation for what went on in the 1960s and 1970s, since this type of research was so moribund during the 1980s. Regardless, it is a pity that the contributions of such outstanding researchers as Pauline, Bourne, Cleverdon, Cuadra, Guiliano and Jones, Keen, Lesk, Rees, Salton, Sparck-Jones, Williams, and many others are largely lost or ignored.

Notes

[1] As a favor, Pauline asked me if I would take a look at the experiment to see if its design was statistically valid. As it turned out, her insight was exactly right even though involving several variables that needed to be controlled. She asked her advisors to discuss the analysis with me, so I attended a meeting at the University of Chicago wearing a business suit and hat. The group was unwilling to accept a non-academic endorsement of her work. Despite the quality and hard work behind the experiment, she failed to get approval for her dissertation. Some wondered why this had happened. Years later, I overheard a conversation on this topic when a graduate student from the same University remarked that Pauline had actually taken a lawyer with her to one meeting. I asked when that had occurred and realized that it was far more ominous than having a lawyer; it was a statistician!

[2] A recent comprehensive history of information retrieval systems (1965-1975) is being recorded by Charles P. Bourne and Trudi Bellardo Hahn. At this writing (1999), the manuscript is 1,400 pages in length.

[3] The issue of relevance simmered for two decades but has recently been rediscovered (e.g., see Schamber, 1994).

References

Cuadra, C. A., & Katter, R. V. (1967). The relevance of relevance assessment. In *Proceedings of the 30th Annual Meeting of the American Documentation Institute* (pp. 95-99). Washington, DC: Thompson.

Rees, A. M., & Schultz, D. G. (1967). *A field experimental approach to the study of relevance assessments in relation to document searching* (Final report. Center for Documentation and Communication Research). Cleveland, OH: Case Western Reserve University.

King, D. W. (1968). Design and evaluation of information systems. In C. A. Cuadra (Ed.), *Annual review of information science and technology* (vol. 3, pp. 61-103). Chicago: Encyclopaedia Brittanica, Inc.

King, D. W., & Bryant, E. C. (1971). *The evaluation of information services and products.* Washington, DC: Information Resources Press.

Schamber, L. (1994). Relevance and information behavior. In M. E. Williams (Ed.), *Annual Review of Information Science and Technology* (vol. 29, pp. 3-48). Medford, NJ: Learned Information, Inc.

The User-Centered Approach: How We Got Here

✦ Raya Fidel ✦

Introduction

I started my professional career in library and information science because of my great interest in knowledge organization. The more experience I gained in the profession, the more I realized how crucial it is to understand which organization would be best for each group of users. This in turn requires an understanding of how users seek information. And so now my focus is on studying information seeking and searching behavior. Throughout the relatively long course of changing my focus, I followed Pauline Cochrane's writings. Now I can say that she has been among the first to have a "user-centered approach" to knowledge organization, and she has used the term three years before it became a mainstream phrase. The following is a short discussion about the user-centered approach which was presented in a workshop in 1997.

What is the User-Centered Approach?

The basic assumption of the user-centered approach to the design of an information system is, rather than teaching a user how to adapt to an information system, discover how users look for information and design systems that conform to the users' searching behavior. That means that information systems are designed according to what users need, not only according to universal rules. It also means that different groups of users may require different types of information systems.

Let me give you an example from my own experience. I worked as a librarian in a geohydrology department at a university. Most of the faculty in that department were well-established scientists. When they wanted a paper from a conference proceedings, they always remembered the scientific body that organized the conference and where the conference took place. They would have requests such as: Find me the paper that Smith presented in the U.S. Geological Survey's conference in Seattle. They rarely remembered the title of the conference or the year (I think it was easiest for them to remember conferences that way because they themselves participated in the conferences and could easily remember where they were held).

Such questions were difficult to answer because the cataloging rules we used at that time (AACR) did not instruct the cataloger to have an entry for the city in which the conference took place. So I searched through all conferences that were organized by the U.S. Geological Survey (and there were many of them) and discovered for each of them where they took place. Soon I developed my own "rule": Whenever I cataloged a volume of conference proceedings, I assigned an added entry for the city in which it took place. That is, I had to "bend" the cataloging rules because they were not the best rules for some of the users in the library.

But we also had students in our department, and they did not go to conferences and therefore looked for conference proceedings in different ways, most of which were accommodated by the standard cataloging rules. This brings up the following point: Whenever we discuss users and their information-seeking behavior, we focus on a specific group of users. My library, for example, had two groups of users: faculty and students. These groups were different because they had different tasks. The faculty needed information primarily for research projects and for teaching. The students needed information to write papers. In addition, faculty members were well established in the scientific community, whereas the students were novices.

Another assumption in the user-centered approach, then, is that each group of users may have its unique pattern of looking for information. That means that when we study users, we want to first define the user groups and then investigate the seeking and searching behavior of that group.

Why is This Approach Necessary?

For centuries, people have used libraries that were designed according to general rules. Further, the rules themselves have evolved to accommodate the changes and developments in information technology. Why all of a sudden the emphasis on the user-centered approach?

There are many reasons. The most obvious reason: the more the system fits a user's needs and seeking and searching behavior, the more likely is the user to find useful information. This is an important reason, and because of it we might advocate the user-centered approach. The question is: why is it more central now than it was ten or twenty years ago?

User needs have always been important, but they have not been addressed as a central issue previously for two reasons: (1) in recent years, an increasing number of users search by themselves without the mediation of a librarian; and (2) the flexibility required to design systems according to individual needs became available only when computers were widely used.

When information systems are not flexible, it is hoped that there is a librarian to mediate between the user and the system. In the past, most library users preferred the help of a librarian when they were not completely sure how to find what they needed. The librarian always knew very well how to search the inflexible system and, for each request, the task was to discover the user's need. Through the reference interview and other means, librarians discovered exactly what a user needed. They then formulated it to fit the system. The inflexibility in the system was compensated for by the professional expertise of the librarian.

Today, many users in the Western world search for information without the mediation of a librarian. The systems are actually not much better than the inflexible card catalog, but there is more flexibility, and users can find *something* about 70 percent of the time. Even though reference librarians are still busy, and probably will always be, it is important to recognize that much of information retrieval is being performed directly by users. Because so much is done without the help of a librarian, it is important to design systems in which users can easily find information that is useful—that is, systems that are responsive to the way users search them.

Fortunately, we can design such systems today much more easily than we could before. At the time when academic libraries used card catalogs or any other form of a printed catalog, it was almost impossible to introduce flexibility into the design of these catalogs. It was best to follow standards because this way one at least knew what to expect from the system. For example, because I knew that each conference proceedings would have an entry under the scientific body that organized it, I could look under "U.S. Geological Survey" and know that the conference I was looking for would be found. In a large university library, it would have been impossible to tailor cataloging to different kinds of researchers and students and type all these different cards.

There is much more flexibility with the computer. One can have all the data associated with a volume of conference proceedings in one place, such as title, year, editor, scientific body, place, or the name of the keynote speaker. When individual users search for such a volume, they can use whatever information they have. Another example is the design of the interface. Many online catalogs have several interfaces: one for the complete novice, one for the experienced searcher, another for the cataloger, and yet another for the librarian working in the acquisition department. This variety of access can be made available only in computerized catalogs. No printed catalog has this flexibility. Today, therefore, we can be more responsive to user needs because we can actually design systems that can meet these needs.

Basic Concepts

The most basic concept in the user-centered approach is *information need*. This is, however, an ambiguous term, and not every one agrees on its definition.

Why do people look for information? Usually because they have to solve a problem or make a decision. Therefore, it is safe to say that the process of information seeking results from some sort of problem solving or decision making.

Consider, for example, a database for a library school. It has information about courses, time schedules, students, faculty, staff, and so on. Suppose a student has to make a decision whether or not to register for a course taught by a Professor Baker. To make this decision, he or she needs some information. The information that is needed we call an *information need*. Unfortunately, this is not that simple because this *information need* has many facets, and it is not always easy to determine what is the objective need. That is, what information will make it possible for the student to make a decision about the course.

Therefore, the following defines a number of basic concepts:

Information Want: The information the user thinks he or she needs. Before a person uses an information system or talks to a librarian, the person has some idea (not always well defined) what information will help to make a decision.

Information Demand: The information the user *says* he or she needs. Users do not always express what they think they need. Sometimes they think they have to present the information system with a request that the system or the librarian will "understand," or they feel uncomfortable to express what they want.

Information Need: The information that is objectively needed to solve a problem. This assumes that through problem analysis and other "scientific" means, it is possible to determine objectively what information will make it possible to make a decision. The purpose of the reference interview, for example, is to do just that: find out what is the objective need and then translate it into a language that the information system can understand.

Let us consider the example of the student who has to make a decision about Professor Baker's course. To make the decision, the student thinks he or she *wants* to know if Professor Baker is a favorable instructor. The student may feel uncomfortable to ask this question directly or may think that the database does not have this information, and he or she may present the request in an information *demand*, asking for a list of the courses that Professor Baker teaches. The student's advisor, however, may discover that what the student really *need*s to know is the average grades that Professor Baker gave last year (because professors who give high grades are usually favorites among students).

This ambiguity in the concept of *information need* makes it difficult to base the design of information systems on this need. What should be considered—wants, demands, or needs? It seems that all should be taken into account, but it is still unclear how this can be accomplished.

Because of this complexity, there were some attempts to adopt more pragmatic approaches that define *information need* according to the use and impact of the information:

Information Use defines *information need* according to how the information is used. For example, suppose the student wants to use the information he or she retrieves from the database to ask other students about Professor Baker. The student's *information need*, then, is a list of students who took Professor Baker's courses.

Information Impact on task performance or decision making. The *information need* is that part of the information that actually affected decision making. If the student looks, for example, at course descriptions and average grade, but the course descriptions have no effect on his decision, then the average grade is his *information need*.

But these definitions have their own various problems. For example, how can one determine that the course descriptions had no effect? After the student reads them, they probably have some effect because the student knows more than he or she knew before, even if it does not seem to have any direct impact. Most problematic, however, is the fact that, according to these two definitions, we can determine what the *information need* was *after* a decision was made or a problem was solved. This is not helpful for designing information systems. In design, it is necessary to know information needs in order to design the system—i.e., *before* the specific information needs are addressed.

Because of the difficulties in defining the concept *information need* and the difficulties in actually understanding how it is being manifested in real life, research focuses on information seeking and searching behavior.

Information Seeking and Searching Behavior relates to how users look for information. Studying this behavior focuses on the *process* of looking for information, not only on the *object* that is being looked for—that is, not only on the information need.

The concept *information seeking and searching behavior* is relatively new. It is not stable yet, and it means different things to different people. I understand *information seeking behavior* to mean what a user does from the moment she or he realizes that a decision is about to be made until the time the decision is made. *Searching behavior*, on the other hand, refers only to the interaction with the information system, which includes the interaction with a librarian.

User Studies as a Tool for the User-Centered Approach

Researchers who study information seeking and searching behavior believe that information systems should be designed to accommodate seeking and searching behavior. This makes sense because individual information needs are difficult to define and are constantly changing. Therefore, it is almost impossible to design long-term systems based on needs. On the other hand, it is likely that we can find patterns in seeking and searching behavior that are common to all users of a certain group. Once these patterns are discovered, one can design a system that accommodates the behavior of users from that group.

To find these patterns, researchers conduct user studies. Such studies explore how individual users behave when they look for information in real-life situations. User studies have several distinct characteristics:

User studies are usually field studies. It is common to distinguish between studies that are carried out in the laboratory, and those that are performed in the "field."

In a laboratory study, investigators select "subjects"—that is, people who will participate in the study. They create an artificial and highly controlled environment in the laboratory and ask the subjects to perform some tasks. Investigators then measure various things. For example, if a librarian wants to compare two online catalogs, he or she can select a group of sixty users and ask them to be subjects. A procedure the librarian might follow is: have two catalogs cover the same database and make up five questions. Ask thirty subjects to search the five questions on one catalog and the other thirty on the other catalog and then compare their searching. The librarian may measure which system provided results faster and/or which system retrieved more relevant items and fewer irrelevant. He can also ask the subjects to complete a questionnaire reporting about how well they liked the system they searched.

Because the study is performed in the laboratory, the librarian can decide which questions to use, he can even instruct subjects how to search (for example, with subject headings or with keywords), and he can compare the results because all subjects search the *same* five questions. Such studies are very promising for evaluating specific features of systems. But they are not very useful if one wants to discover how people look for information because the subjects are assigned questions. They search someone else's questions rather than satisfying their own information needs.

Therefore, user studies are often done "in the field," that is, in the natural environment where users are actually looking for information to satisfy their own needs. There are three major procedures that are used in such studies: questionnaire, interview, and observation. These are described in the next section.

User studies examine both users and nonusers. When researchers study information seeking and searching behavior, they usually focus on people who are already actively looking for information. It is possible, however, that some people with information needs are not looking for information because they do not know how to even start, or they are intimidated by the information system. These are nonusers. It is desirable to design systems that serve even those who do not know how to look for information. Therefore, user studies often include investigations of people who are nonusers.

User studies have to be carried out continuously. User studies are definitely necessary for the design of user-centered information systems. But this creates a dilemma. Information seeking and searching behavior is determined a great deal by the information system itself. Users look for information they think can be found in the system and may avoid looking for data they need if they think it is not in the system. Or they search in a way they think would be fruitful in that particular system, which may not be the way they would prefer to search. Therefore, the patterns of seeking and searching behavior researchers uncover are partly influenced by the system the users searched.

Should a designer of a new system take into consideration patterns of behaviors that were observed under the influence of an old system? Studies of card catalogs in academic libraries, for example, found that most searches were by author and only a small percentage were subject searches. Should a designer of an online catalog assume that there will be a relatively small proportion of subject searches on the new catalog? If the answer is "no," how can designers know which patterns are stable across systems?

The "solution" to this problem is a continuous study. In the life-cycle of an information system, a user study is carried out before the system is being designed. Once the system is designed and is fully operational, the system designer's job is not complete. With the new system, there will be new patterns of seeking and searching. These must be studied so the new system can be improved. And this process is continuous because behavior patterns change with the development of new systems. As a result, no design of an information system is ever complete. Further, no information system is ever perfect—every system can always be improved.

Instruments Employed in User Studies

Because user studies are usually field studies, researchers use one or more of three major instruments:

1. **Questionnaire**. Users answer a list of written questions. An open-ended question leaves some room for interpretation and asks users to respond in their own language. A closed question asks users to answer very precisely or to select one or more answers among a list of possible responses. The question, "Please list the problems you encountered when using the system," is an open-ended question. The question, "Please mark how long you waited for a system response: very little, little, normal, long, very long," is a closed question.

   When composing a questionnaire, researchers have clear and specific ideas of what they want to find out. They also understand that the responses they receive reflect what users *perceive* the situation to be and not necessarily an accurate picture of reality. For example, users may respond that a system was rather slow, but the particular system tested might be the fastest that has been developed.

2. **Interview**. Users answer a list of oral questions. Presenting questions orally is somewhat different than having them in a written form. Usually interviews handle open-ended questions better than questionnaires do. Users might be reluctant to write a lengthy response in a questionnaire, but they might find responding easier when talking to an interviewer. In addition, a skilled interviewer may interact with users during an interview and elicit information that the user initially did not volunteer to report.

   Because interviews facilitate open-ended questions, they can be exploratory in that researchers do not need to have specific ideas about what they will find. But like questionnaires, interviews collect users' *perceptions* of reality rather than *facts* about reality.

3. **Observation**. The researcher is physically present with the users and observes them at the time that they perform their regular job. When studying information seeking and searching, quite often the researcher asks users to think aloud in order for the researcher to understand the users' decisions and actions. In observation studies, researchers collect data by audio taping or videotaping what is occurring in the field, by writing notes, and by collecting paper documents such as search transcripts or filled request forms.

Most observation studies are exploratory because researchers have no control over what information will come their way. On the other hand, such studies collect data about what is actually occurring in the field and are not limited to users' perceptions. The remainder of this discussion will describe various user studies as they have been carried out in England and the United States.

Early User Studies: Correlation Among Observable Variables

Large-scale user studies were first carried out in the 1960s. The purpose of most of these studies was to discover how personal attributes of users correlated with their information-seeking behavior. The basic framework relied on the rationale that if researchers collected enough data, they would be able to predict seeking and searching behavior before systems were in place. For example, suppose we found that engineers who have just graduated from college, who work in teams, and who work in large companies prefer short articles. We could use these data when we design an information system for such users and have only short items.

To find such relationships, large-scale studies used questionnaires and interviews. The questions in these instruments were very specific and precise because they were designed to define variables. After data were collected on the variables, researchers performed statistical analyses to discover the preferences of each group of users. Even though all research at that time focused only on engineers and scientists, there was some inconsistency in the results. Nevertheless, these first studies gave a first glimpse at seeking and searching behavior.

B.C. Vickery (1973) summarized the variables that were examined in his book *Information Systems*. Here are some examples, as he arranged them in five categories.

A. *Environment*

1. Nature of the institution at which the user works (academic or industrial)
2. Size of the institution in terms of employees
3. Duration of the project on which the user is working
4. Rank of user within the institution
5. Nationality of the user

B. *User*

6. Age
7. Education (highest degree, first degree, technical qualifications)
8. Linguistic ability
9. Nature of work activity (management or research)

10. Subject field of work
11. Length of experience in the job
12. Volume of search activity (number of library searches per month, reading hours per week, etc.)
13. Stage of the project

C. Message

14. Subject field
15. Date of publication
16. Type of message (theoretical statements, results and data, method, etc.)
17. Extent of message (full text, abstract, or index record)
18. Perceived complexity of message

D. Channel

19. Type of channel (personal, such as oral or correspondence, or impersonal)
20. Directness of channel (primary or secondary)
21. Bibliographic form of impersonal media (book, journal, report, etc.)
22. Language of medium
23. Perceived accessibility

E. Source

24. Type of source (government department, research organization, etc.)

Vickery also listed the relationships that were discovered:

As far as the *user* is concerned, the volume of search is related to:
• the nature of the institution in which he works
• the size of his work team
• the duration of his work project
• his rank in the institution
• his age
• his education
• the nature of his job
• the subject field of his job
• his scientific productivity
• the bibliographic form of medium used

As for message, the age of message used is related to:
• the nature of the institution in which the user works
• the subject field of the message
• its type
• the form of the secondary medium used

Second Generation of User Studies: Identifying Patterns of Behavior

The early seeking and searching studies aimed at detailed analyses of individual users and their personal attributes, hoping that these would give clues about behavior patterns. The next stage, which started primarily in the United States during the early 1970s, produced studies that examined the patterns themselves rather than the individual user.

These new studies were carried out in locations where users looked for information—i.e., in libraries. There, researchers investigated how users search the catalog. Investigators in these large-scale studies went into a library and interviewed users before and/or after they searched the card catalog and sometimes even looked over users' shoulders to observe how they actually performed searches.

Unlike the studies in the first stage, the aim of these catalog-use studies was to identify patterns of searching in a library of a certain type without taking into account many individual attributes of users. The main targets were academic and public libraries. Examples of such studies were published in Lipetz (1970, 1972) and Tagliacozzo (1972). The first catalog-use studies resulted in a variety of findings. The studies found, for example, that:

- most of the searches were for known-items, for which the user had some bibliographic information;
- undergraduate students searched more by subject than faculty did; and
- most users preferred to search by author name.

These were new insights at the time. It is possible that the librarians in those libraries knew all along that their users prefer to search by author name. The studies, however, used scientific and systematic methods to prove that these are indeed the patterns of searching, and that they are consistent from one library to another. The studies had a major limitation, however. It was not clear how the findings could guide the design of new catalogs—those that would be better for users in these libraries. The lack of "why" questions in the studies was the main reason for this limitation. Catalogs cannot be improved unless designers understand the reasons that caused users to follow certain patterns of behavior.

Let us examine, for example, the finding that most searches were for known items. Given this piece of data, how can a catalog or library services be improved? They cannot without knowing the reason for that pattern. If users prefer known-item searches because most of their assignments in the library require such searches, then an improvement would be to guarantee that such searches are as easy as possible to perform. For instance, an author name can be entered twice: once in a direct manner (e.g.,

Darlene Baker) for those users who do not know that a name is usually inverted, and another in an inverted form (e.g., Baker, Darlene) for experienced users.

But if most of the searches are known-item searches because users gave up on subject searches, the library should take a different approach. Librarians may want to investigate what problems users had in subject searching and act to help users to overcome such problems. Librarians may find, for example, that users avoided subject searching because they could not find the subject headings they needed. Investigating the reasons, it may be found that the terms users looked for were more specific than the subject headings used in the library. Librarians may then create new lead-in terms ("see" references) that point users with specific terms to the broader subject headings they could enter.

User studies that ask "why" questions, and thus aim at a somewhat deeper understanding of user behavior, are not very common even today. But those that do are very insightful and usually provide guidelines that are promising for system improvements.

A Summary of General Results

By the end of the 1970s, many user studies that employed questionnaires and interviews were carried out. At that time, some general patterns of seeking and searching behavior began to emerge. In 1976, Sylvia Faibisoff and Donald Ely presented a summary of research results. The following are some of them:

- people tend to seek out information which is most accessible;
- people tend to follow habitual patterns when seeking information;
- users and potential users of information are often unaware of sources and how to use them;
- face-to-face communication is a primary source of information;
- different types of persons use different sources of information;
- the nature and content of information needed is variable and complex, varying from discipline to discipline and from group to group;
- there is a wide range of need among users in the quantity of information required;
- the quantity of information often exceeds the capability of the individual to use it; and
- the information needs of the individual change at different stages of his or her career and with changes in his or her project.

These generalizations show patterns that are common to information seeking and searching, but they also indicate that behavior is situational–i.e., it depends on the particular situation of a user when he or she searches for information.

For me, the most promising finding here is that people tend to follow habitual patterns when seeking information. I believe that once we identify the seeking patterns for a certain group of users, an information system can be designed to accommodate these patterns. Therefore, studying patterns of seeking and searching behavior is most promising for the development of information systems, and this is the type of research I do.

The CLR OPAC Studies in Early 1980

With the 1980s, the first online catalogs started to appear in American libraries. The Council on Library Resources (CLR) immediately funded a number of studies to help design the future OPAC (online public access catalog). Several teams of researchers investigated users and nonusers, as well as librarians, in a variety of settings and libraries. These studies were different from previous user studies because they employed a variety of instruments and sometimes in combination. The main methods were:

- Focus-group interviews with users and library staff. In such interviews, a moderator leads a group of about five to twelve individuals through an open in-depth discussion (see, for example, Markey, 1983).
- Individual and group interviews with library staff at research libraries (see, for example, Ferguson et al., 1982).
- System monitoring with transaction log analysis. This analysis uses a computer printout that records all the transactions that took place during a search (see, for example, Tolle, 1983).
- Self administered survey online. This survey targeted users after they completed their searches. A screen with an electronic questionnaire appeared at the end of a search, and the user was asked to fill it in. One of the new aspects of such a questionnaire was that the results were automatically transferred to a statistical package which was then used to perform statistical analyses.

An excellent review and analysis of these methods can be found in Cochrane and Markey (1983). The discussion here about the OPAC studies is based on this article.

Examples of Studies that Used a Questionnaire

The results collected with the online questionnaires at the CLR study can illustrate the type of information about users that can be uncovered with a questionnaire. Here are some examples:

1. Demographic characteristics of OPAC users:
—Academic library users visit the library more frequently than do public library or federal and state library users.
—OPAC users visit the library more frequently than do OPAC nonusers.

—A greater percentage of men than women are OPAC users.
—Older adults are likely to be OPAC nonusers.

2. Online searches of the OPAC:
—OPAC users search by subject more than any other search type.
—OPAC searches at academic libraries are course-related and at public libraries are for personal interest.
—At least 40 percent of OPAC users find all that they were looking for or more than they were looking for.

3. Problems with OPAC features:
—Finding the correct subject term.
—Increasing the results when too little is retrieved.
—Reducing the results when too much is retrieved.

Such findings can be very helpful for making decisions about managing a library. For example, a library manager may want to increase the frequency in which women and older adults search an OPAC by reaching out to them and providing more training classes. Or, after realizing that only 40 percent of users find all that they want, a manager can create a new goal for the library—e.g., raise this figure to 60 percent.

Some data, however, are only indications that improvements can be made, but they cannot by themselves show how improvement could be accomplished. For example, a manager may realize that users have difficulties with finding the correct subject term, but the results of the questionnaire cannot provide a suggestion for a solution. Other, more in-depth, methods will be needed for that.

Examples of Studies that Used Interviews

The CLR studies used interviews with groups as well as with individuals. For example, the focus-group interviews revealed the problems users had with OPACs and their databases, what advantages they found, and suggestions for improvements. The following are examples of results relating to existing systems:

1. Problems:
• Terminals were not always available
• Periods of downtime and slow response time
• Commands difficult to use
• Equipment was not useful

2. Advantages:
• Sophisticated search capabilities
• Time saver
• Printout was available, no need to take notes
• Circulation information

3. Improvements:
- New services, such as community bulletin boards, information about the institution
- Enhancement of commands
- New features
- Access at home or locations other than the library

Some examples of results relating to databases are:

1. Problems:
- Difficulties in finding the right subject heading
- Ambiguous codes and abbreviations
- Coverage not current
- Indexing and database not accurate

2. Improvements:
- Useful subject headings and subject headings display
- Shelflist-related displays
- Name and subject cross references
- Holdings information

These and other results were useful in interpreting the findings from the questionnaires. For example, by finding out what users perceived the advantages of the existing systems to be, researchers understood why the attitude of OPAC users was favorable toward the OPAC. Similarly they discovered why users were not satisfied when they examined the nature of the problems users said they had with searching systems and databases.

Examples of Studies that Used Transaction Log Analysis

The use of computer-based systems for information seeking and searching provided another advantage to researchers: users can be monitored without affecting their searching behavior. Because the computer can log every transaction, we can record various pieces of data, such as what terms a user entered, how much time lapsed before another set of terms was entered, how many items were displayed, and which were printed. The CLR studies used analyses of such transaction logs to collect a large variety of data. For example, they collected data about:

- total number of online transactions and/or online search sessions over a given period;
- frequency of commands entered by users;
- average length of an online search session;
- most frequently used access points (author, title, subject, keywords, etc.);

- number of errors by type and number of errors per online search session; and
- average five minutes of catalog activity during a week (number of active terminal, number of logons and logoffs, average response time, etc.).

By themselves, data collected from transaction logs can be essential to support administrative decisions. They can identify the busy and slow hours in the library, the most frequently used features of the systems, and the type of errors made. But in combination with findings arrived at by other methods, the data so collected can help to create a more complete picture of seeking and searching behavior.

For example, transaction log analysis revealed that many users retrieve nothing. It is estimated that currently, on average, 30 percent of the searches in a catalog retrieve zero hits. Obviously, this shows that online catalogs require improvements. But how do you help users avoid zero hits?

If transaction log analysis showed that many errors were spelling errors, a spell checker can be installed to correct such errors. Or, if users frequently entered an author name as a direct entry, rather than inverted, a program should be written to change the order of names in an author search after a zero hit.

Such improvements may eliminate some of the zero hits. It is also likely that many zero hits were the result of a problem mentioned in the focus-group interview: users did not know what subject terms to use. To help users here, we can rely on some of the questionnaire's finding. In an academic library, we can assume that most searches are course related, and that they are subject searches. For each course that is taught, then, we can add relevant vocabulary lists to the online catalog. Once a user types in the title of the course for which he or she is looking for information, the machine can display automatically the relevant lists to help the user find new terms.

Examples of Studies Using Observation

The CLR studies did not use observation. In this method, the investigator is physically next to a user observing him or her while seeking and searching for information. In fact, not many studies to date used this method, primarily because it is labor intensive and because it requires in-depth analysis. One of the earliest examples of an observational study was carried out in England by Tom Wilson. He and his colleagues explored how employees in local social services departments seek information. The aim of the project was to discover patterns in information seeking and searching behavior and to design an information system based on these patterns. The three stages of the study are reported in Wilson and Streatfield (1977), Wilson et al. (1979), and Steatfield and Wilson (1982).

Wilson and his colleagues were interested in information-seeking behavior as part of the communication process in the organization—i.e., for the first time, information seeking was looked upon as a *process*, rather than just a collection of facts.

To explore this behavior, project members spent an entire work week with selected employees of the department. Each project member was assigned to one person and followed him or her all day long. Project members were present when participants talked on the phone, when they participated in meetings, when they talked with a colleague or with their boss, when they went to visit clients, or when they wrote memoranda. Team members were silent but, whenever a communication occurred, they recorded it as a communication event and reported some information about it.

The study included twenty-two employees in various positions in the department and a total of 6,000 communication events. Methods to analyze the data were developed as the analysis was performed, and the findings provided a rich description of the seeking and searching behavior of several user groups. Some of the general findings were:

- 70 percent of information-transfer encounters took up to five minutes. From that the investigators concluded that the working day was fragmented. Therefore, information products should be designed in such a manner that they could be skimmed in less than five minutes.
- 61 percent of the information-transfer encounters were oral communication, face-to-face or by phone. The researchers suggested, then, that the librarian or information specialist should keep direct contact with users.

The team also found patterns that were typical of users in certain positions in the organization and suggested the kind of information services they require. For example, directors need to keep information on a range of subjects which may change frequently. They require, therefore, a personal and individualized information service. Specialists are another source of information for the rest of the staff. They require, therefore, a well organized research library.

Social workers' main difficulty was discovering who are the experts. They need primarily a directory of official and unofficial experts. Tom Wilson and his colleagues actually designed the information system for the social services department. In their evaluation, they found that the new system was much better than the previous one.

Observation can be carried out in various ways. Annelise Mark Pejtersen, for example, observed reference librarians in public and school libraries when they helped users to find books of fiction. Based on the analysis of the data she collected, she designed a retrieval system for fiction with the graphic interface called BookHouse. Other studies are carried out where the investigator is next to a user while the user looks for information and expresses vocally the thought processes. These are taped and analyzed later.

Observation is a powerful method because it records events as they occur and does not have to rely on the user's perception or memory. In addition, it provides for a comprehensive and in-depth analysis of the situation of the user and the process of seeking and searching as a whole. On the other hand, observation is time consuming, and data analysis is labor intensive.

Examples of Studies that Used a Combination of Instruments

Today, it is accepted that the more instruments one employs in combination, the more reliable and insightful a user study is because each instrument reinforces the others. Nevertheless, most user studies are limited to one method, mostly because of practical considerations. An example of an early study that employed a variety of instruments in combination is the study of information transfer among engineers that was conducted by Tom Allen of MIT in the mid 1970s.

This was a complex study that collected rich information and generated important findings. In particular, Allen was interested in the networks that engineers created to disseminate information. His study coined the concept *information gatekeeper* which describes a person who collects information in order to disseminate it to other people. The research project and its results are reported in the book by Allen (1977).

Allen focused on a certain situation where a number of teams had to solve the same problem. A government agency gave contracts to several companies and asked them to propose a preliminary design of a certain hardware product that met certain specifications. This situation was a great advantage to Allen. Because several teams were each working to solve the *same* problem, he could make a comparison among the teams and find out what was common in their seeking behavior and what was different. In addition, when the teams delivered their proposals to the agency, it ranked the teams by performance. Allen then could compare the teams that performed well with those that performed poorly.

The method Allen used was the "case study" method—that is, a detailed analysis of an individual case. Here, each team was an individual case, and he investigated in great detail the process that led the team to the solution.

To investigate the case, Allen broke down the problem that the engineers were supposed to solve into subproblems. He then collected data for each subproblem. For that he used several instruments:

- **Time allocation forms.** At the end of the day, each engineer indicated on a form how much time was spent on: (1) literature search; (2) consultation with colleagues within the organization; (3) consultation with persons outside the organization; and (4) analytic design.

- **Solution development records.** Engineers provided a weekly estimate of the probability that a certain solution would be chosen by the team for a certain subproblem. Suppose a hypothetical team considered two possible solutions, A and B. The solution development record for the first three weeks might be:

	Week 1	Week 2	Week 3
Solution A	0.8	0.75	0.4
Solution B	0.2	0.25	0.6

This shows that Solution A was leading in the first week because the engineer estimated that there was 0.8 probability that it would be selected. Toward the third week, however, Solution B seemed more probable. With these tables, Allen could follow the development of a solution.

- **Interviews.** *Before* the initiation of the project, engineers described what alternatives they considered for solutions. *During* the project, Allen interviewed them by phone if there was a marked shift in the probabilities to find out what was the cause for the shift. *After* the project was completed, he asked the engineers for the cause of each change in probability and what information source was used to induce the change.

Data analysis involved comparing data from teams and uncovering communication and information networks. The data reinforced the previous finding that most of the sources were person-to-person. Allen also showed that several sources were used in solving the same sub-problem. In addition, he found several differences between the lower and higher performing teams. For example, lower performing teams had the heaviest use of literature at the beginning of the project. Higher performing teams had the heaviest use of literature at a point about one-third into the duration of the project and a short period of heavy use at the end of the project.

Conclusion

Researchers in library and information science have been looking for methods to study information seeking and searching behavior for the last forty years. At the start, there was a belief that some universal patterns could describe how users seek and search for information. The way to uncover these patterns was to study as many variables as possible and to find correlations among them. Once these were established, one can create a huge table with all the relevant variables and show how they relate to one another. Such a table could then be used for the design of information retrieval systems.

Today, very few researchers believe in such detailed universal patterns. While all agree that there are some common attributes among all users, it seems that the relationships between this multitude of variables are too complicated and dynamic to be put into well-structured tables regardless of how large they can be. The current trend is to look at specific groups of users and to identify the patterns of seeking and searching behavior that are typical to each group. This means that each group of users may require its own information system.

To design user-centered information systems, developers must investigate the information-seeking and searching behavior of future users. A natural question here is: What is the best instrument to employ in a user study? The only answer is: It depends.

Each instrument provides a different type of results. Therefore, the desired type of results will determine what instruments to use. For example, a questionnaire will probably be the choice if one needs results that are specific and detailed that lend themselves easily to statistical manipulations. On the other hand, an analysis of a user group on which the developer knows very little would require observation.

I hope that this short overview illustrated, however, that a comprehensive and in-depth study always requires a combination of instruments. For example, when exploring a new group of users, an investigator can carry out observation first to discover what questions to ask in a questionnaire. Interviews can help later on in the interpretation of the questionnaire's findings. Suppose an investigator discovered, through observation, that users copied information from the screen rather than printing it. A series of questions in a questionnaire further investigated how users in general preferred to receive the system's output. Suppose the questionnaire revealed that one portion of users preferred to copy and the other to print, interviews with representatives from each camp might then uncover the reasons for these preferences.

We are just starting to adopt the user-centered approach to the design of information systems. Yet, we have a rich experience and tradition of studies and methods. Even though no one study is perfect, and no one method is the best, each contributes to our knowledge and our ability to design new studies. Once we learn how to understand information seeking and searching behavior, we will be able to design systems according to user needs.

References

Allen, T. J. (1977). *Managing the flow of technology: Technology transfer and dissemination of technological information within the R&D organization.* Cambridge, MA: MIT Press.

Cochrane, P. A., & Markey, K. (1983). Catalog use studies since the introduction of online interactive catalogs: Impact on design for subject access. *Library and Information Science Research, 5*(4), 337-363.

Faibisoff, S., & Ely, D. (1976). Information and information needs. *Information Reports and Bibliographies, 5*(5), 2-16.

Ferguson, D.; Kaske, N. K.; Laurence, G. S.; Matthews, J. R.; & Zich, R. (1982). The CLR public online catalog study: An overview. *Information Technology and Libraries, 1*(2), 84-97.

Lipetz, B.-A. (1970). *User requirements in identifying desired works in a large research library. Final report.* Washington, DC: Office of Education (ED 042-479).

Lipetz, B.-A. (1972). Catalog use in a large research library. *Library Quarterly, 24*(1), 129-139.

Markey, K. (1983). Thus spake the OPAC user. *Information Technology and Libraries, 2*(4), 381-387.

Streatfield, D. R., & Wilson, T. D. (1982). Information innovations in social services departments: A report on Project INISS. *Journal of Documentation, 38*(4), 273-281.

Tagliacozzo, R. (1972). Some relations between queries and search-terms generated by catalog users. *Journal of the American Society for Information Science, 4,* 278-280.

Tolle, J. E.; Sanders, N. P.; & Kaske, N. K. (1983). Determining the required number of online catalog terminals: A research study. *Information Technology and Libraries, 2*(3), 261-265.

Vickery, B. C. (1973). *Information systems.* Hamden, CT: Archon Books.

Wilson, T. D., & Streatfield, D. R. (1977). Information needs in local authority social services departments: An interim report on project INISS. *Journal of Documentation, 33*(4) 277-293.

Wilson, T. D.; Streatfield, D. R.; & Mullings, C. (1979). Information needs in local social services departments: A second report on project INISS. *Journal of Documentation, 35*(2), 120-136.

Subject Access in Interdisciplinary Research

✦ Linda C. Smith ✦

Introduction

In a series of lectures presented in 1970, Pauline Cochrane offered an American view of Ranganathan's five laws of library science (Atherton, 1973). According to Cochrane, Ranganathan first conceived of the five laws in 1924. They include: (1) books are for use; (2) every reader his book; (3) every book its reader; (4) save the time of the reader; and (5) a library is a growing organism. With respect to law 4, Cochrane cited the need for more research to understand the match between a user's information needs and the descriptions of information resources. In constructing the catalog and other search tools, do we save the time of the reader? Success in this effort requires knowing more about the reader's information needs and search behavior. Cochrane (1992) revisited the laws two decades later, recommending that they serve as guidelines and criteria for assessing the value of information technology in library and information services. In particular she suggested the need to determine whether information technology improves the timeliness, precision, and comprehensiveness of information provision to users.

This article focuses on how information technology may enable us better to meet the needs of a particular category of information users—those undertaking interdisciplinary research. In a study completed twenty-five years ago, this author investigated the feasibility of developing a mapping of portions of controlled vocabularies as a tool for assisting in cross-database searching (Smith, 1974). At the time, machine-readable databases were in their infancy and corresponded to indexing and abstracting services that were organized largely along traditional disciplinary lines. The purpose of mapping was to allow the researcher to identify correspondences among indexing vocabularies and to make the appropriate translations from one vocabulary to another in seeking to widen the search to locate additional relevant documents. The documents themselves were in print form and needed to be tracked down in library collections once identified through the search of document surrogates in databases or printed indexes.

In 1999 the "information landscape" in which such a researcher undertakes a literature search has changed dramatically due to developments in information technology and electronic publishing. While much of possible interest is accessible from a desktop computer connected to the Internet, the task of threading one's way to items of interest remains quite complex. One must determine where to search, in what sequence, how to formulate an appropriate strategy in each source, and when to stop. Following the emphasis on user orientation in system design shared by Cochrane and Ranganathan, this article begins by characterizing the challenges confronting the interdisciplinary researcher. This is followed by a review of approaches to enhancing subject access in support of interdisciplinary research. Finally, the article concludes with suggestions for future research as we imagine possibilities for subject access in the twenty-first century.

Interdisciplinarity

The simple desire to do interdisciplinary research does nothing to increase one's capacity to utilize information or to lessen the burden of overload (Wilson, 1996, pp. 200-01). Julie Thompson Klein (1996) notes that the perception that knowledge is increasingly interdisciplinary derives in part from the "daily cross-fertilizations of borrowing tools and instruments, methods and techniques, data and information, concepts and theories" (p. 139). Many research problems "fall between the cracks of established disciplines" (p. 140). Klein (1990) provides the first comprehensive study of the concept of interdisciplinarity, synthesizing a wide range of literature regarding interdisciplinary research, education, and practice. She asserts that "there is a subtle restructuring of knowledge in the late twentieth century. New divisions of intellectual labor, collaborative research, team teaching, hybrid fields, comparative studies, increased borrowing across disciplines, and a variety of 'unified,' 'holistic' perspectives have created pressures upon traditional divisions of knowledge" (p. 11). Her characterization of "interdisciplinary individuals" is of particular interest: "They need to know what information to ask for and how to acquire a working knowledge of the language, concepts, information, and analytical skills pertinent to a given problem, process, or phenomenon" (p. 183).

At present, research on information use and information-seeking behavior in interdisciplinary fields is "sparse to nonexistent" (Bates, 1996, p. 156). Scholars in interdisciplinary fields may have to engage in substantially more searching—and of a different kind—than do scholars in a conventional discipline. Palmer's (1996) study of participants in selected interdisciplinary research groups begins to identify the particular problems faced by such researchers: "The sheer magnitude of potentially relevant material seems insurmountable. Literature dispersion is the other distinctive problem experienced by these researchers" (p. 173).

Weisgerber (1993) reports the problems faced by interdisciplinary searchers based on a study undertaken by the International Council for Scientific and Technical Information (ICSTI) Group on Interdisciplinary Searching. They sought to identify, describe, and propose solutions to the principal problems experienced by searchers of multiple bibliographic databases seeking citations to documents that will provide answers to questions of a multidisciplinary nature. They concluded that "access to documents through subject-index terms generated automatically or manually by different database producers presents the greatest challenge in interdisciplinary searching" primarily because of: (1) different missions and the corresponding depth of indexing and its level of specificity in databases covering, to a different degree of detail, various disciplines and subdisciplines; (2) lack of commonly accepted and standardized nomenclature and terminology; and (3) inconsistent use of controlled versus uncontrolled vocabulary in all subject areas compounded by the use of nonstandardized abbreviations, acronyms, and homographs, and by occasional policy changes occurring in individual databases over time (p. 241).

Two possible solutions to this incompatibility—relying on free-text searching (looking for matches with the search terms anywhere in a record) or imposing standards by adopting a single controlled vocabulary—are only partial solutions. Free-text searching does not take full advantage of the knowledge embodied in indexing and also requires users to think of synonyms. Standards do not allow for the diverse needs of users. Alternative approaches, such as creating integrated vocabularies, enhance the possibilities that formerly disconnected information sources will be used in concert, especially to explore interdisciplinary topics. The searcher needs to find ways to take best advantage of all three commonly available subject-searching methods—thesauri, classification schemes, and free-text search—but tools and techniques must be developed to aid in this process.

Enhancing Subject Access

Digital libraries . . . are truly enormous, with records numbering in the millions. They combine formerly distinct intellectual domains into a giant sea of bytes, and place the burden of search and discovery squarely on the user. (Huwe, 1999, p. 68)

In searching "digital libraries" (whether the contents of commercial databases, multiple library catalogs, or the Web), the interdisciplinary researcher confronts two related problems: the scatter of potentially relevant information and the risk of information overload in extending a search across multiple sources without tools that aid in locating items likely to be of particular interest. The successful transition from searching in a single database to searching a multiplicity of networked databases depends on increased understanding of how concepts and terminology relate across user groups and information sources.

Mapping Vocabularies

For cross-database searching, it is necessary to create some device, such as a mapping between controlled vocabularies, to allow translation of a search statement from its initial formulation in one vocabulary to an equivalent statement in other vocabularies. Building such a device may require both manual and automatic approaches to finding correspondences between terms representing concepts. Indexing languages can be thought of in terms of morphology (forms of individual words), syntax (combination of words to form multiword terms), and semantics. Morphological variations in word form which do not alter the meaning of a term for the purposes of information retrieval include singular/plural, spelling variants, abbreviations and acronyms, or differing parts of speech. Syntactic variations include the sequence of terms in multiword headings and coordination of main heading/subheading combinations. At the semantic level, mapping cannot be done automatically because interpretation of the meaning of terms is required. It is necessary to distinguish homographs in order to avoid false retrievals and to link synonyms in order to avoid missing relevant documents. In addition, links can reflect relations between terms such as generic-specific and whole-part. There is a further challenge in maintaining the accuracy and completeness of such a mapping, as controlled vocabularies are not static.

Incompatible indexing languages present a barrier to investigation of interdisciplinary topics across multiple sources. To characterize the extent of compatibility between two indexing languages, it must be recognized that compatibility is a multifaceted concept, including structural compatibility and semantic compatibility (Smith, 1992). Aspects of structural compatibility include morphology and syntax. Semantic compatibility relates to the body of knowledge that can be represented—the range of concepts encompassed (or classes created) and the hierarchical and nonhierarchical relationships displayed among them. The ease with which one indexing language can be matched to another depends on several factors: extent of overlap in subject matter, specificity, degree of coordination of terms, and the extent to which the languages specify relationships among terms. Once a mapping has been developed, it can be used to inform the user of a particular indexing language of corresponding terms that can be used in searching other sources employing different indexing languages.

Lancaster (1988) provides a classification of several approaches to achieving compatibility. They include: (1) intermediate lexicon or switching language—mappings are created between each indexing language and an intermediate lexicon (in order to accomplish the translation from one indexing language to another, terms are first mapped to the intermediate lexicon and then linked to the corresponding terms in one or more other indexing languages); (2) integrated vocabulary—terms are drawn from all participating indexing languages and correspondences identified, creating a conversion table or concordance among indexing languages; (3) microthesaurus—a specialized subset of terms is extracted from, and is therefore compatible with, a larger thesaurus; and (4) macrovocabulary—a superstructure is built to encompass existing indexing languages. Development of such cross-vocabulary tools—associating terms from one domain vocabulary with terms from another domain vocabulary—requires considerable effort. But such tools likely save the time of the searcher and lead to greater success in identifying which sources may yield information of interest and what terms to use in order to extract it. In addition to these mappings between controlled vocabularies, there is a need for an "entry vocabulary" function to map terms from natural language queries onto database controlled vocabularies.

The basic design of controlled vocabularies such as thesauri to date has been as indexing aids with the expectation that searchers would also be able to use them as a guide to searching. However, database producers frequently do not mount their thesauri on search systems. Even if the thesaurus is mounted, the search system may not support the full range of navigational information. Permitting the searcher to switch seamlessly between navigating the thesaurus and searching the database can allow the searcher to use relationships among terms in the thesaurus as a means of expanding the search. Rather than simply making the thesaurus used in indexing available online, it may be necessary to develop tools better suited to support searching. Such an end-user thesaurus differs from a conventional thesaurus in two primary ways: (1) its term inclusion and organization, and (2) its displays (Milstead, 1998, p. 33). It is designed to reflect and organize the total specialized vocabulary of users in a field rather than to provide a limited list of authorized terms. It provides more information about the scope of terms, and its displays are designed around the way in which users approach information.

Available Tools

Some progress has been made in developing tools that may be helpful to the interdisciplinary scholar. These may be developed automatically from database records in machine-readable form, or they may require substantial intellectual effort on the part of human compilers.

Examples of tools built automatically include DIALINDEX and the links displayed by Web of Science. DIALINDEX (Chadwick, 1991) merges the index terms from databases available online through the DIALOG search system. A search of DIALINDEX for a term yields a list of databases containing the term and its frequency of occurrence in each. Because such a search simply does literal term matching and takes no account of either homographs or synonyms, the frequency counts are only rough measures of which databases provide the best coverage of a particular topic. But such a listing can make the searcher aware of databases with relevant material that otherwise might be overlooked.

Web of Science provides a different approach to the literature for the interdisciplinary searcher (Wiley, 1998). It offers new navigational possibilities based on the citation indexing in *Science Citation Index, Social Sciences Citation Index,* and *Arts & Humanities Citation Index.* Following links through citations instead of through subject terms can be particularly valuable because the same theme or issue is often discussed in a different vocabulary from one field to another. In her studies of interdisciplinary researchers, Palmer (1996) has documented the value of "footnote chasing" as a means of identifying pertinent material in peripheral bodies of literature. Web of Science allows the searcher to locate articles that have cited a known relevant article or author as well as locating related articles based on overlap in sources cited. Web of Science takes full advantage of the hypertext capabilities of the Web to allow a searcher to navigate such relationships either within the multidisciplinary scope of a single citation index or across all three indexes.

Many online catalogs have two or more subject indexing vocabularies with overlapping scope. To aid the searcher of such catalogs, mappings have been developed. Olson and Strawn (1997) have created a mapping between Library of Congress Subject Headings and Medical Subject Headings that can be used to generate displays in online catalogs that link these corresponding headings. Chaplan (1995) offers an interesting analysis based on the creation of a mapping between Laborline Thesaurus terms and Library of Congress Subject Headings. Terms were mapped manually, coding each pair for the nature of the match. She estimated that a maximum of 61 percent of the matches could have been found automatically using currently proposed or available strategies. She argues that manual mapping, while labor-intensive, is needed to capture fully the correspondences between vocabularies.

Perhaps the most ambitious mapping project is the Unified Medical Language System (UMLS) Metathesaurus, conceived as a means of navigating among a disparate array of databases organized using different terminologies (Squires, 1993). Sponsored by the National Library of Medicine (NLM), the UMLS Metathesaurus is a synthesis of existing biomedical naming systems, mapping together concepts and terms from important biomedical vocabularies and classifications. Integrating the thesauri maps them to one another thereby creating pointers from every concept in the separate thesauri to the most appropriate equivalent concept in the others. Integration also merges the thesauri thereby creating a more comprehensive knowledge base with a deep level of synonymy. This addresses the UMLS goal of providing an adequate knowledge base for interpreting natural language user queries and linking those queries with appropriate databases. The first Metathesaurus contained 28,816 reviewed concepts from seven sources. The present version incorporates terms from approximately fifty biomedical vocabularies and classifications. The Metathesaurus is organized by concept or meaning. Alternate names for the same concept (synonyms, lexical variants, and translations) are linked together; a number of relationships among different concepts are represented. The 1999 version has 626,893 biomedical concepts with 1,358,891 different concept names. UMLS depends on extensive and intensive human expertise in establishing the links among terms in the various vocabularies (more information about UMLS can be found at the NLM Web site, http://www.nlm.nih.gov/pubs/factsheets/umlskss.html).

The Getty Vocabulary Program has created three resources useful for searching in the arts (see http://www.getty.edu/gri/vocabularies/index.htm): the Art & Architecture Thesaurus (AAT), the Union List of Artist Names (ULAN), and the Getty Thesaurus of Geographic Names (TGN). The AAT is a controlled vocabulary for describing and retrieving information on fine art, architecture, decorative art, and material culture. The ULAN is a database of biographical and bibliographical information on artists and architects, including a wealth of variant names, pseudonyms, and language variants. The TGN contains records for places, including vernacular and historical names. While initially conceived as indexing tools, the Getty vocabularies were not designed specifically to support a particular operating index. Instead they were designed to coordinate or map variant indexing practices across resources (Busch, 1998). The vocabularies provide a clustering of variant or synonymous term or name forms, roles associated with the term, as well as a mapping of the term forms in precoordinated phrases and strings as found or used in a variety of sources. The vocabularies also provide hierarchic (parent-child) and associative (related term/historical) relationships.

On the Internet, one tool to aid searching across multiple resources is a subject gateway (also known as subject-based information gateways, subject index gateways, clearinghouses, subject trees, pathfinders). A gateway is some facility that supports easier access to descriptions and links to network-based resources in a defined subject area (Kirriemuir et al., 1998).

The simplest types of subject gateways are sets of Web pages containing lists of links to resources. Some gateways index their lists of links and provide a simple search facility. More advanced gateways offer a much enhanced service via a system consisting of a resource database and various indexes, which can be searched and/or browsed through a Web-based interface. Each entry in the database contains information about a network-based resource, such as a Web page, Web site, mailing list, or document. Entries are usually created by a cataloger manually identifying a suitable resource, describing the resource using a template, and submitting the template to the database for indexing. The key difference between subject gateways and the popular automated large-scale Web indexing systems, such as AltaVista, is the quality of the results that the end-user receives. This is dependent on the nature of the cataloging process. For interdisciplinary resource discovery, some mechanism must execute a single cross-search of several subject gateways creating a cumulative listing of the results.

Searching

Piternick (1990) suggests that the major trends in vocabulary development at the present time focus on two main areas: the linking of uncontrolled vocabularies (including a searcher's entry terms) with controlled vocabularies to enhance search results, and the linking of vocabularies used by, or appearing in, different databases to facilitate multidatabase searching. Tools to assist in the latter task were described earlier. Buckland (1999) notes that multiple vocabularies are simultaneously present when queries are processed. Even in the most primitive case, with unedited texts searched with unedited queries, there are at least two vocabularies: (1) the vocabulary of the author(s) of the documents searched; and (2) the vocabulary of the searcher. In operational systems, the number of vocabularies is likely to be much larger. An online library catalog would ordinarily include an additional three: (3) the vocabulary of the cataloger, used in creating representations of the documents; (4) "see," "see also," and other syndetic structures that supplement the cataloger's vocabulary; and (5) the vocabulary of the searcher as formulated as a search query. Because there is a multiplicity of vocabularies, there is always a possibility of mismatch. Buckland et al. (1999) note that the number of vocabularies that are accessible but unfamiliar to an individual searcher is increasing steeply. The challenge is to provide automatically the kind of expert prompting that a knowledgeable human search intermediary would provide. They call this type of search aid an Entry Vocabulary Module. This is a set of associations between the lexical items found in the titles, authors, and/or abstracts and the metadata vocabulary (i.e., the category codes, classification numbers, or thesaural terms assigned) based on a measure of association. This dictionary is used to predict which of the metadata terms best represent the topic expressed by the searcher's terms.

Jacsó (1997) contrasts two major approaches to processing searchers' natural language requests. One is to take the request, apply stemming and logical operators between terms, search text fields, and present the results in decreasing rank order determined by various ranking algorithms. The other approach is to offer controlled vocabulary descriptors for the searchers based on the analysis of the question. They can then proceed with the search using the recommended descriptors. He evaluated the implementation of the latter approach by Ovid's Web Gateway and SilverPlatter's WebSPIRS. The study compared direct mapping (checking if the searcher's term is a valid thesaurus term) with derivative mapping (creating a search command from the searcher's question and retrieving records from which subject headings are extracted, ranked, and presented to the searcher). In either case, it is easier for the searcher to recognize pertinent terms than to predict them. Such approaches can combine linguistic analysis (noun phrase extraction) with statistical methods to help searchers. In principle, it would be possible to use the results of such a mapping to allow the system to translate the search query into controlled vocabulary and then to proceed with the search without intervention. In practice, review by the searcher is desirable because not all terms identified in this way are necessarily applicable to the searcher's specific query.

Milstead (1999) provides a helpful review of the efforts of database vendors to assist in cross-file searching. She notes that even different databases from the same producer may each have their own indexing vocabularies developed over a period of many years. She reports on a survey of database producers, search services, and aggregators of full text to determine how each uses vocabulary management to make cross-file searching easier. In various combinations, vendors offer databases produced in-house and licensed from others, aggregated and separately, and via a variety of routes, including third-party search services, proprietary CD-ROMs, or Web sites. More and more they also offer access to a selection of relevant Web sites, which they may index using the organization's regular subject vocabulary. As one example, she cites SilverPlatter Information's Knowledge Cite Library (KCL) (http://www.silverplatter.com/KC/kcintro10_99.html) in which the thesauri from seven database producers have been merged, and the terms have been categorized to permit searching either within a database or across databases. Users can search or browse the thesauri, both merged and singly. A search of a word or a term in the thesauri returns not just terms containing the word but related or approximate terms in other thesauri listed in relevance-ranked order. "See also" references provide hyperlinks between thesauri. Based on a preliminary evaluation, Jacsó (1999) concludes that the mapping of user terms into the controlled vocabulary of various thesauri by KCL is very effective. In summary, Milstead (1999) notes that vendors' use of vocabulary management to facilitate cross-file searching varies from no application, to provision of consolidated thesauri with extensive mapping, all the way to rigorous application of a single vocabulary to the majority of files offered, or even to all files. She concludes that "most vendors seem to recognize the importance of making the boundaries between databases more seamless " (p. 55). Powerful vocabulary tools embedded in a good interface can provide helpful aids to users who know little or nothing about sophisticated searching techniques or complex database structures. At the most basic level, a tool can recognize singulars and plurals or different forms of words. At a more advanced stage, equivalent, broader, narrower, and related terms can appear on screen to suggest additional or different search strategies to users.

Huwe (1999) reviews selected systems that offer global finding aids that make an entire digital collection more accessible without sacrificing the native metadata and thesauri of each individual resource. One system discussed is Northern Light (http://www.northernlight.com), which covers both Web resources and special collections. It is a good example of how structured database families can be paired with the less-organized (but useful) universe of Internet resources. Northern Light sorts its search results into folders based on keywords, sources, and other criteria (Notess, 1998) created dynamically from the search results.

Future Research

Such a holistic view of information retrieval, with no system seen as independent and no database seen in only one version, is very complex (Cochrane, 1981, p. 34).

Information Landscapes

"How will we create network communities and places? Our current landscapes are shallow simple pages of links or cumbersome, non-communicating systems. How to create complete service environments, which are rich in functionality, which mesh with user behaviour and aspirations, and which work across sectors and domains is a challenge" (Dempsey, 1999, p. 3).

Although some progress has been made in developing tools and search techniques that can aid the interdisciplinary researcher in the quest for information of interest, additional research must be undertaken in order to achieve "a holistic view of information retrieval" with "complete service environments." Research must focus on users, systems, and the interface between them. Currently the user of commercial databases is confronted with multiple databases and multiple search systems with varying vocabularies, indexing rules, and access techniques. Likewise, the Web contains a diverse range of scientific material, including Web pages for individuals, projects, universities, and companies; preprints, technical reports, conference and journal papers; teaching resources; and databases (e.g., genetic sequence, molecular structures, image libraries). Just as studies in the 1970s (e.g., National Federation of Abstracting and Indexing Services, 1977) demonstrated both the overlap and unique coverage among different abstracting and indexing services, recent studies by Lawrence and Giles (1999) show that search engines are increasingly falling behind in their efforts to index the Web. Because the overlap among the engines remains relatively low, combining the results of multiple engines greatly improves coverage of the Web during searches. Nevertheless, the functionality of the Internet must be boosted beyond providing mere access to one that supports truly effective searches (Schatz & Chen, 1999). Collections of all kinds must be indexed, from small communities to large disciplines, from formal to informal communications, from text to image and video repositories, and eventually across languages and cultures. Research and development must ensure that the underlying vocabulary management structures and their user interfaces keep pace so that searches give good quality results from the vast amount of material that is available.

Users

As noted earlier, too little is known about information seeking by interdisciplinary researchers. Bates (1996) suggests that scholars and students in interdisciplinary fields "constitute a significant and distinctive class of scholars, much deserving of research on their information needs and information-seeking behavior" (p. 163). Hurd (1992) concurs, observing that while there exists a large body of literature dealing with various aspects of interdisciplinarity, little of that material addresses the nature of problems faced by information seekers whose needs cross the boundaries of traditional disciplines. In particular, we must avoid the temptation to think of vocabulary only as character strings to be manipulated, recognizing that "the meanings of words are constructed subjectively and situationally and the use of vocabulary is social" (Buckland, 1999).

Systems

New approaches are needed in both human-constructed tools for indexing—such as classification schedules and thesauri—as well as in the use of automatic techniques. Beghtol (1998) observes that theoretical perspectives are needed to reorient classification research toward the pluralistic needs of multidisciplinary knowledge creation, electronic dissemination, and extended user groups. Williamson (1998) notes that the challenge for classification systems is not only to serve as a basis for arranging books on shelves and records in files but also to perform a new role in the organization of retrieval from computerized databases and information systems. Thought must also be given to new designs for thesauri. Nielsen (1998) indicates that despite the need for thesauri to serve as guides to the best search terms, the design of thesauri has remained more or less stable. The help that traditional thesauri provide by showing equivalent, hierarchical, and associated relations is valuable. However, the usefulness increases if the thesaurus conceptualizes the specific context of the work domain.

Another type of incompatibility, from the perspective of users, is the problem of accessing databases in languages other than their native language. Multilingual thesauri can support automatic translation of terms from one language to another. In the area of multilingual access, there is a need to follow work in machine translation and machine-aided translation and the potential for its application in facilitating information system use in a variety of natural languages. Hudon (1997) outlines the challenges of integrating the views of different cultures in one gateway to knowledge and concepts via multilingual thesauri.

Given the growing number of systems implementing approaches to aid in vocabulary switching, there is a need to evaluate their effectiveness, particularly from the perspective of the interdisciplinary researcher. Such tools are designed to help users achieve the sometimes conflicting goals of greater precision (by relying on the human judgments represented by the assignment of indexing terms and classification codes) and greater comprehensiveness (by extending a search across multiple resources to encompass different points of view and complementary literatures on a subject).

Interfaces

There is increasing interest in the use of information visualization to enhance navigational support. Card and colleagues (1999) define information visualization as "the set of technologies that use visual computing to amplify human cognition" (p. 640). One possible application is for searching and browsing digital libraries. The apparent attractiveness of visualization and navigation as subject access mechanisms creates a need for considerable research into the usability of systems based on this technology. Visualization is one aspect of interface design. Research and development in information seeking and interface design should develop in parallel as technological developments create new possibilities (Marchionini & Komlodi, 1998).

Those concerned with design of enhancements in information retrieval systems often cite the vision of Vannevar Bush. In his essay "Memex Revisited" (Bush, 1967), he asserted that "a revolution must be wrought in the ways in which we make, store, and consult the record of accomplishment" (p. 75). He suggested that "compact storage of desired material and swift selective access to it are the two basic elements of the problem." As suggested in this paper, the growing emphasis on interdisciplinary research has affected the way in which researchers "make...the record of accomplishment." Greater attention to subject indexing and access in support of interdisciplinary research will in turn affect how we "store and consult" this record.

References

Atherton, P. A. (1973). *Putting knowledge to work: An American view of Ranganathan's five laws of library science.* Delhi, India: Vikas Publishing House.

Bates, M. J. (1996). Learning about the information seeking of interdisciplinary scholars and students. *Library Trends, 45*(2), 155-164.

Beghtol, C. (1998). Knowledge domains: Multidisciplinarity and bibliographic classification systems. *Knowledge Organization, 25*(1/2), 1-12.

Buckland, M. (1999). *Vocabulary as a central concept in library and information science* (Paper for the 3rd International Conference on Conceptions of Library and Information Science [COLIS3], Dubrovnik, Croatia, 23-26 May 1999). Retrieved July 28, 1999 from the World Wide Web: http://www.sims.berkeley.edu/~buckland/colisvoc.htm.

Buckland, M.; Chen, A.; Chen, H.-M.; Kim, Y.; Lam, B.; Larson, R.; Norgard, B.; & Purat, J. (1999). Mapping entry vocabulary to unfamiliar metadata vocabularies. *D-Lib Magazine, 5*(1). Retrieved July 28, 1999 from the World Wide Web: http://www.dlib.org/dlib/january99/buckland/01buckland.html.

Busch, J. A. (1998). Building and accessing vocabulary resources for networked resource discovery and navigation. In P. A. Cochrane & E. H. Johnson (Eds.), *Visualizing subject access for 21st century information resources* (Proceedings of the 34th Annual Clinic on Library Applications of Data Processing, March 2-4, 1997, University of Illinois at Urbana-Champaign) (pp. 148-156). Urbana-Champaign: University of Illinois, Graduate School of Library and Information Science.

Bush, V. (1967). Memex revisited. In V. Bush (Ed.), *Science is not enough* (pp. 75-101). New York: William Morrow.

Card, S. K.; Mackinlay, J. D.; & Shneiderman, B. (1999). *Readings in information visualization: Using vision to think.* San Francisco: Morgan Kaufmann.

Chadwick, T. B. (1991). DIALOG's enhanced DIALINDEX. *Online, 15*(1), 22-26.

Chaplan, M. A. (1995). Mapping Laborline Thesaurus terms to Library of Congress Subject Headings: Implications for vocabulary switching. *Library Quarterly, 65*(1), 39-61.

Cochrane, P. A. (1981). Improving the quality of information retrieval online to a library catalog or other access service...or...where do we go from here? *Online, 5*(3), 30-42.

Cochrane, P. A. (1992). Information technology in libraries and Ranganathan's five laws of library science. *Libri, 42*(3), 235-241.

Dempsey, L. (1999). From files to landscapes: Network information management at UKOLN. *Journal of Documentation, 55*(1), 1-5.

Hudon, M. (1997). Multilingual thesaurus construction: Integrating the views of different cultures in one gateway to knowledge and concepts. *Knowledge Organization, 24*(2), 84-91.

Hurd, J. M. (1992). The future of university science and technology libraries: Implications of increasing interdisciplinarity. *Science & Technology Libraries, 13*(4), 17-32.

Huwe, T. K. (1999). New search tools for multidisciplinary digital libraries. *Online, 23*(2), 67-74.

Jacsó, P. (1997). Mapping algorithms to translate natural language questions into search queries for Web databases. In M. E. Williams (Ed.), *Proceedings of the 18th National Online Meeting* (pp. 189-199). Medford, NJ: Information Today.

Jacsó, P. (1999). Cross-database searching on the Web with term mapping from multiple thesauri. In M. E. Williams (Ed.), *Proceedings of the 20th National Online Meeting* (pp. 217-225). Medford, NJ: Information Today.

Kirriemuir, J.; Brickley, D.; Welsh, S.; Knight, J.; & Hamilton, M. (1998). Cross-searching subject gateways: The query routing and forward knowledge approach. *D-Lib Magazine, 4*(1). Retrieved July 28, 1999 from the World Wide Web: http://www.dlib.org/dlib/january98/01kirriemuir.html.

Klein, J. T. (1990). *Interdisciplinarity: History, theory, & practice.* Detroit, MI: Wayne State University Press.

Klein, J. T. (1996). Interdisciplinary needs: The current context. *Library Trends, 45*(2), 134-154.

Lancaster, F. W. (1988). *Vocabulary control for information retrieval,* 2ᵈ ed. Arlington, VA: Information Resources Press.

Lawrence, S., & Giles, C. L. (1999). Accessibility of information on the Web. *Nature, 400,* 107-109.

Marchionini, G., & Komlodi, A. (1998). Design of interfaces for information seeking. *Annual Review of Information Science and Technology, 33,* 89-130.

Milstead, J. L. (1998). Thesauri in a full-text world. In P. A. Cochrane & E. H. Johnson (Eds.), *Visualizing subject access for 21ˢᵗ century information resources* (Proceedings of the 34th Annual Clinic on Library Applications of Data Processing, March 2-4, 1997, University of Illinois at Urbana-Champaign) (pp. 28-38). Urbana-Champaign: University of Illinois, Graduate School of Library and Information Science.

Milstead, J. L. (1999). Cross-file searching: How vendors help—and don't help—improve compatibility. *Searcher, 7*(5), 44-55.

National Federation of Abstracting and Indexing Services. (1977). *A study of coverage overlap among fourteen major science and technology abstracting and indexing services.* Philadelphia: NFAIS.

Nielsen, M. L. (1998). Future thesauri: What kind of conceptual knowledge do searchers need? In *Structures and relations in knowledge organization* (Proceedings of the 5ᵗʰ International ISKO Conference, August 25-29, 1998, Lille, France) (pp. 153-160). Wurzberg, Germany: Ergon Verlag.

Notess, G. (1998). Northern Light: New search engine for the Web and full-text articles. *Database, 21*(1), 32-37.

Olson, T., & Strawn, G. (1997). Mapping the LCSH and MeSH systems. *Information Technology and Libraries, 16*(1), 5-19.

Palmer, C. L. (1996). Information work at the boundaries of science: Linking library services to research practices. *Library Trends, 45*(2), 165-191.

Piternick, A. B. (1990). Vocabularies for online subject searching. *Encyclopedia of Library and Information Science, 45,* 399-420.

Schatz, B., & Chen, H. (1999). Digital libraries: Technological advances and social impacts. *Computer, 32*(2), 45-50.

Smith, L. C. (1974). Systematic searching of abstracts and indexes in interdisciplinary areas. *Journal of the American Society for Information Science, 25,* 343-353.

Smith, L. C. (1992). UNISIST revisited: Compatibility in the context of collaboratories. In N. J. Williamson & M. Hudon (Eds.), *Classification research for knowledge representation and organization* (pp. 337-344). Amsterdam: Elsevier.

Squires, S. J. (1993). Access to biomedical information: The Unified Medical Language System. *Library Trends, 42*(1), 127-151.

Weisgerber, D. W. (1993). Interdisciplinary searching: Problems and suggested remedies. A report from the ICSTI Group on Interdisciplinary Searching. *Journal of Documentation, 49*(3), 231-254.

Wiley, D. L. (1998). Cited references on the Web: A review of ISI's Web of Science. *Searcher, 6*(1), 32-39, 57.

Williamson, N. (1998). An interdisciplinary world and discipline based classification. In *Structures and relations in knowledge organization* (Proceedings of the 5ᵗʰ International ISKO Conference, August 25-29, 1998, Lille, France) (pp. 116-124). Wurzberg, Germany: Ergon Verlag.

Wilson, P. (1996). Interdisciplinary research and information overload. *Library Trends, 45*(2), 192-203.

Web Search Strategies

✦ Karen M. Drabenstott ✦

Introduction

Surfing the World Wide Web used to be cool, dude, real cool. But things have gotten hot—so hot that finding something useful on the Web is no longer cool. It is suffocating Web searchers in the smoke and debris of mountain-sized lists of hits, decisions about which search engines they should use, whether they will get lost in the dizzying maze of a subject directory, use the right syntax for the search engine at hand, enter keywords that are likely to retrieve hits on the topics they have in mind, or enlist a browser that has sufficient functionality to display the most promising hits. When it comes to Web searching, in a few short years we have gone from the cool image of *surfing* the Web into the frying pan of *searching* the Web.

We can turn down the heat by rethinking what Web searchers are doing and introduce some order into the chaos. Web search strategies that are tool-based—oriented to specific Web searching tools such as search engines, subject directories, and meta search engines—have been widely promoted, and these strategies are just not working. It is time to dissect what Web searching tools expect from searchers and adjust our search strategies to these new tools.

This discussion offers Web searchers help in the form of search strategies that are based on strategies that librarians have been using for a long time to search commercial information retrieval systems like Dialog, NEXIS, Wilsonline, FirstSearch, and Data-Star. Librarians won't recognize some of the Web search strategies that this article recommends because they have been radically altered to take into consideration the new functionality that Web search tools feature. Other Web strategies will be familiar to librarians because they resemble the information retrieval (IR) strategies that librarians have been using since the widespread availability of commercial IR systems in the late 1970s. But the recommendations this article makes about Web search strategies aren't just for librarians—they are for the millions of people who search the World Wide Web everyday; want to find useful information quickly and effortlessly; and use it to address their problems, concerns, needs, and desires.

Definitions

Our first task is to define "search strategy." "A search strategy is an overall plan or approach for a search problem" (Harter, 1986, p. 170). The information retrieval and Web searching literatures confuse search strategy and search tactic or search heuristic. A search tactic or heuristic is "a move made to advance a particular strategy" (Harter, 1986, p. 170). A Web search may involve a single strategy but may also involve many heuristics (or tactics) that the searcher enlists to find the desired information. The Web searching literature is fraught with search heuristics—these are the long lists of "search tips" that authors suggest to help Web users conduct their searches (Classroom Connect, 1999; Crowe, 1999; Gossen, 1997; Grossenbrenner & Grossenbrenner, 1999, pp. 34–35; Scoville, 1996; Tyner, 1998;Wu, 1999).

IR Search Strategies

Charles Bourne and his colleagues Jo Robinson and Barbara Anderson were the original developers of the IR search strategies that have become synonymous with searching commercial IR systems. They gave oral presentations of these strategies at workshops and conferences and left the task of documenting their strategies to the IR professionals who attended their workshops and conference presentations (Markey & Atherton, 1978; Buntrock, 1979; Hawkins & Wagers, 1982; Markey & Cochrane, 1982). Perhaps their intent was to foster refinements to or the development of additional strategies by those who documented their original work. If it was, they succeeded because IR professionals who documented the three original strategies—Building Block, Successive Fractions, and Citation Pearl Growing—added to them based on their own knowledge and experience.

When IR search strategies were developed, most databases were bibliographic databases. These databases consisted of bibliographic records that were surrogates for full-length documents. Surrogates almost always included document titles, citations, abstracts, and index terms from a controlled vocabulary. Over the years, citation databases and full-text databases were added to commercial IR systems. Citation databases featured document titles, citations, and the references that authors cited. Full-text databases featured full-length documents—these were usually newspapers or journal articles. When these new types of databases became available on commercial IR systems, such systems didn't change their functionality because online searchers could use the same functionality that they used to search bibliographic databases to search citation and full-text databases. Strategies for searching commercial IR systems also didn't change because the vast majority of searches that online searchers were doing in bibliographic citation and full-text databases were subject searches.

Since the introduction of commercial IR systems, their functionality has been expressed in a complicated terse language that required aspiring online searchers to seek special training to learn the language and daily practice to master it. Searching commercial IR systems cost money and much of the expense depended on the amount of time searchers spent online. Everyday people couldn't search commercial IR systems themselves. They visited a library or information brokerage and contracted a trained intermediary searcher to perform their search for them. Consequently, searching commercial IR systems has been pretty much limited to individuals—i.e., intermediary searchers—who have special training and experience.

Let's take a look at the six subject search strategies for commercial IR systems that have stood the test of time and continue to be taught to beginning online searchers and presented in the latest online searching textbooks (for example, the second edition of *Online Retrieval* by Geraldene Walker and Joseph Janes [1999] includes these strategies).

Building Block Strategy

Commercial IR systems have always relied on Boolean searching. Boolean searching has made it possible for IR systems to respond to searchers with useful retrievals for complex queries—that is, queries that feature more than one major theme. Of all the search strategies that we will examine here, the Building Block Strategy champions knowledge and expertise in Boolean searching. This strategy requires searchers to analyze their queries and identify the major themes or facets in their queries. Walker and Janes (1993) define facet as "an abstract idea of a thing, instance, phenomenon, etc., regardless of what it may be called in a given situation" (p. 38). A facet (e.g., children) usually has more than one recognizable name (e.g., kids, toddlers, youngsters, etc.). In their presearch analysis, online searchers only need to use one name to represent a facet. Eventually, however, searchers need to represent each facet (e.g., teens) as input to the retrieval system and, to do this, they enter several names (e.g., teens, teenagers, adolescents, youth, young adults) to represent the facet (over the years, the terms "facet," "concept," "concept group," "part," "element," and "component" have all been used interchangeably).

When searchers enlist the Building Block Strategy, they develop each facet of the query separately as if it were a subsearch all on its own and then make the final logical assembly of all the subsearches. This strategy is depicted in Figure 1 for the search request "Should teenagers who commit murder be executed?"

The searcher identifies three facets: teens, murder, and capital punishment. Within each facet box, the searcher lists words and phrases to represent each facet. For example, the words and phrases that the searcher uses to represent the "teens" facet are teen, teens, teenager, teenagers, youth, and adolescents. During the search, the searcher combines the words and phrases for each facet using the Boolean OR operator. The searcher's final step is to combine the OR'd results of the three subsearches, in this case, by the Boolean AND operator. The IR system retrieves documents that bear at least one word or phrase from each of the three facets. Presumably such documents will be about imposing capital punishment on teenagers convicted of murder.

Online searching textbooks promote the Building Block Strategy because it makes full use of the searcher's presearch preparation, tends to read like the original query, and provides a clear trace history—i.e., a record of what happened during the online search that is easy to review and understand at a later date (Markey & Atherton, 1978, pp. 17–19; Meadow & Cochrane, 1981, pp. 137–38; Harter, 1986, pp. 172–76; Walker & Janes, 1993, p. 40).

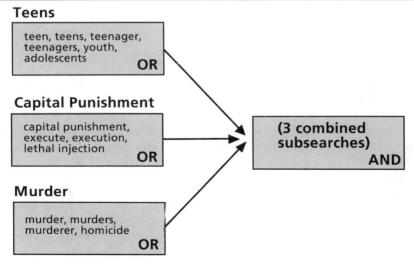

Figure 1. Building block strategy

Most Specific Facet First Strategy

The Most Specific Facet First Strategy is a variation of the Building Block Strategy. It still requires searchers to develop each facet of the query separately as if it were a subsearch all on its own. This development is done prior to the online search. Another task done prior to the online search is the searcher's analysis of the query to determine which facet is the most specific in terms of the database in which she intends to conduct the search. Then the searcher enters the words and phrases for the most specific facet into the retrieval system followed by words and phrases for the second facet and combines the results for the first facet with the second facet. If hits are sufficiently low and on target, then the searcher probably won't impose the remaining conditions to the search. The Most Specific Facet First Strategy is depicted in Figure 2 for the search request "Should teenagers who commit murder be executed?" in a database on criminal justice.

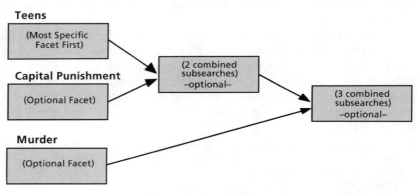

Figure 2. Most specific facet first strategy

The searcher has identified the same three facets: Teens, Murder, and Capital Punishment. Within each facet box, the words and phrases to represent each facet are listed. During the search, the searcher begins with the Teens facet because he hypothesizes before the search that, of the three facets (Teens, Murder, and Capital Punishment), the Teens facet would be the most specific facet for this query in a search of a database on criminal justice. He enters words and phrases representing the Teens facet into the IR system, combines intermediary results using the Boolean OR operator, and evaluates results before entering the second facet. His next step is to enter words and phrases to represent the Capital Punishment facet. He combines intermediary results using the Boolean OR operator and combines results for the Teens and Capital Punishment facets using the Boolean AND operators. He probably doesn't need to enter the third facet (Murder) because the combination of sets for the Teens and Capital Punishment facets reduces results to a manageable number.

Had the searcher conducted this search in a database on education, he probably would have chosen to enter the Capital Punishment facet before the Teens facet because there would have been so much information on teenagers in a database on education. In searches of either criminal justice or education databases, the searcher probably doesn't have to enter a Murder facet because there aren't many offenses except for murder and treason for which capital punishment is imposed and retrieving much material on treasonous teens isn't likely. The searcher does not start the search by combining the Teens and Murder facets because it is hypothesized that much material about teens who have been murdered will be retrieved. So the decisions searchers make about the most specific facet, subsequent facets, and the order of facets are a combination of specificity and logic.

When Charles Bourne and his colleagues originally presented search strategies, they advised searchers to start with the most specific facet first in the Building Block Strategy. The Most Specific Facet First Strategy was a search tactic or heuristic but, through the years, textbooks and manuals have elevated it to search strategy status (Markey & Atherton, 1978, pp. 25–26; Meadow & Cochrane, 1981, p. 136; Harter, 1986, pp. 177–80; Walker & Janes, 1993, p. 40).

Lowest Postings Facet First Strategy

The Lowest Postings Facet First Strategy is also a variation of the Building Block Strategy. It requires searchers to develop each facet of the query separately as if it were a subsearch all on its own and to do this development prior to the online search. Another task done prior to the online search is the searcher's analysis of the query to determine which facet has the fewest postings of all the facets in the query. Some databases publish lists that enumerate postings for words and phrases used in the database so that searchers can consult them prior to the search. Some searchers rely on their extensive searching experience to guess in advance which facet is likely to yield the fewest hits. The lowest posted facet might not be the most important aspect. But, if one facet yields a handful of hits, it is wise to start with this facet because the addition of more facets into the search formulation only reduces the hits further or results in zero hits. The Lowest Postings Facet First Strategy is depicted in Figure 3 for the search request "How effective are squirrels in forest replantation?" in a database on forestry.

The searcher identifies three facets: Squirrels, Seed Dispersal, and Forests. Within each facet box, the searcher lists words and phrases to represent each facet. During the search, the search begins with the Squirrels facet because the searcher didn't find the word "Squirrels" in the database's thesaurus—that is, a list of words and phrases that indexers assign to the

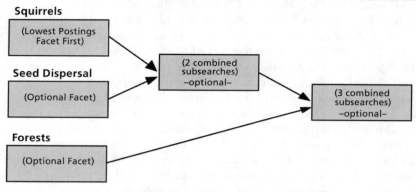

Figure 3. Lowest postings facet first strategy

database's documents to represent their subject contents—and, in fact, when she did find names of animals in the thesaurus, they were assigned to very few documents. In this case, a search for a single facet, Squirrels, might be sufficient, and the searcher can quickly scan titles to determine whether the squirrels are planting the seeds or eating them.

The Most Specific Facet First Strategy started life as a search heuristic, but through the years it has become a full-fledged online searching strategy (Markey & Atherton, 1978, pp. 25–26; Meadow & Cochrane, 1981, pp. 136–37; Harter, 1986, pp. 177–80).

Pairwise Facets Strategy

IR searchers use the Pairwise Facets Strategy to increase their recall in searches for topics that have one or two especially low-posted facets or to produce a high recall search for a query in which all (usually three) facets are roughly equivalent in their precision or specificity of definition (Harter, 1986, p. 180). The Pairwise Facets Strategy is depicted in Figure 4 for the search request "Do flextime work schedules improve the morale of workers in the health-care industry?"

The searcher has identified three facets: Flextime, Employee Morale, and Health-Care Industry. Because of the searcher's knowledge of this topic, he knows that few documents will be retrieved that address all three facets of this query; however, the searcher does think that he will retrieve more than enough documents for two of the three possible pairwise combinations—i.e., Flextime and Health-Care Industry, Employee Morale and Health-care Industry—and relevant documents that will be specific to his interests. The results of the third pairwise combination—i.e., Flextime and Employee Morale—will probably yield too many documents and, surely, documents that are just too broad to be of use because they will address

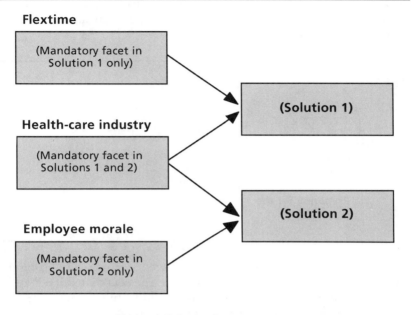

Flextime

(Mandatory facet in
Solution 1 only)

(Solution 1)

Health-care industry

(Mandatory facet in
Solutions 1 and 2)

(Solution 2)

Employee morale

(Mandatory facet in
Solution 2 only)

Figure 4. Pairwise facets strategy

these concepts generally or address them in many industries in addition to
the health-care industry. The searcher's final act is to use the Boolean OR
operator to combine final sets for the two desired pairwise combinations.

Successive Fractions Strategy

The Successive Fractions Strategy is one that Charles Bourne and his
colleagues first introduced and has found its way into online searching
texts and manuals (Markey & Atherton, 1978, pp. 22–25; Meadow &
Cochrane, 1981, pp. 140–41; Harter, 1986, pp. 177–80). Other names for
this strategy—divide and conquer, file partitioning, and big bite—may be
more descriptive of this strategy's overall effect. The searcher makes an
action to take an initial bite of a file and assemble an intermediate set that
satisfies the conditions of the first facet in a multifaceted search. This first
bite may be a sizable portion of the database such as one or more years of
publication, a range of accession numbers, classification number or range,
clearinghouse, document type or availability, or some other characteristic.
When the second facet of a search is applied in a Boolean AND operation to
the partitioned subfile, the result is an even smaller subfile. Remaining
facets could be applied to the subfile using the Boolean AND or NOT
operators until the final subfile reaches a manageable number of hits. The

Successive Fractions Strategy is depicted in Figure 5 for the search request "Has baseball's popularity increased due to the great home run record chase of the 1998 season?"

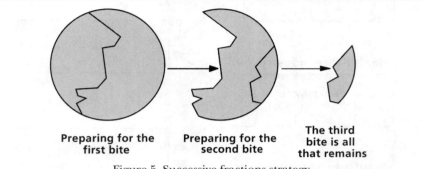

Preparing for the first bite   Preparing for the second bite   The third bite is all that remains

Figure 5. Successive fractions strategy

The searcher has identified four facets: Since Summer 1998, Baseball, Popularity, and Home Run Record Chase. The searcher's first step is to create a set of documents for material written from summer 1998 to the present because the query refers to an event that happened in summer 1998. With intermediate results in hand, the searcher can take a second bite to focus on material that covers Baseball only. Results will probably still include much extraneous material such as the World Series and off-season contract negotiations and trades so the searcher could take a third bite to focus on the Popularity aspect of baseball. A fourth bite representing the Home Run Record Chase might be necessary to produce precise results. The whole idea of the Successive Fractions Strategy is to think increasingly smaller and smaller in terms of the number of retrieved hits and the size of the subfile that the searcher is carving from the original database of hundreds of thousands or millions of items. The searcher stops searching when the subfile reaches a manageable number of hits or achieves a certain level of precision.

Citation Pearl Growing Strategy

The Citation Pearl Growing Strategy, one of the three original strategies that Charles Bourne and his colleagues first introduced, has found its way into online searching texts and manuals (Markey & Atherton, 1978, pp. 19–22; Meadow & Cochrane, 1981, pp. 138–40; Harter, 1986, pp. 183–84; Walker & Janes, 1993, p. 46). The illustration in Figure 6 depicts the dynamic nature of this strategy.

The Citation Pearl Growing Strategy starts with a few documents (pearls) known to be relevant to the information need. Perhaps the searcher

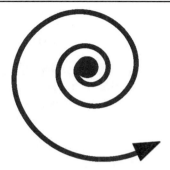

Figure 6. Citation pearl growing strategy

has identified these documents in a previous search or they were the result of a title keyword search in which the titles of retrieved documents matched the specific words in the search query. The searcher reviews retrieved hits and adds their language to the ongoing search to retrieve additional material. After adding such language to the formulation, the searcher again reviews more hits and continues this process in successive iterations until no additional material is found that is appropriate for inclusion.

Let's examine how Citation Pearl Growing can be used in a search for "How safe is the seafood we buy in the supermarket?" The searcher identifies three facets: Seafood, Safety, and Supermarket. He commands the IR system to limit retrieval of these three words to titles of documents so that only the most relevant material is retrieved. He studies words and phrases in retrieved documents, finds terminology that authors use to discuss this topic, and adds the terminology to a second search. For example, he adds words such as "fish" and "shellfish" to the first facet; "tainted," "contaminated," "spoiled," and "cleanliness" to the second facet; and "grocery," "market," and "store" to the third facet. These new search words result in additional useful retrievals which are sufficient for satisfying the search request.

Other Strategies

Through the years, other strategies have been suggested and most resemble one of the six strategies presented here. The Briefsearch resembles a scaled-down Building Blocks Strategy because it requires search words or phrases for each facet of the search request (Markey & Atherton, 1978, p. 11; Harter, 1986, p. 172). The major difference between the two strategies is that the searcher enters a Briefsearch formulation in a single statement. The Building Block Strategy almost always requires the searcher to create and combine several intermediary sets into a final set because the words and phrases for all facets are too numerous to enter in a single formulation.

We described a Briefsearch in the discussion of the Citation Pearl Growing Strategy. It consisted of the three words "seafood," "safety," and "supermarket" that were combined using the Boolean AND operator and restricted to document titles to increase precision.

Citation Indexing Strategies really are specific instances of the Citation Pearl Growing Strategy (Harter, 1986, pp. 185–86). They start with a document in hand that is really relevant. The searcher's next step is to use particular characteristics of this document to find additional ones like it. In the case of the Citation Indexing Strategy for Cited Author, the searcher uses the author's name to find other material she has written because authors typically write on the same subject. In the case of the Citation Indexing Strategy for Cited Works, the searcher queries the database to find other authors who have cited the author of the relevant document in hand because such authors may be writing on the same subject as the author of the original document. Citation Indexing Strategies might have been considered strategies that were separate from Citation Pearl Growing because citation indexing databases contained citation data and bibliographic databases did not, and searchers felt it was necessary to distinguish strategies for citation databases from strategies for bibliographic databases.

Strategies for Searching the World Wide Web

During the early days of the World Wide Web, Web searchers found material on the subjects that interested them using hyperlinks between related documents. This strategy came to be known as "surfing the Web" or serendipity. A few enterprising individuals shared their treasured hyperlinks in lists of "favorite links" on their home pages or became known as trailblazers—"an individual, knowledgeable in a given area who takes on the responsibility of maintaining a Web page focused on that particular area" (Pfaffenberger, 1996, p. 50). Through the years, some trailblazers became affiliated with a subject directory which gathers, publicizes, and indexes the hard work of many other trailblazers. Yet many trailblazers remain lone wolves to the present day. Not long after trailblazers and subject directories came search engines that index sizable portions of World Wide Web content. Some enterprising Web users became so impatient with searching the half-dozen search engines one at a time that they devised meta search engines so they could search Web search engines in one fell swoop and take advantage of the even larger portion of Web content that simultaneous searches of Web search engines made possible.

After hardly a half decade of the World Wide Web's existence, searchers have at their fingertips three basic tools for searching a sizable portion of World Wide Web content or quality Web content: (1) subject directories, (2) search engines, and (3) meta search engines. It should come as no surprise that those who promote strategies for searching the Web recommend using a particular searching tool under certain conditions. We call these Tool-Based Strategies. Other search strategies have been recommended. Pfaffenberger (1996) offers strategies based on the amount of material Web searchers want to retrieve in their searches. Some of the same people who recommend Tool-Based Strategies recommend a Web search strategy that requires searchers to guess URLs. Even some strategies for searching commercial IR systems have been recommended for searching the Web.

This section focuses on Web search strategies. As you read this, remember that, unlike searching commercial IR systems, Web searching is not limited to people with specialized training and experience. Anyone who has access to a computer, network connection, and Web browser can search the World Wide Web. Since search engines process millions of queries on a daily basis, there are many people worldwide searching the Web.

Serendipity (or Surfing Strategy)

World Wide Web searchers have been using the Serendipity (or Surfing) Strategy since the Web began in the early 1990s (Algonquin College of Applied Arts and Technology, 1996). All that searchers have to do is click on hyperlinks in Web pages to find other Web pages. Of course, they have to start their serendipitous voyages at a Web page that features links. Clicking on a Web page's links does not always result in a Web page on the same or related topic as the Web page at hand. In the Web's early days, Web users who took time to compile their own lists of relevant pages on a topic gladly shared such lists with others in the form of "favorite links" on their home pages or they developed trailblazer pages. Although trailblazer pages still populate the Web today, a few Web services now specialize in "starting pages" which are nothing more than lists of interesting links, for example, popular sites that many other Web users visit, cool Web sites, new Web sites, shopping sites, and so on. Such services are comparable to subject directories but, instead of guiding Web searchers to Web sites based on subjects, they use criteria such as popularity or novelty. Serendipity isn't much different from the "New Books" shelves in libraries or the "Staff Favorites" shelves in video stores. The World Wide Web has grown at a phenomenal rate and few now recommend surfing the net because it takes so much time to navigate from link to link, and links often lead Web searchers away from the topics rather than deeper into the topics that interest them.

Tool-Based Web Search Strategies

Tool-B ased Web search strategies encourage searchers to choose among the three major search tools—subject directories, search engines, and meta search engines—based on particular characteristics of their search requests or their overall search objectives. When Web searchers have broad subjects in mind, they are advised to consult subject directories, and when they need information on specific subjects, they are advised to use search engines (Barlow, 1998; Barrett, 1997, p. 63; Black, 1998; Classroom Connect, 1998; Janes, 1999; Kriesel, 1998; Metz, 1998; Notess, 1997, 1999; Scoville, 1996; Skov, 1998; Snell, 1997; Teaching Learning Center, 1999; Telescope, 1996; Tweney, 1996; Tyner, 1998; Webster & Paul, 1996; Wu, 1999). When Web searchers want exhaustive indexing and comprehensive coverage of Web content, they are advised to use meta search engines (Black, 1998; Notess, 1997, 1999; Teaching Learning Center, 1999).

Use Subject Directories for Broad Topics (or Browsing Strategy)

Subject directories feature menus of broad topics such as "Arts," "Computers," "Education," "Government," and "Recreation." Choosing a broad subject such as "Recreation" leads Web searchers through a series of topic menus that eventually ends at narrow subtopic menus and includes such terms as "Baseball," "Basketball," "Fishing," "Football," "Golf," "Hockey," and "Skiing." Some subject directories feature Web pages on listed topics and subtopics at every level and others feature Web pages for subtopics at lower levels only. Advising Web searchers to consult subject directories for broad subjects is wise because directories serve up a series of subjects that become increasingly narrower in scope instead of requiring searchers to put their queries into words (not all subtopics are narrower terms—some address aspects of the broader terms and others describe the types of Web pages that characterize material on the broader topic). Because subject directories supply menus of broad and narrow topics, they should also be especially helpful when Web searchers don't know much about the topics they seek, aren't sure what they're looking for, or don't know how to put their information needs into words.

Use Search Engines for Specific Subjects (or Pinpointing Strategy)

Search engines allow Web searchers to enter words and phrases that they match against a gigantic index of words occurring in millions of Web pages. They retrieve ranked lists of Web pages based on the occurrences of searchers' words and phrases in indexed Web pages. Since search engines often retrieve tens of thousands, hundreds of thousands, and even millions of Web pages, it is impossible for Web searchers to examine every retrieved Web page. Advising Web searchers to consult search engines for specific subjects is wise because specific subjects shouldn't retrieve unmanageable numbers of hits.

But just what is a specific subject and how should Web searchers enter specific subjects into search engines? The answers to these questions aren't simple because not only do they require Web searchers to understand Boolean searching, they require Web searchers to practice Boolean searching and actually enter their queries into search engines using Boolean operators and the particular search engine's strict syntax and search techniques. Although the basic Boolean operators (i.e., AND, OR, and NOT) are usually the same across search engines, search techniques and syntax almost always vary from search engine to search engine making it necessary for Web searchers to develop a basic understanding of Boolean searching and keep in mind all the different search techniques and syntax for a half dozen or so search engines. For example, Web searchers need to have a basic understanding about the technique of truncation—what it is and what it accomplishes. They also need to know how to do truncation. Unfortunately, search engines enlist different approaches to truncation. Some require Web searchers to add a truncation symbol such as an asterisk (*). Others advise Web searchers to enter the basic stems of their search words because they automatically truncate the words that Web searchers enter; in fact, some search engines even search for synonyms for the words that Web searchers enter.

If measured in terms of the number of printed pages or the length of Web pages that manuals, guides, and workbooks on Web searching use to explain Boolean searching, it is not an easy straightforward technique for Web searchers to pick up. In fact, a sizable portion of most sources on Web searching is devoted to Boolean searching and in-depth discussions of the Boolean search capabilities of Web search engines (Glossbrenner & Glossbrenner, 1999, pp. 15–162; Pfaffenberger, 1996, pp. 81–92, 131–94; Barrett, 1997, 49–74; Habib & Bailliot, 1998; Hill, 1997, pp. 45–66; The WebTools Company, 1998; University of California, Berkeley, 1999). Consider that students in Information and Library School programs take a ten- to fifteen-week class to learn how to do Boolean searching in commercial online retrieval systems. And the class includes a fair number of practice searches that the instructor assigns to students, examines, corrects, and discusses in class. Is there any reason to believe that the estimated tens of millions of Web searchers who submit queries to the half-dozen search engines on a daily basis have even a partial understanding of Boolean searching?

Use Meta Search Engines for Exhaustive Indexing and Comprehensive Coverage

The proliferation of search engines spawned the introduction of meta search engines (also called mega search engines, multiple search engines, multi-engine search, and metasearch services). Meta search engines usually feature one of two approaches. Some list search engines and provide forms where Web searchers can enter their queries. Others feature a single search form and submit the queries that Web searchers type into the form to the search engines that Web searchers select or the meta search engine selects for them.

Meta search engines save users from searching several search engines in separate visits. They also attempt the widest possible coverage of Web content because each search engine indexes and searches a different and very large subset of Web content and each search engine indexes and searches its different and very large subset of Web content in different ways. Meta search engines don't have their own index of Web content. They send the queries Web searchers enter either to search engines that the Web searchers select or that the meta search engine selects for them. Those who advise Web searchers to enlist the tool-based Web search strategy for Meta Search Engines promote this strategy for achieving comprehensive coverage of Web content because no one search engine indexes or searches the entire World Wide Web. The same problem that Web searchers face with search engines affects Web searchers who enlist meta search engines—they must understand and know how to conduct Boolean searches to conduct effective searches in meta search engines.

Later in this discussion, research findings are presented to provide strong evidence that most Web searchers haven't a clue about Boolean searching. Yet the tool-based Web search strategies that encourage Web searchers to use search engines and meta search engines require them to understand and know how to perform Boolean searching. We are doing Web searchers a disservice. We need to find alternatives to strategies that require knowledge and mastery of Boolean searching.

Amount Strategies

Bryan Pfaffenberger (1996) recommends three Web search strategies that pertain to the amount of information that Web searchers want to find: (1) the locating strategy which "places emphasis on finding a specific useful piece of information" and requires "a quick, pinpointed search using a high-recall search engine" (p. 82); (2) the sampling strategy which "places emphasis on collecting a few sources of high quality" and requires "a subject tree and a trailblazer page" (p. 82); and (3) the collecting strategy "that seeks to discover and catalog every available Web document pertinent to a subject of professional interest" and requires searchers "to master deep searching . . . performing a search using the tools of information retrieval professionals, such as Boolean operators, truncation, proximity operators, and more" (p. 82). Of Pfaffenberger's three amount strategies, two strategies—the locating and collecting strategies—require knowledge and expertise in Boolean searching. Again, Web searchers aren't trained in Boolean searching and to train the millions of searchers who query search engines everyday would require a superhuman effort. There have to be ways to search the World Wide Web that don't require Boolean searching.

Information Retrieval Search Strategies for Web Searchers

So far, IR search strategies hardly map onto recommended Web search strategies. About the only IR and Web search strategies that resemble each other are Citation Pearl Growing and Serendipity. But IR search strategies have not gone unnoticed by those who promote Web searching. Two IR search strategies—Citation Pearl Growing and Successive Fractions—have been recommended for Web searchers. This section visits these two IR search strategies in the guise of Web search strategies.

Citation Pearl Growing for Web Searchers

Bordonaro (1996) sings the praises of Citation Pearl Growing but warns that following link after link can be time consuming. Her advice is to find a good starting point and she offers many suggestions, for example, sites suggested by colleagues; the Home Page of a public, college, or university library; home pages of colleagues who are familiar with the Web; Home Pages of professional associations; and so on. Solock (1996b) describes a scenario involving a long-time tenured economics professor who realizes he must discover the important material in his field to stay abreast of new developments. He advises this new Web searcher to ask colleagues for recommendations on useful Web sites and use the Citation Pearl Growing Strategy to find additional material.

McQuin (1997) enumerates dozens of Web searching tools to an audience of beginning Web searchers, challenges them to find ones that work for them, and become a "pearl grower, developing a valuable list of tools a set of bookmarks . . . that you find useful . . . . These pearls are more than just bookmarks . . . . Pearls are a collection of particularly valuable sites." Davis (1996) and Friesen and Harapnuik (1995) recognize that Web searchers are a mouse click away from the Citation Pearl Growing Strategy through Excite's "Search for more documents like this one" heading that accompanies all retrieved Web pages. If Excite retrieves an especially relevant document, all Excite searchers have to do is click this heading and Excite uses the terminology in the document to retrieve more documents like the one in hand. Some authors don't come right out and name the Citation Pearl Growing Strategy, instead they advise Web searchers to inspect the words and phrases on relevant Web pages, jot them down, and enter those words and phrases in subsequent searches (Glossbrenner & Glossbrenner, 1999, pp. 17–18). Such advice sure sounds like Citation Pearl Growing.

Kriesel (1998) recommends Citation Indexing as a viable Web search strategy. Citation Indexing is a specific instance of the Citation Pearl Growing

Strategy. Unfortunately, Web search engines don't make Citation Indexing as automatic as searching for documents with the same subject terms (e.g., Excite's "Search for more documents like this one" capability). Web searchers have to be deliberate in their choice of a search engine that allows them to perform Citation Indexing using the search engine's special "link" index. Citation Indexing searches aren't straightforward. Searchers must type the "link" label, a colon (:), and the URL of an especially relevant document. If Web searchers do this complex procedure correctly, they can find all the Web sites that link to an especially useful Web page.

Successive Fractions for Web Searchers

Not all search engines allow searchers to alter the results of their Web searches but some do. For example, Infoseek responds to a query with a list of retrieved hits and, accompanying the dialog box where the searcher enters her query, are two choices for "New search" and "Search within results." If the searcher enters additional words and phrases and highlights the radio button adjacent to the "Search within results" option, Infoseek limits the subsequent search to the occurrences of the newly entered words and phrases in the original set of search results. Since Infoseek combines newly entered words and phrases in a Boolean AND operation with the previous results, this operation can considerably reduce retrieved hits (Glossbrenner & Glossbrenner, 1999, p. 18). Infoseek's query-altering capability remains true to the Successive Fractions Strategy because it takes successive bites from the original results.

Excite's query-altering capability contrasts with Infoseek's capability. Instead of reducing retrievals, Excite responds to the addition of words and phrases to the searcher's original query by expanding results (Black, 1998). However, results from Excite's approach aren't much different than the results from Infoseek's approach because Excite responds to the searcher's entry of additional search words and phrases with an entirely different list of ranked hits. Excite should place relevant items higher on the new list than on the original list because the new list is based on additional words and phrases, and Excite uses this information during the ranking procedure.

URL Guessing Strategy
(or Known-Item Search Strategies)

The strategy of entering a somewhat unique identifier for a particular item is well-known to librarians. For over a hundred years, card catalogs have allowed library users to conduct known-item searches through author searches or title searches. Why use these two characteristics to search for known items? These two characteristics are especially memorable characteristics of library materials—that is, most library users are able to recall the author or title of a book they have read. In the early 1980s, online library catalogs expanded the types of known-item searches available to library catalog searchers. Now online catalog searchers can conduct author, title, author-title, call-number, and several number searches (e.g., ISSN, ISBN, LCCN) and expect that the catalog will respond with the one desired item that matches the search key. In the case of author searches, several items may be retrieved but, since authors often write about the same subjects, additional retrieved items might interest searchers. The "URL Guessing Strategy" can be effective, but it requires Web searchers to know exactly what they want.

Those who recommend that Web searchers consult subject directories for broad subjects and use search engines for specific subjects suggest they guess the URLs for the Web pages they seek (Black, 1998; Notess, 1997, 1999). It isn't necessary for Web searchers to have actually seen or used a particular Web page in the past. They can just use their knowledge of how URLs are constructed to guess a URL for a topic that interests them. For example, if you want to learn about the weather, you could enter a URL bearing the word "weather" (e.g., http://www.weather.com/) or the name of a local television station (e.g., http://www.wdiv.com/) into your browser. Our examples here work because the Web searcher guessed two URLs correctly—for the Weather Channel and for the WDIV television station in Detroit, Michigan, both have extensive weather coverage. In recent years, guessing URLs has gotten much easier because browsers provide a service that tries to match whole and truncated URLs to Web pages with similar URLs.

Forms, Flowcharts, Question-and-Answer, and Step-by-Step Approaches

Not all suggestions about searching the World Wide Web have been formalized into search strategies. Forms, flowcharts, question-and-answer, and step-by-step approaches have been proposed to give guidance to Web searchers. A few sources advise Web searchers to pause before embarking on a Web search and ponder what they want to search, maybe even jot down on paper ideas, synonyms, or the actual query they intend to enter into a search engine (Solock, 1996a; University of California, Berkeley, 1999; Glossbrenner & Glossbrenner, 1999, p. 17). Web searchers can use forms to analyze their search topics into facets and list words and phrases to represent each facet as input to the search engine and combine search terms using Boolean operations (University of California, Berkeley, 1999; Franklin D. Schurz Library, 1998).

Powell and Tate (1997) depict Web searching in a flowchart format. They advise Web searchers to obtain a basic understanding of Web searching and research before searching the Web using familiar URLs, consult subject directories, and submit their specific search requests to Web search engines. UC Berkeley Library's extensive tutorial on Web searching features a six-pass approach that begins with meta search engines, proceeds to major search engines, subject directories, specialized subject directories, and major search engines that feature Boolean searching, and ends with sources that are not available through Web searching (University of California, Berkeley, 1999, Strategies). Although the tutorial does not recommend that Web searchers consult subject directories because of their "inefficiency and frustrating results" (University of California, Berkeley, 1999), it features subject directories and specialized subject directories in the third and fourth passes of the tutorial's six-pass approach.

At the AskScott Web site (Nicholson, 1997), Web searchers respond to questions about their information needs, and AskScott suggests Web searching tools that it feels are right for the job. Not only does AskScott question searchers about the subjects that interest them, it asks them about the form of information sought (e.g., news, maps, computer programs, poetry), and eventually suggests promising Web searching tools. Web pages by Debbie Abilock (1999) and Bruce Grossen (1997) aren't as sophisticated as AskScott's question-and-answering service, but they too serve up suggestions for promising Web searching tools using hyperlinks that describe various scenarios.

But What Do Web Searchers Really Do?

The foregoing discussion on search strategies is instructive for telling us what strategies are suggested for Web searchers and what strategies search engines do automatically. This discussion doesn't tell us what Web searchers really do. All the talk about search strategies may be a moot point if Web searchers don't really use the search capabilities that are at their fingertips and make these strategies possible.

Despite the novelty and popularity of the World Wide Web, there isn't much research on Web searchers. The World Wide Web is hardly a half decade old, and it takes considerable time to design a credible study, collect data, analyze the results, and present them formally. Also, it is difficult to observe and interview Web searchers because they aren't centered in one particular place; instead they're scattered around the world and search the Web from their homes and businesses—places that would be difficult and expensive for researchers to cover in a systematic and comprehensive way. The researchers who conducted the studies covered here did the best they could to overcome these limitations. Despite their limitations, these studies paint a good picture of what Web searchers really do.

David Nicholas (1995) studied journalists at the *Guardian*, one of Great Britain's daily newspapers, who searched FT PROFILE, an information retrieval system that covers national and regional newspapers in the United

Kingdom and compared their searches to the searches of *Guardian* librarians. Granted, journalists and librarians weren't searching the Web but Nicholas's study was included here because it was conducted about the time search engines became popular, and his findings were comparable to the findings of other researchers who have studied end users–i.e., searchers of information retrieval systems who have no formal training in system use.

Nicholas (1995) found that journalists were "economical" in terms of the number of words and phrases they entered into FT PROFILE. "Single term searches were the most common (36 percent fell into this category) and two-thirds of all searches were expressed in two terms or less" (p. 389). Of the many commands available to them, journalists typically used the same four commands. They often used these commands to conduct searches using the Successive Fractions Strategy—that is, they began their searches with a one- to two-word query, then used commands and additional search words and phrases to narrow their initial results. Librarians typically used eight commands—twice as many different commands as journalists used. But "journalists tampered more with their searches—over 14% of their searches involved five steps or more, while the equivalent figure for librarians was under 9%" (p. 389). The researcher suggests that journalists' tampering was connected with the poor quality of the initial query which, because it was poorly constructed, required changes. Nicholas (1995) concluded that "journalists' searches were typically straightforward and simple in that they contained few terms and commands. The hallmark search is a stripped down or bare essentials one, which gives very early contact with the data and then maximum time online to browse and display records" (p. 395).

Researchers at Virginia Polytechnic Institute (VPI) (Abdulla et al., 1998) analyzed transaction logs from five separate server files that represented accesses from Web users across Korea, VPI's library, VPI's Computer Science Department, a high school in Virginia, and America Online. Accesses of Web search engines and subject directories made up a substantial portion of Web use and ranged from a low of 4 percent (Korean users) to a high of 20 percent (high school users). Restricting their analysis to Web searchers' queries, the VPI researchers concluded that queries weren't very complex. One-third of queries consisted of one word and another one-third consisted of two words. Queries in the Korean log were even shorter—over half consisted of a single word. Few queries included Boolean operators or advanced searching features such as truncation, proximity operators, or nested Boolean logic.

Jansen et al. (1998) analyzed the activity of about 18,000 visitors to the Excite search engine on March 10, 1997. Their results about query length were not much different from those of Nicholas and the VPI researchers. About one-third of the queries consisted of one word and another one-third consisted of two words. About one-twentieth of user queries involved the "Search for more documents like this one" capability which automatically invoked the Citation Pearl Growing Strategy. The researchers performed analyses that made it clear that Excite searchers rarely used the system's Boolean searching capabilities and, when they did, they used them incorrectly. Here are results that indicate how infrequently Web searchers do Boolean searches (Jansen et al., 1998):

- Of the three Boolean operators that Excite accepts (i.e., AND, OR, and AND NOT), Excite users enlisted the Boolean AND operator most frequently—in 6 percent of all queries.
- Less than one-half of 1 percent of Excite searchers' queries bore the OR or AND NOT operators.
- When Excite searchers used the Boolean AND or OR operators, they used them incorrectly in over one-third of their searches.
- When Excite searchers used the Boolean AND NOT operator, they used it incorrectly in about two-thirds of their searches.
- Excite searchers used nested Boolean logic in less than 1 percent of their searches and when they used this capability, they used it wrong about one-third of the time.
- Of the 6 percent of Excite queries that contained the shortcut Boolean AND operator (a plus sign, +), over one-half used it incorrectly.
- Of the 5 percent of Excite queries that contained the shortcut Boolean AND NOT operator (a minus sign, -), almost all used it incorrectly.
- Of the 5 percent of Excite queries that contained phrases (enclosing a string of words in a quote), less than 8 percent of queries used phrase searching incorrectly (pp. 5-6).

At Central Connecticut State University (CCSU), Tomaiuolo and Packer (1997) recruited ten students with no formal training in search engine use, assigned them seven topics to search in the AltaVista and Opentext search engines, and examined their retrievals to determine if they retrieved the benchmark Web site(s) that expert searchers had retrieved for the same topics. About three-quarters of students' searches were successful. The CCSU researchers didn't conduct an extensive analysis of students' queries, but they made a few observations about the effectiveness of students' queries in which they "simply picked out the main concepts of the topic and entered them" (p. 46). The few students who entered advanced searching techniques added truncation (an asterisk, *), phrases (strings surrounded by quotes), or the shortcut Boolean AND operator (a plus sign, +) to their AltaVista queries. These techniques are the very ones that AltaVista presents in the form of search tips near the dialog box into which searchers enter their queries. Students' success led the CCSU researchers to conclude that "it is natural for end-users to want to search without applying difficult command languages . . . . Within the context of this experiment, natural language searching apparently works as well, in many cases, as the more precise methods that the investigators employed" (p. 46).

What do Web Searchers Really Require of Searching Strategies?

Research findings from studies of Web searchers make it clear that Web searchers simply choose the main concepts of their topics and enter them in queries consisting of one to two words; they rarely use Boolean searching or advanced techniques and, when they do, they use such techniques incorrectly. Despite these findings, Web searchers conduct surprisingly effective searches—they retrieve some of the same useful hits that experts find, sometimes additional useful hits that experts don't find and, when they find promising retrievals, they are especially good at separating useful hits from undesirable ones.

Tenopir and Cahn (1994) offer a good explanation for why Web searchers are so successful. They gathered six search requests, conducted searches for these requests using the Boolean searching techniques of DIALOG and NEXIS, then simplified their original searches to conform to the simplified syntax of Dialog's "Target" and NEXIS' "Freestyle" which conduct searches that aren't that much different from the search engines on the World Wide Web because they use statistical techniques to retrieve and rank retrievals. The final results were pretty surprising. Dialog's precision was 61 percent and Target's was 56 percent; NEXIS's precision was 64 percent and Freestyle's was 53 percent. The author cannot help but be tempted to generalize the Hawaii researchers' results to Web searching. If we use the number thirty to represent the maximum number of hits that Web searchers usually display (Jansen et al., 1998), this means Boolean searching would retrieve nineteen relevant hits and statistical search engines would retrieve seventeen relevant hits of thirty total hits. A difference of two relevant hits separates results for the Boolean and statistical approaches to searching, which is not much at all.

Why do statistical search engines do so well? Susan Feldman (1998) sums it up best:

> These systems are doing what you as searchers have learned to do yourselves. They look for terms that can distinguish one document from another, they ask for the terms to appear close together in the document, they stem words, and they count words that appear in the title more heavily than those appearing in the rest of the text.... Some systems also try to match query concepts .... They enlarge a search beyond the boundaries that the query originally defined. (pp. 40-41)

Let's take a closer look at six criteria most search engines use to determine whether a document is retrieved and how high it is ranked in the list of retrieved hits:

1. Occurrence of search words in Web page titles: Web pages bearing titles matching search words get more weight than titles in which search words are absent.
2. Occurrence of search words in retrieved Web pages: Web pages bearing all search words in queries receive higher weights than Web pages bearing fewer than all search words.
3. Proximity of search words: Web pages bearing search words adjacent or near one another get more weight than pages in which search words are separated by a sentence, paragraph, or more.
4. The frequency of search words across all indexed Web pages: Search words that occur infrequently in Web pages receive higher weights than frequently occurring search words.
5. Frequency of search words in each Web page: The more frequently search words occur in documents, the more weight given to the documents.
6. Order of search words in queries: The initial search words receive higher weights than the trailing search words in queries.

There may be more ranking and retrieval criteria but these six are important ones. Since most search engines don't openly divulge their secrets about how they rank retrievals, it is difficult to say which criteria play a greater role in ranking and retrieval. What we do know is that Boolean-based searching only allows searchers to have control over the first three listed ranking and retrieval criteria. And, in some cases, control is minimal. For example, Boolean searchers can specify how close search words can be. If searchers are too stringent in their use of proximity operators, they may fail to retrieve any documents at all. In contrast, statistical-based retrieval doesn't require searchers to specify how close search words must be, but it takes word proximity into consideration during ranking and retrieval. Furthermore, some search engines stem search words and some even add related terms based on statistical associations between co-occurring words. Boolean searchers must indicate truncation using the particular search engine's truncation technique, and they must enter related terms on their own because the system doesn't do it automatically for them.

Statistical-based retrieval assumes much of the burden of ensuring high precision results. It uses the same criteria as Boolean searching offers to expert searchers to serve up the most relevant retrievals. And it uses additional criteria to retrieve and rank retrieved hits. Let's give credit to statistical-based retrieval. Its results are comparable to the results of Boolean searching, it enlists the same criteria as Boolean searching and more to serve up the most relevant retrievals, and it doesn't require end-users to have knowledge of Boolean operators and searching techniques.

It's time for those of us in the business of recommending strategies for searching the World Wide Web to take heed. Print and Web-based books, articles, manuals, and tutorials that teach Boolean searching to Web search-ers are doing them a disservice. The vast majority of Web searchers aren't going to learn Boolean searching or use it correctly. Strategies for searching the Web must let statistical-based retrieval do its job. Such strategies should not require searchers to remember subtle differences between search en-gines. And they should be devised with the expectation that searchers sim-ply pick out the main concepts of their topics and enter them in queries consisting of one to two words.

New Search Strategies for Web Searchers

Here are six new subject searching strategies for Web searchers and a set of scenarios in which Web searchers need to call on using one of the six subject searching strategies to search for known items. The strategies re-quire little if any knowledge of Boolean searching. The few search tech-niques that are recommended should work across several search engines so that Web searchers don't have to memorize the specific techniques that work in each search engine. About the only search techniques that expert searchers use that Web searchers need to master are facet analysis and a rudimentary understanding of truncation.

Let's first tackle facet analysis. Facet analysis is really important. Search-ers should perform a facet analysis on every search they undertake. What they need to do is analyze their search request before rushing to enter their query into a search engine's dialog box. This analysis requires them to identify the major concepts present in their search requests. Some requests have one facet. An example is "I want to know about smoking." The one facet in this request is "smoking." Some requests have two facets. An ex-ample is "Does smoking cause cancer?" The two facets in this request are "smoking" and "cancer." Other requests have more than two facets. An ex-ample is "To what extent do teens know that smoking causes cancer?" The three facets in this request are "smoking," "cancer," and "teens." Web search-ers don't need to know Boolean searching to combine facets and the search words and phrases that represent facets into Boolean queries. Search en-gines don't require Boolean queries. And the search strategies that we present in this section don't require Web searchers to know Boolean search-ing. What Web searchers do need to know is how to perform a facet analysis and substitute search words and phrases for the facets they identify in their search requests. Search engines pretty much do the rest. Discussions of recommended Web strategies in this section include sample searches, facet analysis, and suggested words and phrases for searching Web search en-gines.

The next thing considered in this discussion relates to truncation. Some Web search engines require searchers to be explicit about truncation and tack an asterisk (*) or some other symbol onto search words and phrases to indicate where they want truncation to begin. Other search engines urge searchers to enter word stems instead of plural forms and truncation symbols because they do the truncation themselves and search for both singular and plural forms of the word. In an attempt to reach a happy medium, our examples show singular forms of search words and phrases unless their plural forms are uncommon plurals—e.g., child and children, goose and geese. In this case, we use whatever form we believe will be characteristic of retrievals. If Web searchers prefer one search engine over all others, they should commit its truncation procedures to memory and adjust accordingly.

The major objective underlying the new search strategies in this section is to "let the system do the walking" (Feldman, 1998, p. 46). Web search engines are programmed to do exactly what expert searchers have been trained to do themselves. Our search strategies let them do their job.

There is no order to these search strategies. Web searchers should keep knowledge of these strategies in the back of their minds. Let's say they conduct an initial search using the Kitchen Sink Strategy. They assess the results and realize that the Big Bite Strategy would be a much better way to proceed. Then they should start all over again and this time use the Big Bite Strategy.

We've added a graphic to make these strategies more memorable. The graphics enlist a wildlife metaphor that depicts Stanley the Squirrel who spends his days foraging for food, burying his finds, or devouring them on the spot. Stanley experiences the bad times—weathering a tumultuous thunderstorm late at night—and the good—cavorting with his mates in the forest. What does our "Stanley the Squirrel" metaphor have to do with searching the Web? Let's find out. We've covered so much ground to get to this point.

A Shot in the Dark Strategy

Few queries will fit this strategy. It requires an information need with a single facet. This facet names a single concept, condition, place, person, program, device, or idea in one word. To be successful as a viable Web search strategy, this word must be so specific, so identifiable, and so unique that it retrieves few hits on the Web and, if it retrieves many hits, it should be easy to separate the relevant ones from the nonrelevant ones. Since the World Wide Web has grown so huge, search requests for the Shot in the Dark Strategy are really hard to come by. Here are a few: Guadalcanal, Pompeii, Madonna, Goroka, scabies, Kikuyu, cartomancy, Clydesdales, and Subud. The reason why we've named this strategy "A Shot in the Dark" is because the Web searcher's action of entering a single word to represent her interests is like taking a shot in the dark. Rarely will you hit your

Figure 7. Shot in the dark strategy

target. But follow our advice about entering words that are so unique and so distinctive that you just might get lucky and hit your target. About the only search-engine-specific detail that searchers might want to remember is to capitalize the first letter in proper nouns and capitalize any other characters that are typically capitalized in the word—e.g., QuickTime, NeXT, and xRes.

Madonna is a celebrity who is almost universally recognizable in Western culture. A search for "Madonna" yields over a million hits and many are home pages of individuals who collect information, images, and links to other Madonna Web sites. If Web searchers want to learn something about Madonna, this search yields plenty of links for hours and hours of reading, viewing, and fun. If Web searchers are overwhelmed, they might want to consider transforming their Shot in the Dark Strategy into a Big Bite Strategy to focus results on an aspect of Madonna's life or career—e.g., her pregnancy, motherhood, movie roles, and so on.

Figure 7 depicts the Shot in the Dark Strategy. Here we find a late night thunderstorm has awakened Stanley the Squirrel with such a start that he almost leaps out of his nesting cavity. Search results of Shot in the Dark Strategies can be just as tumultuous. Use this strategy when your query consists of a single facet and can be expressed in a single word that is very unique. Failure to use a unique word will result in lists of millions of hits that may startle you as much as the thunderstorm has startled Stanley.

The Bingo! Strategy

When playing Bingo, your objective is to cover five numbers in a row. You can cover them up, down, across, or diagonally. For those of you who have played Bingo, you know how frustrating it can be when you have covered only four of the five numbers in a row. You hang on the caller's every last syllable waiting for him to call your uncovered number. Suddenly he calls your number and you've got Bingo!

We use the name Bingo! for a Web search strategy that requires a phrase—a series of words in a particular order. This phrase describes a single facet but, unlike the Shot in the Dark Strategy, the facet can't be named in a single word, and instead it requires a phrase bearing two, three, four, or as many as five words. The phrase could describe a concept, condition, place, organization, institution, person, program, device, or idea. There are only two search-engine-specific details that Web searchers need to keep in mind. First, they should capitalize proper nouns and any other characters that are typically capitalized in the phrase—for example, "University of Michigan," "Monica Lewinsky," and "QuickTime VR Authoring Studio." Second, if Web searchers are positive that no intervening word will ever occur in the phrase, they can enclose it in quotes. For example, placing the queries "Hillary Clinton" and "Charlie Parker" in quotes may seem perfectly reasonable at first glance; however, these bound phrases miss Web documents bearing the phrase "Hillary Rodham Clinton" or "Charlie 'Bird' Parker." Granted, Web searchers will still retrieve plenty of useful retrievals for the former but they just might miss ones for the latter that were really useful. If you think an intervening word is likely, don't put quotes around your phrases.

Line up your search words so they make a phrase that represents a single simple concept, enter them into a search engine, and you just might be exclaiming "Bingo!" when you hit the jackpot with relevant retrievals. There are so many concepts that are expressed as bound phrases—"secondhand smoke," "Gypsy Rose Lee," "border gardens," "Buffalo Bills," "fox squirrels," "miniature roses," "west coast jazz," "space shuttle," "congenital heart disease," "adult education," "cabbage diet," "Earth Day," "Human Genome Project," "Doug Flutie," "American Greetings," and so on. You'll find yourself using the Bingo! Strategy for many of your single-faceted queries.

If you search Hotbot using the Bingo! Strategy, choose the "exact phrase" option from the drop down menu right under the search dialog box. You can also delete the quotes around your query because choosing the "exact phrase" option tells Hotbot how to handle your query.

If the phrase you have in mind has two valid forms due to one-word and two-word variations, enter each form in separate searches. For example, if you're interested in second-hand smoke, your first query would be "secondhand smoke." Take time to examine your retrievals. If you haven't found enough, your second query would be "second hand smoke."

Figure 8 depicts the Bingo! Strategy. On a clear summer day, we find Stanley relaxing under a tree. He's playing Bingo!, and from the look of the pieces on his playing board, he has lined up several acorns and has just won Bingo! When you enlist the Bingo! strategy, you'll have a search request that can be represented in a single facet. To search for this in a search engine, line up the words so they form a phrase and type them into the search engine's search dialog box. It is hoped that you, too, will be exclaiming Bingo! when your results describe exactly what you're looking for.

Figure 8. Bingo! strategy

Everything But the Kitchen Sink Strategy

Here's a Web search strategy where Web searchers throw "everything but the kitchen sink" at the search engine. You've got a complex topic in mind that features two, three, maybe as many as four facets. Throw words and phrases from all the facets at the search engine and try the best you can to put the most important words and phrases first.

Perhaps you're interested in Congress' efforts to limit the amount of violence that children see on television. This topic has four facets: Congress, Limit, Children, and Television Violence. In fact, those words and phrases are really good ones for searching this topic. The next step is to determine the most important idea. "Television violence" is important and so is

"Congress." Let's put "Congress" first in the query. So far the query reads "Congress television violence limit." Can you think of one or two synonyms for the query's words or phrases? "Television" and "tv" are synonymous. Perhaps the word "control" might be another way of expressing "limiting" the amount of violence on television. Let's put those words at the end of the query since the query already contains words to represent those ideas. Our final query is "Congress television violence limit tv control." Search for this query in AltaVista, Excite, Lycos, Northern Light, or other search engines and examine the results.

Should you use Hotbot, choose the "any of the words" option from the drop down menu right under the search dialog box. Hotbot's default "all of the words" option requires matches of all the words in your query. That's usually pretty hard to do. Hotbot's "any of the words" option tells Hotbot to match any of the words in our query. Since Hotbot ranks retrievals based on many of the same criteria that expert searchers use, it does a really good job placing the most relevant retrievals on the first few pages of retrieved hits.

Except for Hotbot, our search didn't require any special knowledge of a particular search engine. We didn't add any special symbols or Boolean operators to the query. We just let the search engine do its job.

Web searchers might find it disconcerting that their Kitchen Sink queries don't make sense. They have no syntax and they sure don't read like an English-language sentence or phrase. They're just a bunch of words and phrases that stand for the key concepts in the search request. Web searchers may need time, experience, and success with the Kitchen Sink Strategy to adjust to this new approach to searching Web search engines. They'll have to learn to resist transforming their Kitchen Sink queries into phrases that read like questions or search requests. Search engines don't need the prepositions, articles, conjunctions, and other grammatical devices that make Kitchen Sink queries understandable to people.

Here's a second search request that was used in an extensive Web searching manual on the World Wide Web (The WebTools Company, 1998). It really isn't a search request, it is a scenario that describes an event that is the impetus for a person searching for information on the Web:

> Jan is an office worker in downtown Minneapolis. While on lunch break one fine spring day, Jan's eye is caught by a flash in the sky above. Jan sees a bird about the size of a crow diving at high speed and catching in mid-air what appears to be a pigeon. The bird then swoops out of sight. Jan is captivated by the mostly gray and white bird with the crooked black and yellow beak. Jan has never seen this bird before and wonders what it is doing in the city. That night, Jan decides to find out more about this mystery bird on the Internet. Where does Jan begin?

Our first task is to eliminate all the filler about Jan and her reaction to the event. Then, the most important ideas emerge from the scenario. These ideas are the bird, the fact that Jan is in a downtown urban area when she sees the bird, and the bird's action of diving for the pigeon—its prey. This topic has three facets or important ideas: Bird, Urban, and Prey. In fact, those words and phrases are really good ones for searching this topic. Some readers probably wonder why we used the word "prey" instead of "pigeon." Jan's objective is to identify the bird that hunted the pigeon. If we add the word "pigeon" to the query, we'll retrieve many Web pages about pigeons in downtown urban areas—something we definitely don't want. We substituted the word "prey" for the word "pigeon" because that's truly what the pigeon was to our mystery bird—its prey.

The next step is to determine the most important idea. "Bird" is really important. Unfortunately, it is pretty vague but, since Jan doesn't have a clue as to the bird's identity, and in fact, her objective is to identify the bird, the word "bird" has to suffice here. So far the query reads "bird urban prey." Can you think of one or two synonyms for the query's other words or phrases? "Downtown" and "city" may be interchangeable with "urban." Let's add them at the end of the query which now reads "bird urban prey downtown city." Search for this query in AltaVista, Hotbot, or Infoseek, or the other search engines and examine the results (don't forget to change Hotbot's default "all the words" option to "any of the words" option). If you're not a birder, you'll have to examine retrieved Web pages and look for clues in the text and graphics to identify Jan's mystery bird. Jan gave you lots of hints—the bird hangs out on downtown buildings, hunts and eats pigeons, is mostly gray and white with a crooked black and yellow beak. If you're stumped, check this paper's references beginning with the name "Mason" for the answer.

Let us examine another search request: Are the reasons why men have eating disorders the same as the reasons why women have such disorders? This topic has three main concepts: Men, Eating Disorders, and Women. In fact, those words and phrases are really good ones for searching this topic. The next step is to determine the most important idea. Since men are less likely than women to have eating disorders, let's put Men first (for a change). So far the query reads "men eating disorders women." Can you think of one or two synonyms for the search request's main concepts? Instances of eating disorders are "anorexia," "bulimia," and "obesity." We can really go bonkers and enter synonyms for men and women like "woman," "girls," "males," and so on. The query "men eating disorders women anorexia bulimia males" will probably suffice (some searchers might be tempted to enclose the words "eating disorders" in quotes to indicate that they want the search engine to consider this a phrase and that's fine). Try searching for this search request in a major search engine. However, the answer to the search request won't immediately hit you over the head. You've got to read relevant retrieved Web pages and answer the question using the material you've read.

Figure 9 shows the Everything But the Kitchen Sink Strategy. Stanley is thrown to the ground when he opens the door to his cache—everything but the kitchen sink tumbles to the ground and on top of Stanley. He has stored so much junk in his cache that it can't hold it securely. The search requests submitted to Kitchen Sink Strategies won't feature as much stuff as Stanley keeps in his cache, but they will consist of several facets and require you to think of unique words and phrases to represent each facet.

Figure 9. Everything but the kitchen sink strategy

Here's one last search request to illustrate the Kitchen Sink Strategy (this query came from a list on Search Voyeur). "Are people with hearing impairments poorer drivers than people without such impairments?" This topic has two key concepts: Driving and Hearing Impaired. It is difficult to determine which concept is more important. For now, we'll leave a word or phrase that represents the Driving facet as the first word in the query. There are lots of synonyms for Driving—e.g., "driver," "drive," "car," "auto," "automobile." The search word "deaf" could be used in addition to "hearing impaired." Let's line up words and phrases in the query and see what we've got. How about "driver driving deaf hearing impaired car." Enter this query into Excite or Infoseek. If you don't find anything useful, change the order of search words so that "deaf" or "hearing impaired" comes first. If you still don't find anything useful, switch to another search engine and search there. Don't hesitate to switch around the initial words in the query. Using several search words like "car," "auto," and "automobile" isn't a good idea because the Web has so much information on buying and selling cars. Sometimes search engines won't cover your topics. For example, searchers interested in this search request might want to follow up search engine searches with searches of medical or health sciences databases.

Big Bite Strategy

There will be many times when you use the Shot in the Dark or Bingo! Strategy and you retrieve so many hits that you can't quite find what you want. Maybe the particular angle you want on your topic isn't among the hits you see listed on the first few pages of hits. Or maybe what you are retrieving covers your topic generally and doesn't get as specific as you'd like. In these situations, it is time to think about switching to the Big Bite Strategy.

In the Big Bite Strategy, the Web searcher takes an initial bite of the file. If you've already conducted a search using the Shot in the Dark or Bingo! Strategy, you've taken your first bite. The next step is to take a second bite of the file by searching for a second facet and then review retrieved material to determine if it isn't more to your liking. Let's use an example. Say that you took your first bite in a Shot in the Dark Strategy for "Madonna." You reviewed retrieved hits and found that they were about Madonna, her life, music, movies, and so on. You realize you are interested in her new role as a mother. Now you've introduced a second facet into the mix. If you are searching Infoseek, that's all you have to do is click on the "Search within results" radio button and enter additional words and phrases into the search dialog box such as "Lourdes mother motherhood." If you're searching the other search engines, you'll have to ensure that your original query still resides in the search dialog box and then add the additional words and phrases to it (most search engines leave your original query on the results page so you can add more terms to it).

Let's use the Shot in the Dark Strategy to perform a search for "Bonsai." After reading some retrieved Web pages, you decide you want to know about caring for your Bonsai indoors instead of outdoors. Execute the Big Bite Strategy by adding words to represent the Indoors facet such as "indoor," "inside," and "house" into the search engine. Your Big Bite query might read "bonsai indoor inside house." Try searching for this topic in Infoseek or Northern Light and see if you can focus your initial results on caring for Bonsai inside the house.

The Big Bite Strategy can stand on its own two feet, that is, you can decide right from the start that the Big Bite Strategy is the right one for your situation. Let's say you are interested in the rabies outbreak that began in New England in the early 1990s and is spreading westward. This search request has several facets—Rabies, New England, Spread, and Westward. You begin your search with the one word "rabies" to represent the rabies facet, scan results, and determine that they cover too much general material on this disease and really don't focus on the spread of this disease westward. Adding words to represent the "spread" and "westward" facets such as "spread west westward Michigan Ohio" really focuses retrieved hits on the spread of rabies to Midwestern states. Try searching for this search request in AltaVista using the Big Bite Strategy and see how many facets you need to introduce before you start retrieving relevant material.

Figure 10 shows the Big Bite Strategy. We find Stanley balanced on a tree branch and biting into a huge hamburger. Stanley has taken a second bite and has a few more big bites to go to completely devour the hamburger. Chances are that Stanley won't finish the burger but, instead, satisfied from his mid-day feast, he'll stretch out on the branch and take an afternoon snooze. The Big Bite Strategy requires that Web searchers take an initial bite of a file, examine results, and take successive bites until search results express the specific topic they have in mind. Web searchers might not need to take as many bites as they have facets because they are retrieving useful material.

Figure 10. Big bite strategy

Citation Pearl Growing Strategy

The Citation Pearl Growing Strategy is extendable to Web searching. In Excite and Infoseek, the Citation Pearl Growing Strategy is automatic.

All Web searchers have to do is find an especially relevant document and click on Excite's "Search for more documents like this one" heading or Infoseek's "Find similar pages" heading that accompanies all retrieved Web pages for Excite or Infoseek to use the terminology in the document to retrieve more documents like the one in hand. In other search engines, Web searchers need to be deliberate about executing this strategy. For example, let's say you watch the movie "Twister" and want to learn more about the people who study tornadoes. In Alta Vista, a search for "tornado" using the Shot in the Dark Strategy produces results that aren't too promising except for a Web site called "The Tornado Project Online!" which features links to much information on chasing tornadoes. Besides featuring links to Web-based newsletters, FAQs, and tours for storm chasers, this site is superb for providing useful words and phrases like "chasing," "stormchasing," "stormchasers," "storm chasers," "intercept team," "whirlwind gang, " "Whirlwind Tours," "Cloud 9 Tours," and "Silver Lining Tours." Collect these words and phrases and use them in subsequent searches. (In fact, within a matter of minutes, you'll be overwhelmed by the amount of information on this subject that you have at your fingertips.) Your subsequent searches might take many forms—for example, Kitchen Sink Strategies, using the word "tornado" and words for a Chasers facet:

- tornado chasing
- tornado chaser

Subsequent searches also might take the form of "Bingo!" Strategies, using phrases for various tours and formal and informal groups of stormchasers:

- "storm chasing"
- "storm chasers"
- "intercept team"
- "whirlwind gang "
- "Whirlwind Tours"
- "Cloud 9 Tours"
- "Silver Lining Tours"

So, what might start as a search using the Citation Pearl Growing Strategy actually grows into many subsequent searches enlisting several different strategies. But what got these searches started was a highly productive Citation Pearl Growing Strategy. In fact, whenever you conduct a Web search, always keep in mind the Citation Pearl Growing Strategy. Be on the lookout for words and phrases in useful retrievals that have potential as words and phrases in subsequent searches. Jot these words and phrases down on your computer's notepad or make a mental note of them so that you can come back to them after following initial hits and hyperlinks.

Let's examine a second search that is aided by the Citation Pearl Growing Strategy. You develop an interest in mushrooms and want to learn more about identifying wild mushrooms. The only search words that come to mind are "mushroom hunting." Those words are sufficient for retrieving a few Web pages bearing the very title "Mushroom Hunting." Scanning these pages leads to additional words and phrases, e.g., "mushrooming," "mushroom clubs," "mycological associations," "mycological clubs," and "edible mushrooms." Within a short period of time, your knowledge of this subject mushrooms through subsequent searches in search engines and following hyperlinks in retrieved hits.

Whenever you identify a really relevant Web site, you can use Citation Indexing, a type of Citation Pearl Growing, to find additional Web sites on the same topic. For example, in a search for hunting mushrooms, the North American Mycological Society's Web page proves to be especially helpful. Enter its URL into AltaVista using the "link" search capability and you retrieve page after page of Web sites that link to this society's Web page. Searchers must be deliberate about conducting searching using Citation Indexing. In AltaVista, you first enter the "link" label into the search dialog box, followed by a colon (:) and the text portion of the URL. To search for links to the North American Mycological Society's Web page, enter the following query:

- link:www.namyco.org

Results of the "link" search capability aren't always helpful. For example, the search on chasing tornadoes results in the really useful site entitled "The Tornado Project Online!" (URL: http://www.tornadoproject.com/). Entering its URL into AltaVista using the "link" search capability (link: www.tornadoproject.com) results in a long list of Web pages, but most are about weather generally or cite "The Tornado Project Online!" because it is a cool site and it appeals to kids.

AltaVista isn't the only search engine with a "link" search capability. The "link" search capability of Infoseek works just like AltaVista's capability. Hotbot has a "link" search capability that works a little differently. Just enter the text portion of the URL into Hotbot's search dialog box and choose the "links to this URL" from the pulldown menu just below the search dialog box.

When your search results in very few hits, use Citation Indexing to find more based on searching the URL for one or two really relevant hits. It doesn't always lead to additional material, but you'll be thankful when it does.

Figure 11 illustrates the Citation Pearl Growing Strategy. Stanley is surfing the waves. He searches for a wave that grows into a huge swell and rides the wave for as long as he can. Citation Pearl Growing isn't much different. Find a relevant hit and use its words and phrases to find additional ones like it. Sometimes you can rely on a particular search engine's special features to help you find additional material and other times you have to do some searching on your own using one of the Web search strategies discussed earlier.

Figure 11. Citation pearl growing strategy

Getting a Little Help from Your Friends Strategy

Did you ever have a situation when you didn't know how to phrase your query? Maybe you had a general notion what you wanted but putting it into words just wasn't possible. Well, it's time to "get a little help from your friends."

Maybe you find yourself in the position of wanting to find something specific about a subject area but you have no experience or knowledge about the subject generally. Perhaps you want to learn about investing in the stock market but you don't know anything about the stock market and you don't even know where to start. Again, "your friends" could help you out.

How about the situation in which you know you want some information about something like "earthquakes," but you really don't know what it is about earthquakes that you want to explore. In fact, if you could just see some stuff about earthquakes, you'd know what you'd want. (This situation could be compared to shopping for a top to match a skirt or slacks—you know what you want, you can't quite say what it is, but you'll sure know it when you see it.)

These three situations are perfect candidates for calling "your friends" for help through the Getting a Little Help from your Friends Strategy. Just who are your friends? They are the Subject Directories that serve up lists of broad subjects. Clicking on a broad subject leads to lists of subtopics that become increasingly narrower in scope upon each successive mouse click on listed subtopics. (Some subtopics aren't narrower terms—they address aspects of broader terms or the types of Web pages that characterize material on the broader topic but, for the sake of simplicity, we'll call them narrower terms.) Because subject directories supply menus of broad and narrower topics, they are especially helpful when you don't know how to put your information needs into words, when you are searching for something specific in a subject area unfamiliar to you, or when you need good stuff served up so you can find what you're looking for.

I don't want to play favorites so I won't recommend one friend over another. Of course, Yahoo! always comes to mind because it is one of the longest-lasting subject directories and it covers so many subjects. The Mining Co.'s recommendations on Web searching were really terrific for researching this paper. Here are the "friends" I call on periodically. They aren't able to come through for me all of the time, but I keep coming back to them because they've helped me in the past:

- Argus Clearinghouse (www.clearinghouse.net/)
- Canadian Subject Guide (www.nlc-bnc.ca/caninfo/esub.htm)
- Einet Galaxy (www.einet.net/)
- Infoseek (infoseek.go.com/WebDir)
- Internet Public Library (www.ipl.org)
- Librarian's Guide to the Internet (sunsite.berkeley.edu/InternetIndex/)
- Looksmart (www.looksmart.com/)
- Magellan (magellan.excite.com/)
- The Mining Co. (miningco.com/)
- Webcrawler (www.Webcrawler.com/)
- Yahoo! (www.yahoo.com/)

When these "friends" recommend Web sites, they react somewhat differently. Yahoo! merely lists titles of Web sites under the broad subjects or narrow subtopics; it accompanies a few listed titles with a phrase or sentence describing its contents. The Argus Clearinghouse rates individual subject guides on particular subtopics, cites authors of the guides and their affiliations, lists a few keywords describing the guide, and provides the guide's URL so searchers can click on it to travel to the guide. Webcrawler usually provides one-paragraph reviews for listed "Top Sites" and one-sentence descriptions for listed "More Sites."

"Getting a Little Help from your Friends" is the same as the Browsing Strategy that so many Web searching manuals and books recommend. There's a scenario that Jack Solock (1996b) describes in which a tenured economics professor is one-upped by a student who is hip to the Web—it seems that the professor knows all about searching traditional resources in economics—e.g., books, journals, encyclopedias, and yearbooks—but hasn't a clue about what can be found on the Web. Solock suggests that this professor begin at the Argus Clearinghouse where there are hundreds of subject guides on academic, popular, and esoteric subjects including economics. The authors of the dozens of subject guides on economics did the professor's job for him—they sorted through the thousands of economics Web pages and found the best ones. The Argus Clearinghouse saved the professor the hassle of finding all the good stuff on his own. Now he can study recommended sources and one-up his student in the future. What a great reason to "Get a Little Help from your Friends!"

Figure 12 shows the Getting a Little Help From Your Friends Strategy. On an autumn day, Stanley is hard at work burying nuts for the winter. Some of his friends—Missy Mouse and Ricky Rabbit—are helping Stanley gather and guard his nuts. Others— Ozzie Opossum and Rascal the Raccoon—are nearby and ready to help in case Stanley needs them. Subject directories are your friends. Their keepers will always be hard at work assigning the latest Web pages to categories of broad and specific topics. When you need help—you can't find the right words to express what you're looking for, you don't know the subject, or you just can't put into words what you're looking for—call on subject directories to help you gather material on your topics of interest.

Déjà Vu Scenarios (Searching for Known Items)

How many times have you retrieved a really good Web site, failed to bookmark the site, and never been able to find the site again? Or perhaps a colleague suggested you visit a site, mentioned its name, and cited its URL. A few days later you're poised to visit the site but you can't recall its exact title or URL. These scenarios describe situations in which you need to perform searches for known items. That is, you know the item exists because you've seen it before or a colleague brought it to your attention. You now need to retrieve the item a second time so you can read or consult it again.

No one search strategy can solve the problem of searching for known items. You need to call on one of the foregoing strategies based on the amount of information you have in hand (or in mind) about the Web site you want. Because you've seen the item you want sometime in the past, we call the scenarios that lead up to known-item searches Déjà Vu Scenarios. But Déjà Vu describes scenarios not search strategies. Your selection of a search strategy to help you out in a Déjà Vu situation depends on how much information you recall about the known item.

Figure 12. Getting a little help from your friends strategy

Of all the Web search strategies this article describes, the strategies you use to search for a known item are more likely than all other strategies to leave you empty handed. There are reasons for this and to describe them, let's think back to the good ol' days, that is, the days of authors, books, and library catalogs. Most of us remember the books we've read recently. If asked, we can quickly recall their authors and titles. In fact, books display authors and titles quite prominently on the book jacket, spine, and title page. Over the years, librarians have made sure that the library catalog features author and title access points because readers are quick to recall these memorable characteristics of books, and they recall them with amazing accuracy.

The people who contribute pages to the World Wide Web don't take credit for their work in the same way as book authors. Rarely can you find an author's name listed prominently on a Web page. If there is a person's name or organization's name cited on the Web page, it is often given at the bottom of the page in small print and you don't know whether this person or organization is responsible for the Web page's text, its design, or merely supports it through some financial arrangement. If you do remember a name on a Web page, then there's the problem of whether you remember the full name or only part of the name.

For names of persons or organizations, use the Shot in the Dark or Bingo! Strategy. If you recall only the person's last name or one word in the name of an organization, use the Shot in the Dark Strategy. If the person's name or the organization's name is quite common—e.g., "Miller," "Black," "Financial," "Computing"—you probably shouldn't even try searching because you've got to recall a unique name to have any success at all. For example, I might be able to find Web pages by Solock or Abilock, but I won't find Web pages by Crowe, Fox, and Berkeley. Even names like Bordonaro and Pfaffenberger retrieve hundreds of hits. If you're game, that's all you have to do is launch the search engine of your choice and type the one-word name into the search dialog box. Examples are:

- Solock
- Bordonaro
- Abilock

If you recall the full name of a person or organization cited on a Web page, you have a better chance of finding the one Web page you want. Use the Bingo! Strategy and line up the words that make up the name in the search engine's search dialog box. Your decision to place quotes around the name depends on how sure you are about the name. If you recall only the first and last names and think that you've forgotten the person's middle name, then don't place quotes around the person's name. If you only recall the really unique or unusual words in an organization's name, don't place quotes around the name. Here's some examples of the author names for the Bingo! Strategy:

- Karen Bordonaro
- Bryan Pfaffenberger
- Dylan Tweney
- "Edward A Fox"

If searching for an author's name fails, try to remember the Web site's title. When Web search engines index Web titles, they file titles into a special "title" file. The title that they file is the page title which appears on the title bar of most browsers. This isn't the title you see prominently displayed on the Web page in bold type. In fact, many of the titles which are displayed prominently on Web pages are image files. If Web search engines index image files at all, they index them in their special "image" file, not in their special title file because they can't distinguish between images that proclaim titles and images that illustrate Web pages. Page titles on a browser's title bar do not display prominently. In fact, they are so understated on the title bar that it is doubtful that Web searchers pay much attention to them. Sometimes title bar titles are exactly the same as titles that display prominently on Web pages. If you're lucky to have paid attention to a Web page's title bar title or if both title bar title and display title are the same, you can use a search engine's title file to search for a Web page with a particular title.

When you are poised to enter title words and phrases into a particular search engine's search dialog box, the Shot in the Dark, Bingo!, or Kitchen Sink Strategies can help you out. Choose the most appropriate strategy in view of the number of words in the title and how accurately you think you recall them. If the title consists of only one word or you only recall one word in the title, use the Shot in the Dark Strategy. If the one-word title or the only title word you can recall is quite common—e.g., "roots," "jukebox," "financial," "computing"—you probably shouldn't even try searching because you've got to recall a very, very unique title word to have any success at all. Don't bother capitalizing title words. Here are examples of searches for really unique title words. These examples begin with the "title:" label to tell the search engine to search its special title index:

- title: jukejoint
- title: proletariat
- title: sukkot

If the title consists of several words, you need to ask yourself some questions. Do I remember all the words or just some of the words in the title? Do I remember the title words in the right order or am I unsure of the right order of the title words? Your answers to these questions dictate which strategy you use. If you remember some or all of the words in the right order, use the Bingo! Strategy—type the words into the search engine's search dialog box—and surround them in quotes. Don't bother capitalizing title words. The examples below begin with the "title:" label to tell the search engine to search its special title index:

- title: "how search engines work"
- title: "starry night"
- title: "the squirrel page"
- title: "stratford festival"

If you don't remember the right order of the words in the title but you are fairly sure of some of the words in the title, use the Kitchen Sink Strategy and type as many substantive words as you can remember into the search engine's search dialog box. Omit nonsubstantive words like "the," "of," "for," "we," "is," and so on. Don't put quotes around your title and don't capitalize title words. The examples below begin with the "title:" label to tell the search engine to search its special title index:

- title: rouge river observatory (to retrieve the Web site for the Rouge River Bird Observatory)
- title: munch scream (to retrieve the Web site entitled "Edward Munch: The Scream")
- title: blue mountain cards (to retrieve the Web site for Blue Mountain Arts' Animated Greeting Cards)

- title: librarians movies (to retrieve the Web site entitled "Librarians in the Movies—An Annotated Filmography")

It's conceivable that you cannot recall a name or title associated with a Web site but you can remember its URL or at least the most substantive words in the URL. Our third and last known-item search approach requires searchers to enter some or all of the substantive words in a URL into a search engine's dialog box. Since URLs consist of a string of characters separated by punctuation, there really aren't any phrases in URLs. URLs are made up of segments separated by punctuation such as periods or slashes. If you remember two or more segments in a URL, preface every segment you remember with the "url:" label. The examples below show URLs bearing one segment and more than one segment:

- url: benmiller (to retrieve the Web site for the Benmiller Inn, Goderich, Ontario)
- url: midamconf url: football (to retrieve Mid American Conference football Web pages)
- url: searchenginewatch (to retrieve the Search Engine Watch Web page)
- url: ski url: ca (to retrieve Canadian Web pages with the word "ski" in the URL)

Guessing URLs isn't the most productive way to search. But, if you have nothing else to go on, you just might get lucky guessing URLs.

If known-item searches fail to yield the Web site you want, switch to a different search engine. There's a really good chance that the search engine you are searching doesn't index the Web site you want and no amount of searching, creativity, or perseverance will turn up the site you want. Always keep known-item searching in the back of your mind as a prelude to Citation Pearl Growing. Let's say that a search in Lycos produces the Web site of your dreams. Copy its URL or its title bar title onto your computer's note pad. Switch to the Infoseek search engine. Then search for this perfect Web site's URL or title in Infoseek. If you find it, click on the "Find similar pages" heading accompanying the hit to tell Infoseek to use the Web site's terminology to find more Web pages like it. You can also use the "link:" label followed by the perfect Web site's URL to find other Web pages that cite it.

Known-item searching is complicated. If you want to retrieve a Web page you've retrieved in the past, known-item searching enables you to search for the Web site's author, title, or URL (see Table 1). To search for a title or URL, you'll have to use a search engine's "title:" label or "URL:" label to limit retrievals to the search engine's special title or URL index, respectively. Your decision to use the Shot in the Dark, Bingo!, or Kitchen Sink Strategies is based on the amount of information you recall about the known item. If you come up empty-handed, switch to a different search engine.

Table 1. Six New Subject Strategies for Web Searchers:
Déjà Vu Scenarios for Known-Item Searching on the Web

Information in Hand	No. of Search Words	Web Search Strategy	Explanation
author	1	Shot in the Dark	For one-word queries; queries must be very unique names to have any hope of success
author	More than 1	Bingo!	For full or partial names of persons or organizations; enclose phrase in quotes only if you are sure you know the full name
title	1	Shot in the Dark	For one-word titles; titles must be very unique to have any hope of success; use the "title:" label to restrict hits to title bar titles on Web pages
title	More than 1	Bingo!	For phrases in full or partial titles; enclose title in quotes only if you are sure you know the full title or a phrase in the title; use the "title:" label to restrict hits to title bar titles on Web pages
title	More than 1	Kitchen Sink	For substantive words in titles; do not enclose title words in quotes; use the "title:" label to restrict hits to title bar titles on Web pages
URL	1 segment	Shot in the Dark	For one segment; use "URL:" label to restrict hits to URLs
URL	More than 1 segment	Shot in the Dark	For more than one segment; repeat "URL:" label preceding each segment to restrict hits to URLs

There's a chance the search engine you just searched did not index the one item you want to retrieve. Give known-item searching your best effort but be prepared to be disappointed because finding the one item you want among hundreds of millions of indexed Web pages is like finding a needle in a haystack.

Summary

Table 2 presents six new subject searching strategies and organizes them according to the number of facets in Web searchers' search requests.

TABLE 2.
Six New Subject Searching Strategies for Web Searchers

No. of Facets	No. of Search Words	Web Search Strategy	Explanation
1	1	Shot in the Dark	For one-word queries; queries must be very unique words to have any hope of success
1	More than 1	Bingo!	For phrases; enclose phrase in quotes if you know the exact words in the phrase
More than 1	More than 1	Big Bite	Enter words and phrases for each facet in the search request successively and monitor number of hits and relevance of top-ranked hits
More than 1	More than 1	Kitchen Sink	Enter words and phrases for all facets in the search request at the same time
More than 1	More than 1	Citation Pearl Growing	Enter words and phrases for some or all facets in the search request at the same time; inspect results and use relevant terminology in retrieved relevant hits in subsequent searches
1 or more	N/A	Help From Your Friends	Choose a broad topic that represents the subject area, field of study, or discipline that describes your interests; choose narrower topics as needed to arrive at a narrower subtopic that expresses your interests

When Web searchers have a search request in mind that bears one facet, they have the choice of Shot in the Dark, Bingo!, and Help From Your Friends Strategies. The Shot in the Dark Strategy handles one-word queries and the Bingo! Strategy handles phrases. The Friends Strategy can help Web searchers find Web content on their topics of interest regardless of their number of facets. Since the Friends Strategy calls on Subject Directories to serve up menus of broad and narrower topics, Web searchers don't even have to transform their search requests into queries. They can just launch the Subject Directory of their choice and start browsing.

When Web searchers have a search request in mind that bears two or more facets, they have the choice of Big Bite, Kitchen Sink, Citation Pearl Growing, and Help From Your Friends Strategies. The Big Bite Strategy allows Web searchers to be deliberate about their searches; they enter words and phrases for each facet in the search request successively, monitor the number of hits and relevance of top-ranked hits, and stop before their retrievals are reduced to zero. Since Web searchers who choose the Kitchen Sink Strategy enter words and phrases for all facets in the search request at the same time, top-ranked hits are likely to be on target because ranking algorithms strive to place documents bearing as many search words as possible at the top of the heap. The objective of searchers who enlist the Citation Pearl Growing Strategy is to identify really relevant hits and use them to find additional ones. Some search engines (Infoseek and Excite) feature a type of automatic Citation Pearl Growing Strategy. Accompanying hits are headings on which searchers click to command the system to use the terminology in the selected hit to find additional ones. Searchers can also examine hits on their own, find relevant terminology, and use the terminology in subsequent searches. The strategies they use for subsequent searches may be any of the strategies listed in Table 2.

Table 2 search strategies aren't really new. Charles Bourne and his colleagues were the first to develop the Citation Pearl Growing and Big Bite Strategies. They used the name Successive Fractions instead of Big Bite but we prefer "Big Bite" because it conjures up a more interesting image than "Successive Fractions." Search engines' ranking and retrieval capabilities make it possible to combine Building Block, Most Specific Facet First, Lowest Postings Facet First, and Pairwise Fractions Strategies from IR system searching into the Kitchen Sink Strategy for Web searching. Just like intermediary searchers formulate queries that represent several facets for the Building Blocks Strategy, Web searchers formulate queries that represent several facets for the Kitchen Sink Strategy. Web searchers then leave the dirty work of determining specific words and phrases, low-posted words and phrases, word proximity, occurrences of search words and phrases in some or all documents, and so on to the search engines' ranking and retrieval capabilities. Shot in the Dark and Bingo! Strategies could be compared to the one-facet Building Block searches that intermediary searchers have been doing over the years. About the only thing that's new in Table 2 is the Help from Your Friends Strategy. Commercial IR systems have never supported browsing subject directories. In fact, expert searchers have always avoided any type of browsing because it increases connect time due to the time spent online to navigate, compare, evaluate, and persevere. Now that one of the major IR systems (Dialog) has switched to a pricing scheme that is not dependent on connect time, subject directories are certainly a possibility for future development.

Subject searching isn't the only type of searching that Web searchers do. On occasion, they need to find a Web page that they have seen before or that a colleague has brought to their attention. This type of searching is called known-item searching because searchers know the item exists. Table

1 presents Déjà Vu scenarios for known-item searching and organizes them according to the type of known-item information searchers have in hand.

Web searchers who have author information in hand have two strategies for finding known items based on whether the author information consists of one word or more than one word. If they recall a Web page's title bar title, they have three strategies from which to choose based on whether the title information they recall consists of one word, a phrase, or just the substantive words in the title. Web searchers can search for URLs using the Shot in the Dark Strategy. Search engines usually reserve special indexes for title and URL information so Web searchers are advised to preface their title search or URL search with the "title:" label or "url:" label, respectively, to limit searches to these special indexes.

Conclusion

Web searching is different from searching commercial IR systems. We can learn from search strategies recommended for searching IR systems, but most won't be effective for Web searching. Web searchers need strategies that let search engines do the job they were designed to do. This article presents six new Web searching strategies that do just that.

References

Abdulla, G.; Liu, B.; & Fox, E. A. (1998). *Searching the World-Wide Web: Implications from studying different user behavior.* Retrieved February 6, 1999 from the World Wide Web: http://video.cs.vt.edu:90/~abdulla/Webnet98/query2.html.

Abilock, D. (1999). *Choose the best search engine for your information needs.* Retrieved February 6, 1999 from the World Wide Web: http://www.nueva.pvt.k12.ca.us/~debbie/library/research/adviceengine.htm.

Algonquin College of Applied Arts and Technology. (1996). *Web search strategies. Search strategies.* Retrieved February 6, 1999 from the World Wide Web: http://www.smpcollege.com/online-4styles~help/cite6.html#1.

Barlow, L. (1998). *The spider's apprentice. 3. How to plan the best search strategy.* Retrieved February 6, 1999 from the World Wide Web: http://www.monash.com/spidap1.html.

Barrett, D. J. (1997). *NetResearch: Finding information online.* Sebastopol, CA: Songline Studios.

Black, L. (1998). *Research strategies.* Retrieved February 6, 1999 from the World Wide Web: http://bvsd.k12.co.us/curriculum/research/strategies.html.

Bordonaro, K. (1996). Pearl growing on the Web. *The 'Net Homesteader, 1*(3). Retrieved January 13, 1999 from the World Wide Web: http://sunyoclc.sysadm.suny.edu/tnh3.htm.

Buntrock, R. E. (1979). The effect of the searching environment on search performance. *Online, 3*(4), 10–13.

Classroom Connect. (1999). *Hints and tips for searching the Internet.* Retrieved February 6, 1999 from the World Wide Web: http://www.classroom.com/resource/searchingfaq.asp.

Crowe, E. P. (1999). *Search the net in style: Seek and ye shall find* (clnet Special Reports). Retrieved February 6, 1999 from the World Wide Web: http://www.cnet.com/Resources/Tech/Advisers/Search/index.html.

Davis, E. T. (1996). *A comparison of seven search engines.* Retrieved February 6, 1999 from the World Wide Web: http://www.iwaynet.net/~lsci/Search/paper.htm.

Feldman, S. (1998). Where do we put the Web search engines? *Searcher, 6*(10), 40–57.

Franklin B. Schurz Library, Indiana University, South Bend. (1998). *Search strategy worksheet.* Retrieved February 6, 1999 from the World Wide Web: http://www.iusb.edu/~libg/srchwrk.html.

Friesen, N., & Harapnuik, D. (1995). *Online searching and the Internet: The WWW database; search engines.* Retrieved February 6, 1999 from the World Wide Web: http://www.ualberta.ca/~nfriesen/536/srchengs.htm.

Grossen, B. (1997). *Search engines: What they are, how they work, and practical suggestions for getting the most out of them: III. Getting the most out of search engines and related services.* Retrieved February 6, 1999 from the World Wide Web: http://Webreference.com/content/search/.

Habib, D. P., & Balliot, R. L. (1998). *How to search the World Wide Web: A tutorial for beginners and non-experts.* Retrieved February 6, 1999 from the World Wide Web: http://www.ultranet.com/~egrlib/tutor.htm.

Harter, S. (1986). *Online information retrieval: Concepts, principles, and techniques.* Orlando, FL: Academic Press.

Hawkins, D. T., & Wagers, R. (1982). Online bibliographic search strategy development. *Online, 6*(3), 12–19.

Hill, B. (1997). *World Wide Web searching for dummies.* Foster City, CA: IDG Books.

Janes, J. W. (1999). Introduction. In G. A. DeCandido (Ed.), *The Internet searcher's handbook,* 2d ed. New York: Neal-Schuman.

Jansen, B. J.; Spink, A.; Bateman, J.; & Saracevic, T. (1998). *What do they search for on the Web and how are they searching: A study of a large sample of Excite searches.* Unpublished manuscript submitted to SIGIR '98 (21st Annual International ACM SIGIR Conference on Research and Development in Information Retrieval, Melbourne, Australia, August 24–28, 1998. 15 p.).

Kriesel, R. W. (1998). *Suggested Internet research strategies. Keywords. Subject trees.* Retrieved February 6, 1999 from the World Wide Web: http://www.concentric.net/~Rkriesel/Search/Strategies.html.

Markey, K., & Atherton, P. (1978). *ONTAP: Online training and practice manual for ERIC data base searchers.* Syracuse, NY: ERIC Clearinghouse on Information Resources.

Markey, K., & Cochrane, P. (1982). *ONTAP: Online training and practice manual for ERIC data base searchers,* 2d ed. Syracuse, NY: ERIC Clearinghouse on Information Resources.

Mason, H. (1998). *Ontario Peregrine Falcon Newsletter,* number 4, fall 1997. Retrieved February 6, 1999 from the World Wide Web: http://www.cciw.ca/glimr/data/peregrine-falcon/intro.html.

McQuin, D. L. (1997). *The little search engine that could.* Retrieved February 6, 1999 from the World Wide Web: http://www.isd77.k12.mn.us/schools/jefferson/lsengine.html.

Meadow, C. T., & Cochrane, P. A. (1981). *Basics of online searching* (Information Science Series). New York: Wiley.

Metz, T. (1998). *Tips for using Web search tools.* Retrieved February 6, 1999 from the World Wide Web: http://www.library.carleton.edu/Websearch/tips.html.

Nicholas, D. (1995). Are information professionals really better online searchers than end-users (and whose story do you believe?). In D. A. Raitt & B. Jeapes (Eds.), *Online Information 95* (19th International Online Information Meeting Proceedings, London, 5–7 December 1995) (pp. 383–397). Oxford: Learned Information.

Nicholson, S. (1997). *AskScott: Your guide to finding it on the Internet.* Retrieved February 6, 1999 from the World Wide Web: http://www.askscott.com/index.html.

Notess, G. R. (1997). Internet search techniques and strategies. *Online, 21*(4), 63–66.

Notess, G. R. (1999). *Search engine showdown: Internet search strategies.* Retrieved February 6, 1999 from the World Wide Web: http://www.notess.com/search/strat/.

Pfaffenberger, B. (1996). *Web search strategies.* New York: MIS Press.

Powell, J. M., & Tate, M. A. (1997). *Web search strategies: A synthesis.* Retrieved February 6, 1999 from the World Wide Web: http://www.science.widener.edu/~withers/strat.htm.

Scoville, R. (1996). Special report: Find it on the net! *PC World Online.* Retrieved February 6, 1999 from the World Wide Web: http://www.pcworld.com/reprints/lycos.htm.

Skov, A. (1998). Internet quality. *Database, 21*(4), 38–40.

Snell, J. (1997). When hits are misses. *MacUser, 12*(9), 86.

Solock, J. (1996a). Searching the Internet. Part I. Some basic considerations and automated search indexes. *InterNIC News, 1*(6). Retrieved February 6, 1999 from the World Wide Web: http://www.scout.cs.wisc.edu/scout/toolkit/enduser/archive/1996/euc-9609.html.

Solock, J. (1996b). Site-ation pearl growing. *InterNIC News, 1*(3). Retrieved February 6, 1999 from the World Wide Web: http://internic.net/nic- support/nicnews/archive/june96/txt/enduser.txt.

Teaching Learning Center, Community College of Denver. (1999). *Searching the Web.* Retrieved February 6, 1999 from the World Wide Web: http://ccdWeb.ccd.cccoes.edu/tlc/search.htm#.

Telescope: How to find and search for information on the Internet. (1996). *Lesson 2: browsing or pinpointing: Strategies for finding.* Retrieved February 6, 1999 from the World Wide Web: http://www.clis.umd.edu:8000/students/projects/Telescope/lesson2.html.

Tenopir, C., & Cahn, P. (1994). Target & freestyle: DIALOG and Mead join the relevance ranks. *Online, 18*(3), 31–47.

Tomaiuolo, N. G., & Packer, J. G. (1997). Web search engines: Key to locating information for all users or only the cognoscenti? In D. A. Raitt & B. Jeapes (Eds.), *Online Information 96* (20th International Online Information Meeting Proceedings, London, 3–5 December 1996) (pp. 41–48). Oxford: Learned Information.

Tweney, D. (1996). Searching is my business: A gumshoe's guide to the Web. *PC World Online.* Retrieved February 6, 1999 from the World Wide Web: http://www.pcworld.com/software/internet_www/articles/dec96/1412p182a.html.

Tyner, R. (1999). *Sink or swim: Internet search tools & techniques.* Retrieved January 25, 1999 from the World Wide Web: http://www.ouc.bc.ca/libr/connect96/search.htm#tips.

University of California, Berkeley. (1999). *Finding information on the Internet: A tutorial.* Retrieved January 25, 1999 from the World Wide Web: http://www.lib.berkeley.edu/TeachingLib/Guides/Internet/FindInfo.html.

Walker, G., & Janes, J. (1999). *Online retrieval: A dialogue of theory and practice,* 2d ed. (Database Searching Series). Littleton, CO: Libraries Unlimited.

Walker, G., & Janes, J. (1993). *Online retrieval: A dialogue of theory and practice* (Database Searching Series). Englewood, CO: Libraries Unlimited.

Webster, K., & Paul, K. (1996). Beyond surfing: Tools and techniques for searching the Web. *Information Technology.* Retrieved February 6, 1999 from the World Wide Web: http://magi.com/~mmelick/it96jan.htm.

The WebTools Company. (1998). *Tutorial: Guide to effective searching of the Internet,* Parts 1–7. Retrieved February 6, 1999 from the World Wide Web: http://theWebtools.com/searchgoodies/tutorial.htm.

Wu, H. (1999). Internet searching tips. Retrieved February 6, 1999 from the World Wide Web: http://www.jsr.cc.va.us/lrc/netrain2/tips.htm.

Enhancing Subject Access to Monographs in Online Public Access Catalogs: Table of Contents Added to Bibliographic Records

✦ Vinh-The Lam ✦

Abstract

S ubject access to monographs through online public access catalogs (OPACs) has always been a major concern for large research and/or academic libraries. Academic library practice of providing subject access to monographs has proven inadequate, especially in the case of composite works. Many techniques have been proposed to enhance subject treatment of monographs in OPACs. This article briefly reviews these efforts in the past and presents the case of adding Tables of Contents as one of the most useful and probably also one of the most cost-effective ways of improving subject access to monographs in an academic environment.

Introduction

Several decades ago, Ranganathan affirmed as the First Rule of Library Science that "Books Are For Use." In order to help users make good use of books, the library catalog should be able to provide a good representation of the books' contents. This goal for the catalog has always been elusive. The library world has struggled to make it a reality. With the first-generation online public access catalog (OPAC) in the late 1970s replacing the traditional card catalog, librarians had great hopes for improved access in general and improved subject access in particular. But before long the library community realized that the OPAC was, in this area of subject access, not much better than its predecessor and with all the same limitations.

Inadequacies of LCSH

By the 1970s, Library of Congress Subject Headings (LCSH) had been used to provide primary subject access in large research and/or academic libraries for some eighty years. In spite of its firmly established place in these libraries, LCSH had serious weaknesses which were identified by various authors and researchers between the 1950s and the late 1970s. These were grouped together with suggested improvements by Pauline Atherton and Monika Kirtland in their 1981 *Critical Views of LCSH: A Bibliographic Survey* (see Cochrane, 1986, pp. 5-7).

Among the most serious weaknesses of LCSH were inconsistent form of headings, lack of clarity in subdivision structure, lack of currency of heading terms, and lack of specificity of heading terms. The impediment in OPAC access and retrieval was created not only by these internal weaknesses of LCSH but also by subject cataloging practices. The limited number of subject headings assigned to monographs as well as the practice of providing a more general subject heading for a monograph that covers several more specific topics resulted in very inadequate subject access to monographs. Even now, LC still instructs its catalogers in its *Subject Cataloging Manual: Subject Headings* (1996) as follows: "Assign to the work being cataloged one or more subject headings that best summarize the overall contents of the work and provide access to its most important topics. Assign headings only for topics that comprise at least 20% of the work. The number of headings that are required varies with the work being cataloged. Sometimes one heading is sufficient. Generally a maximum of six is appropriate. Do not assign more than ten headings to a work" (pp. 1-2). The reality turned out to be that "an average of only two headings per book is provided. . . ." (Byrne & Micco, 1988, p. 440). Catalog use studies have shown that subject searches account for more than half (52 percent) of all catalog use, and the failure rate in this category of search is 50 percent (Matthews, 1985, p. 8).

Exploring Ways to Improve
Subject Access in the OPAC

Pauline Atherton Cochrane, one of the pioneers in the history of information retrieval and library automation, has called the 1970s "The Development Decade" and the 1980s "a time for reassessment" (Cochrane, 1985, p. viii). A series of research projects were carried out, mostly during the 1980s, with the objective of improving and assessing the online public access catalog.

The most noted, and probably the most comprehensive, project to look into improving subject access for the OPAC was Pauline Atherton's Subject Access Project (SAP) for the Council on Library Resources in 1978 (Cochrane et al., 1978). In this important research work, Atherton and her colleagues tried to provide increased subject access to an online database called BOOKS. Subject terms, selected according to clearly defined rules from tables of contents and end-of-book indexes, were added to bibliographic records in BOOKS. The average number of selections per book was 32.4. The research findings were a clear indication of better subject access (see Table 1):

TABLE 1. Subject Access Project Findings.

	Marc	Books
Number of Searches	90	90
Number of Relevant		
Items Retrieved	56	131
In Social Sciences	31	61
In Humanities	25	70
Number of Known Relevant		
Items NOT retrieved	117	42
Average Precision Rate	35%	46%
Search Time	.27 Hour	.14 Hour
Social Sciences	.15 Hour	.08 Hour
Humanities	.12 Hour	.06 Hour

The most significant finding was that increased recall did not necessarily mean a decreased precision as many other researchers have feared. Basically, Atherton's SAP technique clearly demonstrated four benefits from such a database: (1) greater access, (2) greater precision, (3) less cost, and (4) the ability to answer questions that are otherwise impossible using regular catalog information. Many research studies in the 1980s explored ways of enhancing subject access to monographs and almost all pointed to the addition of contents terms as the best way.

A study by Karen Markey in 1983 found that one of the most desired new capabilities of an OPAC was to search a book's table of contents, summary, or index. In 1987, Karen Calhoun and Karen Markey, comparing the search value of some of the content components, found that notes in MARC tags 505 and 520 (Contents Note and Summary Note) accounted for the largest percentage increase in the number of unique words with an average of 15.5 new subject terms per record. And in 1989, Florence DeHart and Karen Matthews confirmed the benefits of searching chapter titles (in Van Orden, 1990, pp. 27-32). In a landmark paper from this period, Carol Mandel, having determined the main value of enriched records was to provide access to parts of books, suggested eleven alternative ways to provide such information. Basically, she envisaged three ways of carrying out these eleven alternatives: (1) creation of separate databases of monographs; (2) content indexing, including monograph content indexing in LC MARC records; and (3) adding monograph content indexing in either utility databases or online catalogs. For each of these three ways, she proposed using controlled and uncontrolled vocabulary. For the uncontrolled vocabulary scenario, SAP technique was proposed as the mechanism for content indexing of a select set of monographs. Although Mandel identified three ways of doing this in her matrix, a closer look revealed that, in fact, there were only two ways: either providing monograph content information in separate databases or right in the bibliographic records. In the conclusion of her paper, Mandel (1985) said: "The possible alternatives suggested in this paper need to be tested and weighed against cost-effectiveness and need. Should we enhance the MARC record to improve subject access? We won't know until we try" (pp. 5-15). People did try.

One of the most important experiments in this area in the 1980s reaffirmed the findings from Atherton's research. This experiment, called the Enhanced Subject Project (ESP), was carried out at the Australian Defence Force Academy (ADFA) library. After having considered several methods, ADFA library staff decided to choose Atherton's SAP technique. Supplementary terms selected from tables of contents of books and, where needed, the index (on an average of twenty to twenty-five per book) were keyed into field 653 in the bibliographic records for these books. The first report, after six months into the experiment, with more than 6,000 books receiving ESP, was published in 1988. "The Enhanced Subject Project has demonstrated that the use of contents terms is a viable and cost-effective technique for dramatically increasing the number of subject access points to the contents of books without a serious increase in false drops" (Byrne & Micco, 1988, p. 440).

Five years later, with ESP now applied to close to 40,000 records, or about 25 percent of ADFA's collection, another report was made public and the benefits of ESP reconfirmed. Halfway around the world, Atherton's SAP technique was put into practice in Sweden. Irene Wormell reported on the application of SAP technique in indexing Swedish government official reports for the SOU database (SOU stands for Statens Offentliga Utredningar = Government Official Reports) at the Library of the University of Lund. Of particular interest was the use of SAP technique in capturing terms used in tables and graphs included in these reports for indexing purposes. Wormell (1983) found that the captions of tables and graphs were "usually more self-explanatory than the fancy titles or chapter headings of the reports" (p. 15). Wormell concluded that "SAP-indexing is a new way to produce subject description for monographs and, at a moderate cost, retrieve those specific parts of publications which are not usually accessible in traditional IR-systems" (p. 15).

In the late 1980s, as many American university libraries started to enrich bibliographic records by adding either abstracts or tables of contents, the OCLC Office of Research, using recall and precision as evaluation measurements, conducted a research project to evaluate retrieval effectiveness of an online test database of about 4,900 records which contained both abstracts and tables of contents. Ten records were randomly selected from the database to generate twenty queries, which were then translated into Boolean form and used to search the database. The searches were done at four levels: level 1 using an index containing title and subject heading fields, level 2 is level 1 plus tables of contents, level 3 is level 1 plus abstracts, and level 4 is level 1 plus both tables of contents and abstracts. The findings showed that recall improved as additional content information was added to the records but this increase in recall was accompanied by a decrease in precision (see Table 2) (Dillon & Wenzel, 1990, pp. 43-46):

TABLE 2. Results of an OCLC Office of Research Project to Evaluate Retrieval Effectiveness of Approximately 4,900 Records

| | Average | |
	Recall	Precision
Level 1	0.17	0.71
Level 2	0.26	0.59
Level 3	0.29	0.60
Level 4	0.34	0.60

Recently, at the University of Minnesota Bio-Medical Library, a project was undertaken to enhance online bibliographic records for the reference collection monographs with meaningful tables of contents and summaries. "Of the 1,100 enhanced records, 33% were enhanced with tables of contents, 39% with summaries only, and 20% with both a table of contents and summary. Overall, for this project, the benefits of adding the content-bearing data to the records outweighs problems with precision" (Makinen & Friesen, 1995, pp. 244-46).

Discussing Standards for Subject Access Enhancements

In 1991, the Library of Congress issued MARBI Discussion Paper No. 42 in which tables of contents were listed as one of the four additions (the other three are: indexes, abstracts, and book reviews) to be considered for OPAC bibliographic records. MARC field 505 (Formatted Contents

Note) was singled out as the location for this addition. "Contents could be represented by titles and possibly authors of chapters or by chapter number, full title, and page numbering" (*Content Enriched and Enhanced Subject Access in USMARC Records,* 1991, p. 2).

After responses and comments to this Discussion Paper were received and analyzed, it became clear that the majority of respondents opted to go with tables of contents. MARBI Discussion Paper No. 46, therefore, limited itself in discussing issues related to the enhancement of bibliographic records with table of contents (TOC) information. It provided a good discussion on how to change field 505 to accommodate TOC information. Basically, it recommended that field 505 become a repeatable field with two subfields—$a for authors of chapter titles and $t for chapter titles. It also raised some concerns about name authority control for these enhancements ("Enhancing USMARC Records with Table of Contents," 1991, pp. 105-13).

One of the disadvantages of the addition of TOC information to the bibliographic records is that it makes the latter too lengthy and too hard to read. Recently, the Library of Congress Cataloging-In-Publication (CIP) Office started providing electronic CIP. Part of this program was the provision of lengthy TOC information in separate files which were linked to the bibliographic records through a URL (Uniform Resource Locator) in field 856. These files are now accessible at the following URL: http://lcweb.loc.gov/catdir/toc/. LC seems to follow, though not completely, Mandel's suggestion of providing monograph content indexing in separate databases.

Current Developments in TOC

After the release of these two MARBI discussion papers, the main concern for most libraries was the cost involved in implementing these enhancements. Many libraries will not have the money and/or the staff to do this, considering the financial constraints of the 1990s. It appeared that the solution ought to be sought in finding a way to automatically capture content-bearing information for inclusion into the online catalog. The new scanner technology was tested successfully at the School of Library Science and Documentation, Colegio Maximo de Cartuja, Granada, Spain, in the mid-1990s. In this research project, the OCR (Optical Character Recognition) scanner technology was used to extract tables of contents from composite monographs. This information was then automatically converted into SGML (Standard Generalized Markup Language) format by a commercially available application called Rainbow Maker. Finally, these SGML-tagged information components were processed into MARC format for inclusion into the online catalog, using another application designed by the Electronic Text Center of the University of Virginia

called "tei2marc" (tei stands for Text Encoding Initiative). The researchers then created two test databases: each containing 200 records for items
in the fields of librarianship, documentation, and applied computer science. The first one was directly from the regular online catalog and the
second from the enhanced online catalog. Twenty queries were searched
against the two test databases. It was found that "the system with enriched
records is more effective in satisfying user needs than the operating one.
For fixed recall points, average precision for the catalog system with enriched records is between 21 percent and 45 percent better than that of
the opearating catalog system. The best results appear for the midrange
recall values" (Peis & Fernandez-Molina, 1998, pp. 161-72).

Just as the cataloging operation was made more efficient through cooperation and/or centralization almost a century ago, the implementation of enhanced subject access with TOC information in individual libraries may be outsourced to vendors. One vendor is currently providing
this service at a reasonable price—$1.00 U.S. per record. The technolo-
gies helping make this dream come true are electronic scanning of TOC
data by the vendor and electronic transfer of data from the vendor to the
individual libraries via FTP (File Transfer Protocol). This vendor proposes
to use the repeatable local field 970 to store TOC data. Recently, it has
started to perform authority control for authors' names provided in these
fields. Hence, enhanced subject access to monographs in large academic
and/or research libraries is now possible at a reasonable cost. A new concern arises though. Claus Poulsen, in his study on the number of composite works in the library collection and the number of articles or citable
works in these books, found that: "The proportion of composite works is
between 10% and 20%. The number of articles in the composite works
varies from 20 to 30 articles per book. This implies that the libraries under
consideration can add access to between 200% and 600% more works to
their catalog without buying one more book, just by adding the tables of
contents of their composite works" (Poulsen, 1996, p. 137). Academic and/
or research librarians now have to find solutions to the potential challenge of information overload. It is really unfortunate that current developments in this area do not use Atherton's SAP technique. Convenience
and low cost have been given preference over a good and proven technique. First of all, SAP technique requires some intelligent human intervention while the current TOC services are totally mechanical. The use of
scanning technology precludes the elimination of fancy, but mostly irrelevant, if not misleading, terms used in chapter headings in the TOC of
many books. And, of course, the index for TOC terms will be swamped
with generic and totally useless terms like "foreword," "preface," "introduction," "afterword," and so on taken automatically from the TOC by
scanners. With the SAP technique, all of these useless terms would be
eliminated. Second, SAP technique not only makes use of terms from the

TOC but also includes terms taken from the index of books, which are far more content-specific. To illustrate these points, let us examine how SAP technique was actually used for one book in the famous 1978 project conducted by Atherton:

> Turney-High, Harry Holbert, 1899-
> *Primitive war: its practice and concepts* / by Harry Holbert Turney-High; foreword by David C. Rapoport; afterword by Harry Holbert
> Turney-High.—2nd ed.—Columbia, S.C. : University of South Carolina Press, 1971.
> Its one-page TOC looks like this:

Contents
Foreword

Preface to the First Edition
Part I. The Practice of Primitive War

The index has a total of 11 pages (pp. 278-288).

The following represents the record for this items in BOOKS:
RSN - 00670542
SNO - 0978
CCN - GN497 T87 1971
ME - Turney-High, Harry Holbert, 1899-
TI - Primitive war; its practice and concepts.
Foreword by David C. Rapoport.
Afterword By Harry Holbert Turney-High.
IM - Columbia, University of South Carolina Press, 1971
COL - 288 p.
PY - 1971
LCH - War

CT - *PRACTICE OF PRIMITIVE WAR (P. 5-140);
WEAPONS (P. 5-20);
THEORY OF WAR (P. 21-38); FORMATIONS (P. 39-60);
DISCIPLINE AND COMMAND (P. 61- 90);
FUNCTIONAL DESIDERATA (P. 91-106);
INTELLIGENCE SURPRISE AND COUNTERSURPRISE (P. 107-122);
BATTLE PLANS (P. 123-140)
CT - *CONCEPTS OF PRIMITIVE WAR (P. 141-253);
SOCIO PSYCHOLOGICAL MOTIVES (P. 141-168);
ECONOMIC MOTIVE (P. 169-186);
MILITARY VALUES (P. 187-204); MILITARY ATTITUDES (P. 205-226);
WAR AND ORGANIZATION OF SOCIETY (P. 227-253)
CT - *SURVIVAL AND REVIVAL OF PRIMITIVE WAR (P. 254-265)
IT - AFRICA ; DAHOMEAN ; ENEMY LIFE VALUATION OF (P. 220-226);
EURASIA
IT - GIBEAH CAMPAIGN AGAINST (P. 32-38); GREAT PLAINS AMERICAN
IT - HEAD TAKING (P. 196-200)
IT - HEBREWS EARLY MILITARY OPERATIONS (P. 31-38); IROQUOIS; JIBARO
IT - LAND ECONOMIC (P. 182-186); LIFE ATTITUDES REGARDING (P. 210-215)
IT - MELANESIA; METHODS TACTICAL (P. 21-38); OCEANIA; OJIBWAY
IT - OMAHA; PLANS PRINCIPLE OF SIMPLICITY OF (P. 123-137);
POLYNESIANS
IT - SAMOAN; SEX MOTIVE (P. 151-164); SLAVING (P. 178-182)
IT - SOCIAL ORGANIZATION (P. 227-253); SOCIOLOGY (P. 227-253)
IT - TENSION RELEASE (P. 141-145); WOMEN (P. 151-164); ZULU (Atherton
et al., 1978, p. 101).
(CT = Contents Terms from the TOC; IT = Index Terms from the Index)

We can see clearly that useless terms (foreword, preface, afterword, bibliography, index) and non-specific terms, such as "form and function," "military horizon," "certain," from the TOC chapter headings were dropped in the Contents Terms (CT). At the same time, the Index Terms (IT) really provided highly content-specific subject access points. There should be no doubt about the superiority of SAP technique.

Small Survey at Two Canadian Universities

The author of this article did a search on the OPACs of the University of Saskatchewan (U of S without TOC) and the University of Western Ontario (U of WO with TOC) on August 12, 1998. The main reason for choosing these universities is that they are quite similar in terms of monograph holdings (1.5 million and 2.1 million respectively) (*American Library Directory 1997-98*, 1997, pp. 2353, 2467) and holdings per medical student (266 and 267 respectively) (Maclean, 1997, p. 59). The search was done in the Keyword Index, and the search term was "Prostate Cancer." The search result was: 16 items retrieved from the U of S

OPAC and 101 from the U of WO OPAC. Only two items appeared on both lists. Of the ninety-nine items on the U of WO list that do not appear on the U of S list, seventy-four do not contain the term "Prostate" in their titles. A second search on the U of S catalog, using Title Index for these seventy-four items, revealed that U of S had twenty-six of the same items. The twenty-six items were retrieved in the first search because U of WO catalog records had TOC information. If the U of S OPAC had TOC information, a keyword search would have retrieved forty-two items, an increase of 163 percent.

Conclusion

It is too early for a final assessment of subject access enhancement by TOC in OPACs. Some academic libraries that have TOC in their OPACs, however, report some positive preliminary results: "Recall has obviously been greatly enhanced. Overall, I think students are glad that we have TOC information. They can see what is in a book and even how many pages each chapter covers. That has been very much appreciated by many students whom I have helped" (Zimmerman, W., personal e-mail communication to the author, September 29, 1998). "That it is a way of being more precise, and is helpful for those users to work from their office, and identify before going to the library, which library materials are worth examining" (Palmer, D., personal e-mail communication to the author, September 23, 1998).

Some decisions have to be made regarding the indexing of this information. Most libraries have decided to have section/chapter title information put in both keyword and title indexes. With search words found in TOC data now highlighted in most systems, it is no longer confusing for users searching the title index. At Hong Kong University, it was decided to have a separate index for TOC. These libraries also have witnessed some impact on their cataloging procedures. "The chief impact for cataloging procedures has been in ensuring that staff are aware of the span of records (based on CAT DATE) that have been extracted and sent for TOC processing. If changes are to be made to records being processed for TOC, staff need to wait or repeat the changes once the records are reloaded into the database as they overlay the existing bibliographic records. We have "protected" all TOC 9XX fields so that they cannot be erased by any future overlay process" (Kennedy, W., personal e-mail communication to the author, Sept. 29, 1998).

Subject access enhancement with complete TOC information is now a reality. However, the verdict on its value is still pending. We should expect some large-scale evaluation of this new feature of OPACS in the forseeable future.

References

American Library Directory 1997-98 (50th ed., vol. 2.). (1997). New Providence, NJ: R.R. Bowker.

Byrne, A., & Micco, M. (1988). Improving OPAC subject access: The AFDA experiment. *College & Research Libraries, 49*(5), 440.

Cochrane, P. A. (1985). *Redesign of catalogs and indexes for improved online subject access: Selected papers of Pauline A. Cochrane.* Phoenix, AZ: Oryx Press.

Cochrane, P. A. (1986). *Improving LCSH for use in online catalogs: Exercises for self-help with a selection of background readings.* Littleton, CO: Libraries Unlimited.

Cochrane, P. A. et al. (1978). *Books are for use: Final report of the Subject Access Project to the Council on Library Resources.* Syracuse, NY: Syracuse University, School of Information Studies.

Content-enriched and enhanced subject access in USMARC records. (1991). (MARBI Discussion Paper No. 42, rev. Feb. 7, 1991). Washington, DC: MARBI.

Dillon, M., & Wenzel, P. (1990). Retrieval effectiveness of enhanced bibliographic records. *Library Hi Tech, 31*(3), 43-46.

Enhancing USMARC records with table of contents (MARBI Discussion Paper No. 46). (1991). In M. Ra (Ed.), *Advances in online public access catalogs* (Vol. 1, pp. 105-113).

Makinen, R. H., & Friesen B. (1995). Enhancing online bibliographic records to improve retrieval of reference collection monographs. *Bulletin of the Medical Library Association, 83*(2), 244-246.

Mandel, C. A. (1985). Enriching the library catalog record for subject access. *Library Resources & Technical Services, 29*(1), 5-15.

Matthews, J. R. (1985). *Public access to online catalogs*, 2ᵈ ed. New York: Neal-Schuman.

Peis, E., & Fernandez-Molina, J. C. (1998). Enrichment of bibliographic records of online catalogs through OCR and SGML technology. *Information Technology and Libraries, 17*(3), 161-172.

Poulsen, C. (1996). Tables of contents in library catalogs: A quantitative examination of analytic catalogs. *Library Resources & Technical Services, 40*(2), 137.

Subject cataloging manual: Subject headings, 5ᵗʰ ed. (1996). Washington, DC: Library of Congress, Cataloging Policy and Support Office, Vol. 1, section H 180, pp. 1-2.

Table of Contents Information (a one-page document from LC's Electronic CIP).

Universities 97: The seventh annual ranking. (1997). *Maclean's, 110*(47).

Van Orden, R. (1990). Content-enriched access to electronic information: Summaries of selected research. *Library Hi Tech, 31*(3), 27-32.

Wormell, I. (1983). Factual data retrieval according to SAP technique. *International Forum on Information and Documentation, 8*(3), 15.

Objects for Distributed Heterogeneous Information Retrieval

✦ Eric H. Johnson ✦

Introduction

The success of the World Wide Web shows that we can access, search, and retrieve information from globally distributed databases. If a database, such as a library catalog, has some sort of Web-based front end, we can type its URL into a Web browser and use its HTML-based forms to search for items in that database. Depending on how well the query conforms to the database content, how the search engine interprets the query, and how the server formats the results into HTML, we might actually find something usable. While the first two issues depend on ourselves and the server, on the Web the latter falls to the mercy of HTML, which we all know as a great destroyer of information because it codes for display but not for content description. When looking at an HTML-formatted display, we must depend on our own interpretation to recognize such entities as author names, titles, and subject identifiers. The Web browser can do nothing but display the information. If we want some other view of the result, such as sorting the records by date (provided it offers such an option to begin with), the server must do it.

This makes poor use of the computing power we have at the desktop (or even laptop), which, unless it involves retrieving more records, could easily do the result set manipulation that we currently send back to the server. Despite having personal computers with immense computational power, as far as information retrieval goes, we still essentially use them as dumb terminals. This is the price we pay for the expedience of having a "thin" client. The server works much harder than it ought to, and the client hardly does anything. The so-called "client-server" setup, as manifested on the World Wide Web, is really an old-fashioned "host-terminal" setup but with more bandwidth, more computational power, and prettier displays. Unfortunately, most of that computing power goes to the GUI. It does not do much toward enhancing the usability of retrieval software or make it able to recognize the elements it displays so you can do something with result sets besides look at them.

Bibliographic standards and metadata initiatives go a long way toward giving client programs the means to identify entities within result sets and records. This potential has existed ever since the MARC record came about in the 1960s, even though it was the 1980s before desktop computers could have made use of it themselves without reliance on a host computer. More recently, XML (eXtensible Markup Language) provides an even more flexible means to encode records with machine-identifiable entities. XML has captured the attention of developers everywhere and will soon dominate other document-based formats.

When searching online, either with a vt100 terminal or with the World Wide Web, we connect to only one source and search it before moving on to other sources. However, we really ought to be able to search any combination of databases simultaneously. Online services, such as Dialog, provide heterogeneous data access by coordinating different database formats at the server end, giving us a single interface with which to search these databases. However, we really ought to search any collection of databases directly from our desktop without having to go through a central coordination center.

Yee and Layne (1998) offer their view on heterogeneous data access: "Perhaps the ultimate solution is to try to standardize bibliographic practice over all these systems or develop highly sophisticated mapping programs that could automatically translate queries from one system to another" (p. 2).

History tells us that the former will never happen (though we should have only a handful of formats), so instead we should focus on building what they refer to as "mapping programs." Instead of building programs that map from one particular system to another, the approach described here builds an object layer on top of existing systems and uses a specialized client utilizing those objects to provide unified ways of querying and viewing distributed heterogeneous databases.

Sparing You the Details

To retrieve information from any online database (a library catalog or an abstract database, for example), you must perform the following four general actions:

- connect to it;
- query it;
- view result sets from queries; and
- select and view individual records from result sets.

Each of these involves complicated sequences of operations at the machine level which vary depending on the types of databases and protocols involved. However, as the user, you should not have to worry about these details. As far as retrieval interaction goes, you should only have to think about the four actions listed above and even less if possible. Ideally, they should seem to flow together into a seamless whole that does not distract from the intent and goal of your retrieval task.

The retrieval client software, in giving you simplified views of databases and making it easy for you to retrieve information from them, ought to shoulder much on your behalf. One simple action on your part may require it to issue a different query to each database, which most likely reside on different remote servers, and then collate and organize the results as they asynchronously come back from each server, all within the span of a few seconds. The databases may each have different communication protocols, index structures, query languages, and record formats, all requiring the retrieval client software to perform complicated conversions and translations. Yet the retrieval client software must hide all of this thereby providing a clear view of the bibliographic landscape unfettered by technical details of the retrieval software.

The use of *objects* helps system designers and implementers deal with much of the complication that arises in building heterogeneous information retrieval client software and other types of nontrivial software. Thinking about information retrieval client software in terms of the objects it manipulates, and that you manipulate in the GUI, greatly simplifies the concepts involved. It will also help me keep my promise about sparing you the details.

The idea of software objects provides a convenient metaphor to objects in the physical world. Like objects in the physical world, we can think of software objects as having properties and displaying behavior. By setting an object's properties and invoking various kinds of behavior (technically known as *methods*), we can make it do useful work for us. An object also hides (by way of *encapsulation*) its inner workings so we only have to worry about it in terms of its properties and methods. This mostly benefits the software developer, though the user benefits as well through greater software reliability.

Database, Query, and Result Set Objects

So what do the objects in a heterogeneous retrieval client look like? Starting with the databases from which we would like to retrieve information, reconsider the four general actions described above. We can start by thinking of these as *methods* to invoke on the databases, regardless of their type. Whether we have a Z39.50 database, a WAIS database, or even a legacy BRS database, we want to consider the method of connecting to them all in the same way: just connect to it please, and spare me the details. We don't even want to know what kind of database it is, other than some information about its content (the database object can provide this description as a property, manifested as a text paragraph). The database object might also have a yes/no property that indicates whether or not we connected to it successfully. This object view of databases effectively puts wrappers around them, giving them all the same methods for us to invoke and with the same labels and exhibited behavior, even though their internal mechanisms may differ greatly.

Once connected to a database, we can actually use it by sending queries to it, the second general action. But a query has properties and a structure of its own; representing it as a property or a method of the database will not do. We must therefore represent queries as objects and further as objects of a class quite different from databases.

Thinking of a query as an object may seem strange, especially if you usually think of a query as a sort of command. When we query a database, we command it to send us records matching the description in the query, therefore using it as an action. This happens when, for example, we use the FIND command as specified in ANSI/NISO Z39.58 (Common Command Language for Online Interactive Information Retrieval). Some examples of the FIND command and their explanations taken from Appendix B of the Z39.58 standard follow:

> "FIND ecosystems"
> searches for the word "ecosystems" in the default index
> "FIND conversion tables"
> searches for "conversion" immediately preceding "tables" in the default index
> "FIND SU library automation"
> searches the subject index(es) for "library" immediately preceding "automation"
> "FIND chopin AND etudes"
> searches for records with both "chopin" and "etudes" in the default index
> "FIND AU william shakespeare AND TI julius caesar"
> searches for records with "william" immediately preceding "shakespeare" in the author index and with "julius" immediately preceding "caesar" in the title index
> "FIND AU (asimov OR bradbury) AND SU science fiction"
> searches for records with "asimov" or "bradbury" or both in the author index and with "science" immediately preceding "fiction" in the subject index.

Queries can get much more complicated than these, and involve operators for value ranges and character masking as well as the Boolean operators shown in the last three examples. Booleans and parentheses allow any level of nesting so you can make queries as complicated as you want. Qualifiers, such as *AU* for author and *SU* for subject, indicate which index to search.

But now these things that we think of as actions must be taken and somehow cast as objects. Suppose "FIND" is deleted at the beginning of each example above, removing the verb from the command in each case. Then we no longer have commands as such but rather descriptions of the result sets we want from the database:

ecosystems

conversion tables

SU library automation

chopin AND etudes

AU william shakespeare AND TI julius caesar

AU (asimov OR bradbury) AND SU science fiction

Each of these descriptions retrieves records as effectively as its corresponding command. They differ in that the command form represents an *action on* a database, whereas the descriptive form *describes* the records we want from the database. At some point the client performs a command based on the description because the server expects it in that form, but we don't have to know about that part.

From your point of view as the user, each description takes the form of an object which, unlike a command, does not depend on other commands or actions to precede it. The retrieval client software automatically takes care of such dependencies when it sends the query to the server. In this way, the query has *persistence,* which allows you to keep it for as long as you find it useful.

When the retrieval client software submits the query object to the database, it invokes a method defined by the database object that accepts the object query, converts it into the form expected by the server, and submits it to the server. After, we hope, a short time, the server returns a response. If the response indicates no errors and a number of records retrieved, the database object requests a set of brief records from the server (though with some protocols, like Z39.50, the server may return a small set of initial records with the response). The database object then converts the records into a result set object and returns it to the client.

A result set object has the same kind of structure regardless of the type of database it comes from. A result set basically consists of a table and parameters that describe its content, methods for sorting the table on selected fields, and a method for fetching a brief record's corresponding full record from the database object. An empty result set contains no table, but it has encoded parameters explaining its emptiness (typically that the server returned no hits for the query submitted). A database object returns a result object for every query object submitted to it.

Having queries and result sets as objects solves a number of data management problems that plagued system developers during the days of procedural programming languages. Queries and result sets have nontrivial structures, yet the object management system allows the developer to treat them as simple variables. This still leaves the problem of how to manage all the database objects, query objects, and result set objects the retrieval client software generates during a session.

A number of internal data structures take care of this, but the GUI objects that present the databases to you and allow you to manipulate queries and result sets provide the clearest manifestation of how the retrieval client software organizes them. The *search document* provides the principal way of organizing queries and result sets for both you and the client. Figure 1 shows a search document with queries in the top half and a result set in the bottom half. The search document stores a reference to each query object in it, along with a reference to the corresponding result set. Each query has a selector next to it; the search document uses radio buttons as query selectors to indicate the mutually exclusive display of each result set. Selecting a query by clicking on the radio button next to it makes the search document display that query's corresponding result set. In this way you can observe any query's result set, even though you can only see one result set on the document at a time. The search document

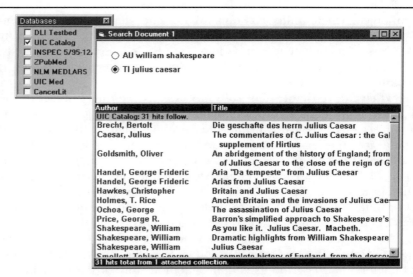

Figure 1. Database selection window (upper left), and search
document with two queries. The selected query, TI julius caesar,
displays the result set in the lower part of the search document

provides a persistent place for queries to reside. As long as a query resides on a search document, you can select it and view its result set.

The repository selection window at the left in Figure 1 indicates the databases selected for retrieval with the search document. You select a database to search by clicking the checkbox next to the name of the database. You can select multiple databases to search. You can also select databases after you have created queries, and the search document will manage connecting to the database and sending the queries to it for you. In this way, database, query, and result set objects exhibit not only persistence but also *persistent concurrency:* changes in the state of one invoke changes in all dependent objects, with all server connections, queries, and data management tasks handled automatically. You only need to manipulate the objects, and the retrieval client software handles the updating for you. Provided that network delays remain short and failures do not occur, you should only perceive a very short time lag between when you change an object and see the result of that change.

Using drag and drop, you can directly combine persistent query objects to form new queries. Consider the two queries on the search document in Figure 1, *AU william shakespeare* and *TI julius caesar.* Searchers often reduce the size of large result sets by specifying more than one index to search, with the stipulation that each record in the result set match all the criteria in the query (in other words, they perform an *AND* query). You can do this in this user interface by dragging one query and dropping it next to another one (see Figure 2).

You can also add to a query that already has a combination of terms. The query object over which you drag a new search term suggests a

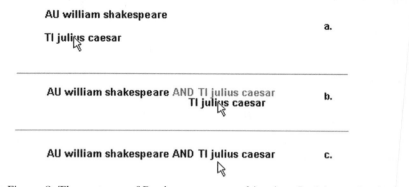

Figure 2. Three stages of Boolean query combination. In (a), you begin dragging one query toward another. In (b), the other query responds to the query dragged over it by "pencilling in" the combination as a Boolean AND query. In (c), you release the mouse button to complete the combined query. One drag-and-drop motion accomplishes all three

reasonable default location for it based on its qualifier. For example, dragging an author term over a query that already has at least one author causes the query to suggest adding it to the author clause in conjunctive normal form (see Figure 3).

AU (asimov OR bradbury OR clarke) AND SU science fiction
AU clarke

Figure 3. Query with conjunctive normal form
penciling in dragged-over Author term

This makes it very easy to construct Boolean queries in conjunctive normal form, commonly used by searchers when querying more than one field while hedging each field with more than one search term. Searchers often have trouble writing the correct Boolean syntax for these types of queries, and experienced searchers, though they have no difficulty understanding the syntax, still find it tedious to construct when they have to type it all out. Even novice users who do not really understand Boolean syntax and would have difficulty writing a correct Boolean query can construct useful queries with the default user interface behavior illustrated here.

However you construct a query, you can always edit it directly in the query area, just as you edit text in a GUI-based word processor. If you are so inclined, you can even type complex Boolean queries without resorting to keyword indexes, thesauri, or any of the on-screen qualifier and descriptor selection features described later. But anytime you want to use them they are there for you, no matter what method you used to construct the query.

When you change a query object, either by dropping another term on it or editing it directly, the search document, in an effort to maintain persistent concurrency of the objects, automatically submits it to the database object to get the new result set.

Qualifier Objects and Qualifier Sets

The content of the database determines what qualifiers you can provide in a query. Any bibliographic database should support title (TI), author (AU), and subject (SU) qualifiers at the very minimum. Typical bibliographic databases support those and other access points, including publisher and publication date.

Sources for qualifiers include such metadata initiatives as the Dublin Core. A qualifier set consists of one or more *qualifier objects*. A qualifier object contains a unique identifier for the qualifier (used internally by the retrieval client software), a display name, and a mnemonic (such as *SU, TI,* or *AU*) for use in queries.

Qualifier sets provide database objects with qualifier objects. A repository uses a qualifier set by selecting a subset of qualifiers from it, similar to how it might pick attributes from an attribute set such as bib1 if it used Z39.50. Z39.50, however, only allows a repository to use one attribute set, while here a database can use more than one qualifier set. This allows a database to use qualifiers and qualifier sets in a modular way. It also means that a qualifier set does not have to attempt to define every possible qualifier that a database in that domain might need. It can just define a few base qualifiers (such as the thirteen in the Dublin Core), and repositories can get additional qualifiers from other qualifier sets or even define their own qualifiers when needed.

Modular qualifier sets help solve a couple of long-standing problems posed by heterogeneity. First, no predefined set of qualifiers conceived by a standards committee can cover all the indexes a database might want to provide searchers. Second, particular databases need to indicate mappings of certain qualifiers to others or use a certain qualifier as default when it does not define a qualifier specified by a query. The use of hierarchy in a qualifier set can allow a database object to deal with the latter aspect of this problem very effectively, even allowing it to automatically manage vocabulary switching when accessing databases with controlled indexing vocabularies. The remainder of this section describes this latter use of qualifier hierarchies in some detail.

Z39.58's requirement that unqualified queries use a default index provides a "base level" of searching supported by all databases. For example, the qualified query *TI julius caesar* searches the title index for "julius caesar" while the unqualified query *julius caesar* searches the default index for "julius caesar." The repository defines the default index; in most cases it may be a full-text search, in some others a title keyword search, for example.

The use of a default index allows a database search engine to deal somewhat gracefully with qualifiers it does not define. For example, suppose you submit the query *AB telecommunication networks* (search the abstract index for the phrase "telecommunication networks") to an online catalog that does not have an abstract index. While it could rightfully return an error telling you that it does not support abstract searching and may not even have an abstract field as part of its record scheme, it could instead adapt the query by removing the qualifier, thereby searching for "telecommunication networks" in its default index. As a courtesy, it should inform you that it had to alter the query in order to use it and describe how it altered it.

By degrading the precision of queries in this way, a database can use a query that it would otherwise have to reject due to unsupported qualifiers.

If a database supports all the qualifiers in a query, then of course it does not have to degrade the query and can evaluate it to its full precision.

Now the question arises as to why you would submit a query with an *AB* qualifier to a database that does not support searching on an abstract index or otherwise does not have the abstract as part of its scheme. This can happen when you have a retrieval client that can submit a single query to multiple databases and the databases have different schema (as often happens in a world of heterogeneous databases). For example, you may form the query *AB telecommunication networks* when searching a database of abstracts. If it retrieves some useful abstracts for you, you may decide to expand your result set by submitting the query to an online library catalog. Typical library catalogs, however, only provide author-title-subject indexes. In keeping with the requirements of Z39.58, the database object representing the library catalog may provide title keywords as a default index, in which case it would convert a query into the base form *telecommunication networks* and maybe retrieve some catalog records for you. Otherwise you must manually select a more appropriate qualifier for searching the catalog (depending on circumstances, you might want to manually select a different qualifier anyway, but this way provides you with a useful default).

Library catalogs and abstract databases have fairly simple schema, and converting qualifiers between them does not pose much of a problem, either conceptually or in a retrieval system implementation, which can merely decide if it can support a particular qualifier or not. With full-text and scientific data, however, database schema can get quite complicated and require more sophisticated ways of resolving qualifier incompatibilities. We therefore need a more systematic way of understanding how different qualifiers relate to each other and how a database can degrade the precision of a query with as little damage to it as possible.

A hierarchical relationship exists between a qualified query and the default base level form of that query. If a database does not recognize a qualifier, it can always remove it from the query, reducing it to a base level query. In this hierarchy, the base level sits at the root, and the qualifiers we have discussed so far sit one level above it.

In terms of the tree shown in Figure 4, a database tries to match each qualifier in a query to one of the qualifiers in the left-hand (leaf) nodes. Any qualifier it cannot find in a leaf node gets eliminated, effectively reducing it to the default base (root) level. With this more formalized notion of qualifiers as nodes in a tree structure, we can extend it to cover more sophisticated relationships between qualifiers than merely their presence or absence.

Many online catalogs extend the idea of an author search, allowing you to search for either a personal author (e.g., Hunter S. Thompson) or a corporate author (e.g., Atomic Energy Commission). The Dublin Core

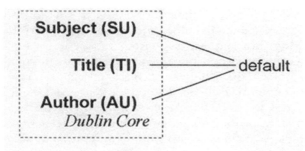

Figure 4. Subset of the Dublin Core with three qualifier objects

supports neither of these; it only supports author. However, we can define qualifiers for personal author and corporate author that extend the author qualifier, having the author qualifier as their common root. This changes the tree to look like Figure 5.

The tree in Figure 5 gets its structure from the qualifier identifiers. The Dublin Core qualifiers shown have Subject, Title, and Author as their respective identifiers, which happen to correspond to the display forms of their names. The author extension qualifiers have Author.Personal and Author.Corporate as their respective identifiers, which the qualifier manager uses to build the tree; the identifier Author.Personal, for example, identifies it as a child of Author. The mnemonic forms AU.P and AU.C function as shorthand representations of the qualifiers. The display forms Personal Author and Corporate Author make for nicely displayed human-readable names in context menus and identity popups, described later.

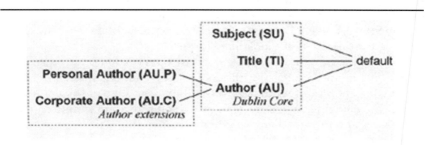

Figure 5. Dublin core subset with author qualifier extensions

Suppose that we have queried a database that supports personal and corporate authors with the query *AU.P thompson, hunter s,* the qualifier meaning *author—personal,* the dot separating the two levels of qualification displayed in the tree in Figure 5. Now to expand our results, we connect to another database that does not happen to support the personal/corporate distinction but only supports the basic query for *author.* This database cannot perform the search as specified by the qualifier, but it does not have to cut the qualifier out completely and resort to the default base level query. Instead it cuts the qualifier back one level, changing it from *AU.P* to *AU* and then checks to see if it supports the resultant qualifier. It does support *AU,* so it performs the query *AU thompson, hunter s.,* still a perfectly good author query which will return a useful result set.

Thus, if a database object cannot handle the qualifiers in a query given to it, it automatically performs *qualifier precision reduction* to reduce the qualifier to the level of precision that the database can handle. If it cannot match a qualifier, it tries removing the finest level of precision that the qualifier has and then attempts to match it again. This continues until the qualifier matches one of the qualifiers supported by the database or the qualifier disappears altogether, yielding a default base level query.

The opposite circumstance may also occur. Suppose you form the query *AU thompson, hunter s.* using a database supporting only the general kind of author query. Then you connect to another database that supports the personal/corporate author distinction. When it receives the query, it will have no way of determining whether *thompson, hunter s.* refers to a person or a corporation. Therefore the database must support a generalized author index which merges personal and corporate authors, or the database object must form the query *AU.P, AU.C thompson, hunter s.* (equivalent to the Boolean query *AU.P thompson, hunter s. OR AU.C thompson, hunter s.*) before submitting it to the database server.

Qualifier precision hierarchies can support multiple levels of reduction. Consider a qualifier set designed for online retrieval of SGML full-text documents, where the markup indicates the detailed structure of each document. Such a qualifier set would provide qualifiers for parts of the document markup not covered by qualifiers in the Dublin Core. The qualifier tree for this set might look like Figure 6.

This allows you to create a very precise query based on the structure of the document. Databases with less precisely defined structures could use qualifier precision reduction to use the query. Like in the author example, the database object specifying this hierarchy must support queries made with any intermediate qualifiers, besides the leaf and root node qualifiers.

Notice how the full-text qualifier structure in Figure 6 makes no use of the Dublin Core Subject qualifier. Full-text databases do not often have terms from a controlled indexing vocabulary attached to them, so in a strict sense a subject search on such a database has no meaning. However, a database object can map a qualifier it does not explicitly support to one

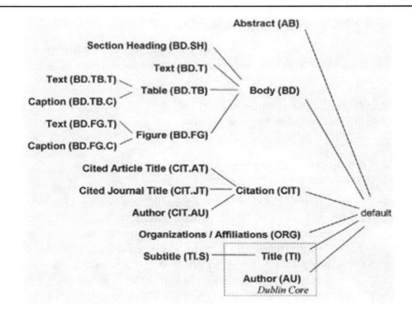

Figure 6. Qualifier tree for SGML full-text document structure

it does in anticipation of the use of that qualifier by a searcher. In this example, the database can map the Subject qualifier to the Abstract qualifier so that Subject terms get searched for in the abstract. This appears to work reasonably well for full-text databases that cover the same domain as a given indexing vocabulary.

The Subject-to-Abstract mapping constitutes an explicit nonhierarchical mapping between qualifiers rather than a precision reduction. The database object handles this mapping and includes Subject in its qualifier structure. Figure 6 therefore only shows qualifiers directly supported by the database; from the point of view of the searcher, it also supports Subject and any other qualifiers the database object maps to directly supported qualifiers.

Subject Qualifier Extensions and Controlled Vocabularies

Weibel et al. (1995) extend Dublin Core elements by specifying particular *schema* associated with those elements. For the Subject element, acceptable schema include LCSH, Compendex, and INSPEC, each referring to the controlled vocabulary of the same name. Examples include:

Subject: scheme=LCSH: Internet (Computer network)
Subject: scheme=INSPEC: information retrieval systems

OCLC's use of schema corresponds exactly to the use of qualifier extensions as described in the previous section. This means that we can submit queries such as:

SU.LCSH Internet (Computer network)
SU.INSPEC information retrieval systems

Or with abbreviated qualifiers:

SU.LC Internet (Computer network)
SU.INT information retrieval systems

The semantics of Subject qualifier extensions differ from those of qualifiers such as Author or Title. Author and Title qualifier extensions, as well as qualifiers and extensions used for full-text databases, refer to refinements of structure within the database. Personal Author (AU.P) and Corporate Author (AU.C), for example, refer to separate author indexes in the database, which represent a refinement of a single author index having both kinds intermixed. The INSPEC Thesaurus (SU.INT) and the Compendex Thesaurus (SU.COT) on the other hand, do not represent refinements of database structure in the same way as with Author extensions. Each Subject extension represents a controlled vocabulary that a database may use to index its records.

A database can still apply precision reduction to a Subject qualifier it does not support, yielding an unextended *SU* qualifier. In the case of the full-text qualifiers described above, the database searches the abstract for a phrase matching the Subject term, in effect using a non-controlled indexing vocabulary. Such a database would also apply precision reduction to queries like *SU.INT information retrieval* and *SU.COT information systems*. In such cases, Subject qualifiers behave the same as any other qualifier.

More interesting Subject qualifier behavior arises when a database has records indexed using a particular controlled vocabulary, such as Compendex, and you submit a term from a different vocabulary in the same subject domain, such as from INSPEC, and the database has access to a metathesaurus containing both and can convert terms from one vocabulary into the other. Such a database would therefore directly support queries with the qualifier *SU.COT.* If it gets a query with the unextended Subject qualifier *SU,* it would attempt to match the term to the controlled vocabulary (in effect, reversing the idea of precision reduction). If, however, it gets a query with the qualifier *SU.INT,* having a qualifier extension different from the one it supports, it asks the metathesaurus object if it contains the vocabulary so indicated.

If the metathesaurus contains both vocabularies, the database object proceeds to ask it to convert the given term in the given vocabulary to the corresponding term(s) in the supported vocabulary. Ideally, the metathesaurus responds with one term, and the database object can then submit the modified query with the appropriate term to the database server. If the metathesaurus responds with more than one term (it is hoped a very small number of them), the database object constructs a Boolean *OR* with each term and submits that to the database server. This may reduce the precision of the result set.

The worst case occurs when the metathesaurus cannot match the given term and returns a null result. In this case, the database object applies precision reduction to the qualifier and treats it as a plain *SU*. However, in this case, the metathesaurus has already indicated that the supported vocabulary does not have a term corresponding to the given term, and the database object will most likely waste its time attempting to submit the given term in a query using the supported vocabulary. At this point it may submit the term to the default index.

If the metathesaurus does not support the given vocabulary, the database object applies precision reduction to yield an *SU* qualifier and proceeds as before.

In the GUI, subject thesaurus windows use extended Subject qualifiers to identify the thesauri they display. When you drag a term from a thesaurus display and drop it onto a search document, it carries the extended Subject qualifier with it to use in the query on the search document. Other term suggestion windows use qualified terms in similar ways (see Barnes et al., 1998 for details and illustrations).

Language Translation

Internationalization (sometimes abbreviated as *I18N* because of the 18 letters between the first *i* and the last *n*) brings with it the retrieval problem of using the same query across heterogeneous databases which contain items in different human languages. Assuming that a given database uses the same human language throughout, the problem of translating query terms to each database's human language resembles the problem of translating controlled vocabulary terms.

If each database has a property identifying its human language, using a standardized set of language identifiers (e.g., English.Am for American English or English.Br for British English), then each database object can translate query terms with a conversion dictionary. Conversion dictionaries work much the same way as metathesauri but afford considerably greater liberty of use since they do not deal with controlled vocabularies but rather with natural language words and phrases.

Making Qualifiers Usable and Queries Readable

Including qualifiers in query syntax dredges up an old usability problem that normally occurs only in command-line interfaces: to properly form a query, you must type the correct qualifiers for the indexes you want to search as well as getting various other syntactic elements correct for more sophisticated queries. An earlier section covered how drag and drop manipulation of query objects simplifies Boolean combination of existing queries but did not mention where the qualifiers for the queries came from.

Unless you want the database to use the default index, you must provide the correct qualifier for a query to search the index appropriate to the kind of search you want. Most GUI-based interfaces would solve this problem by providing pull-down menus or command buttons with which to select qualifiers. This type of interaction requires that you select the qualifier before you type the query, but because a search term may have more than one qualifier or even no qualifiers at all, the search term ought to be typed first and then qualified afterward. Figure 7 illustrates how to qualify a search term.

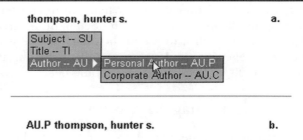

Figure 7. Selecting a qualifier. In (a), you activate the context menu for the query and select a qualifier, either from the top-level menu or from any submenus. In (b), the qualifier adds itself to the query

The software client automatically generates qualifier context menus directly from qualifier trees and uses the display name and mnemonic of each qualifier to build each menu item.

While you might accept using *AU.P* for personal author, especially if you can select it from a menu, longer qualifier mnemonics can get cumbersome and difficult to remember. Default qualifier semantics follow the dot structure of their identifiers: *AU.P* derives from *Author.Personal*. The full-text qualifiers in Figure 6 illustrate the problem with longer qualifier names and deep qualifier trees. The full-text qualifier *Figure Caption,* for example, because it lies in the third level of the qualifier tree, has the default mnemonic *BD.FG.C*–difficult to remember and not very pretty to look at. A qualifier object allows you to define an alternate mnemonic for it that you can use instead of the often cryptic dot format. *FIGCAP* serves as a much nicer mnemonic for Figure Caption than does *BD.FG.C*. Figure 8 shows the full-text qualifier context menu with alternate qualifier mnemonics for some of the second and third level qualifiers. Compare them to the standard mnemonics for the same qualifiers in Figure 6.

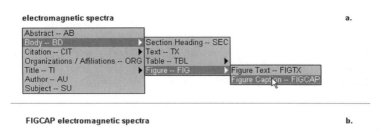

Figure 8. Selecting a full-text qualifier with alternate mnemonics. You perform the same actions described in Figure 7. Alternate mnemonics, while more legible than standard mnemonics with dot notation, qualify the query in exactly the same way

When a qualifier has both a default and alternate mnemonic defined, it prefers the alternate. Base level qualifiers such as Subject, Title, and Author generally have reasonable default mnemonics, so they don't need alternate mnemonics.

If you use a particular set of qualifiers often, which happens when you frequently search the same databases, you can type the qualifiers and the entire query directly instead of using qualifier menus and drag-and-drop combinations of queries. You can also ignore case when typing. This article has used the typographic convention of qualifiers and operators in ALL CAPS and search terms in lowercase, while Z39.58 requires case-insensitivity for all queries. Thus:

FIGCAP, TBLCAP electromagnetic spectra AND INT fourier transform spectra

means the same as:

figcap, tblcap electromagnetic spectra **and int** fourier transform spectra

which you can type easier, even though you would have a harder time reading it later.

Since the query object recognizes the structure of the query, you can have it displayed using various typographic conventions, even though you may not have used those same conventions when it was typed. You might, for example, have it display all qualifiers and operators in ALL CAPS, regardless of the case used when you typed it. Or you could have it apply different styles of text in different parts of the query, so that only qualifiers and operators appear **bold**:

figcap, tblcap electromagnetic spectra **and int** fourier transform spectra

Even with more readable alternate mnemonics, you may not remember the meaning of certain mnemonics when examining the query again later. Depending on the complexity of the query and the number of qualifiers and operators used, you may have trouble discerning the query structure as well, even though there may be typographic cues to different parts of it.

The example query used here has three parts, consisting of the first term, a Boolean operator, and a second term. Each term has subparts consisting of qualifiers and search words. The query object knows about each of these and where they begin and end in the displayed form of the query and can therefore indicate the location of each and the scope of qualifiers and operators. It can do this unobtrusively as we perform simple interaction, such as moving the mouse over it.

In Figure 9(a), you move the mouse over the first term (you do this with no buttons pushed; you do not do a drag operation, you merely move the mouse there). In response, the query object highlights the term and shows the display form of each qualifier in the text area below the query (if you have ever experienced using "tool tips" in a Windows application, this should look familiar). Notice how it highlights the subparts differently, with the qualifiers having a darker highlight and the text shown in white. This matches the color scheme of the "tool tip" area to indicate that the tool tip area describes the qualifiers. It also highlights the search words in the term but not as intensely. This indicates that the search terms lie within the scope of the qualifiers, but that the tool tip only describes the qualifiers and not the search words.

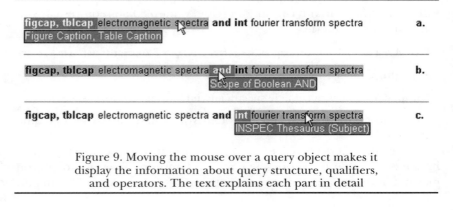

Figure 9. Moving the mouse over a query object makes it
display the information about query structure, qualifiers,
and operators. The text explains each part in detail

In Figure 9(b), you move the mouse over the Boolean operator. In response, the query object highlights the operator and the terms within its scope (in this case both terms in the query). This helps especially in more complicated queries, where multiple operators and nested parentheses can make it difficult to discern the query structure.

In Figure 9(c), you move the mouse over the second term. As in 9(a), the query object highlights the term and shows the display form of the qualifier.

Other mouse actions do other things to query objects. Clicking on a query term allows you to edit it or to change the qualifiers attached to it. Dragging a query term allows you to combine it with other queries, as shown in Figures 2 and 3. Clicking on a Boolean operator allows you to choose other Boolean operators from a popup list. Dragging a Boolean operator allows you to combine it and the terms in its scope with other queries.

Many in the library science community, especially those who build user interfaces for information retrieval systems, argue against the use of Boolean operators because they confuse novice users. However, the dynamic behavior of the user interface objects described here, combined with feedback from the persistent concurrency between them, warrants reexamining this premise. Direct manipulation of query terms with drag-and-drop allows you to dynamically construct Boolean queries with the query objects themselves providing the correct syntax. You select qualifiers from context menus and recognize when the results of queries you have combined yield a useful result set. Unless you choose to compose it directly, a Boolean query happens as a response to your actions rather than as a conscious effort at composition.

An expert searcher can type complete Boolean queries directly, and at any point use drag-and-drop to arbitrarily combine them into sophisticated queries without having to re-key anything. Experts and novices alike can alternate between typing and direct manipulation, whichever happens to better suit their circumstances. By observing how query objects automatically compose Boolean syntax when combined, and seeing the immediate feedback from persistent concurrency, novices can quickly learn how to compose Boolean queries. Evaluating how well this works in practice will require usability studies.

Searching Multiple Heterogeneous Databases Simultaneously

The real value of qualifier objects, and especially of database objects that define qualifier trees, comes to the fore when we search multiple databases simultaneously. This has already been alluded to in a previous section, and now I want to describe an actual scenario.

Figure 6 illustrates a qualifier tree for a database of full-text documents. Compare it to the qualifier tree for a database of abstracts, say for INSPEC, as shown in Figure 10.

Note that the two share some qualifiers, in particular the *Abstract* qualifier and the *Title* and *Author* qualifiers from the Dublin Core. When you select both for use with a search document, it provides a qualifier context menu derived from the union of the two trees (see Figure 11). Now you can build queries using qualifiers from either or both databases, and each database will still use its own qualifier tree to reduce the query for use with its own indexes. For example, you can type the query:

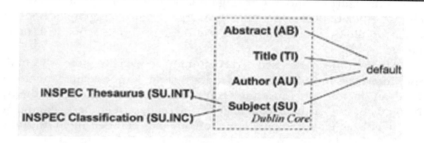

Figure 10. Qualifier Tree for a database of INSPEC abstracts

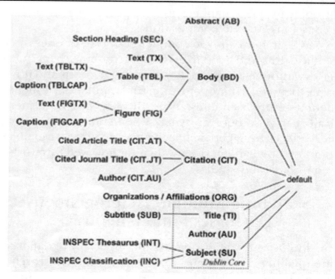

Figure 11. Qualifier context menu

ABelectromagnetic spectra AND TI emission

and the database objects for both the full-text and the INSPEC databases will submit the query unchanged, as each supports both the Abstract and Title qualifiers.

However, suppose you used the INSPEC Thesaurus to get a controlled vocabulary term, *optical dispersion*. When you transfer the term from the thesaurus browser, it brings the INSPEC Thesaurus (INT) qualifier with it, forming the query:

INT optical dispersion

Now we have a query that the INSPEC database can handle but the full-text database cannot. The INSPEC database object has the qualifier *INT*, so the query goes to the INSPEC database server unchanged. The full-text database object, however, must convert the query before it can send it on to the database server, because its qualifier tree contains nothing resembling *INT* as a qualifier.

The search document carries out the first step in a qualifier conversion by converting the alternate mnemonic, if the term contains one, to the standard form, in this case *SU.INT*. Then the search document passes it on to the database object, which traverses its qualifier tree, looking for a match. The full-text database object contains no qualifier that matches *SU.INT*, so it applies precision reduction to the qualifier, yielding *SU*. Recall that even though the full-text database does not directly support subject searching, the database object can contain a mapping from *SU* to some other qualifier, such as *AB*, which this database object has. Applying this mapping to the reduced query qualifier yields the query:

AB optical dispersion

which the full-text database object then sends to the full-text database server. The full-text database object also notifies the search document of this conversion so that it can inform you that the full-text database could not perform the subject search directly, and that it searched the abstracts instead. The qualifier tree structures and mappings allow all this to happen automatically.

Suppose you enter a query that the full-text database can directly support but the INSPEC index cannot. For example,

FIGCAP electromagnetic spectra

which the search document converts to the default qualifier form

BD.FG.C electromagnetic spectra

before passing it on to each database object. The full-text database object handles it directly, passing it on, unaltered, to the full-text database server. But now the INSPEC database server has the problem: the INSPEC database qualifier tree has no match to the qualifier *BD.FG.C* or the reduced form *BD.FG* or even *BD*. Therefore it reduces the query to the default, unqualified state, submitting only the phrase

electromagnetic spectra

to the INSPEC database server and hoping for the best.

Database objects apply qualifier reduction and mapping to each term of a Boolean query independently. Following the above examples, consider the Boolean query

INT optical dispersion AND FIGCAP electromagnetic spectra

The full-text database object would submit it to the full-text database server as

AB optical dispersion AND BD.FG.C electromagnetic spectra

while the INSPEC database object would submit it to the INSPEC database server as

SU.INT optical dispersion AND electromagnetic spectra

Query terms with multiple qualifiers, such as this one from a previous example

FIGCAP, TBLCAP electromagnetic spectra

have a logically equivalent Boolean form using an OR, which the search document generates before sending the query to each respective database object. This example yields

FIGCAP electromagnetic spectra OR TBLCAP electromagnetic spectra

which the full-text database object sends to the full-text database server as

BD.FG.C electromagnetic spectra OR BD.TB.C electromagnetic spectra

The INSPEC database object, however, supports neither qualifier, so direct conversion yields the query

electromagnetic spectra OR electromagnetic spectra

which by idempotence reduces to

electromagnetic spectra

More complicated queries with complex Boolean structures and qualifiers derived from multiple heterogeneous databases can emerge from each database object looking quite different from each other even though they perform the nearest equivalent query on each respective database.

Conclusion

The objects described in this article have developed from my attempts at building object-oriented retrieval interfaces as well as my thinking about how retrieval systems will work in a universally networked world of heterogeneous data sources. Many more kinds of objects are necessary for data display and transfer operations that I do not describe here; I purposefully limited my focus to objects that deal specifically with database heterogeneity.

Operating systems and GUIs will continue to become increasingly object and document oriented, and information retrieval interaction must fit into this model. Users of the next generation of operating systems will expect seamless interaction between information retrieval and other tasks and will at best feel troubled by retrieval systems that work like command-line interfaces with GUI window-dressing, as Web-based retrieval interfaces largely do now.

Furthermore, if they must use a different user interface for each database they access, they will opt for lowest-common-denominator services that provide simple searching across these databases, even if the searches do not have the level of completeness and precision offered by indexes specific to each database. The object-oriented approach described here attempts to preserve the best of multiple database searching with access to each database's specific indexes.

References

Barnes, B.; Johnson, E. H.; Young, J. B.; & Cochrane, P. A. (1998). Generalized software requirements to access thesauri and classification schemes for user-based image collections. In *9th ASIS SIG/CR Classification Research Workshop* (Pittsburgh, PA, October 25, 1998). Chicago: ASIS.

National Information Standards Organization. (1994). *ANSI/NISO Z39.58-1992, Common command language for online interactive information retrieval.* Bethesda, MD: NISO Press.

Weibel, S.; Godby, J.; & Miller, E. (1995). *OCLC/NCSA Metadata Workshop Report.* Retrieved February 9, 2000 from the World Wide Web: http://www.oclc.org:5047/oclc/research/conferences/metadata/dublin_core_report.html.

Yee, M. M., & Layne, S. S. (1998). *Improving Online Public Access Catalogs.* Chicago: American Library Association.

Curriculum Vita for Pauline Atherton Cochrane

Work Experience

The design and implementation of plans for information systems and services for diverse users—in both the laboratory and real-world setting; evaluation of information systems and services; staff supervision, training and recruitment; preparation of budgets, proposals, progress and final reports, manuals and handbooks, publicity; information policy formulation and development of national standards; academic administration; and teaching and advising students.

1998
Professor Emeritus, Graduate School of Library and Information Science, University of Illinois at Urbana-Champaign

Spring Continuing Education Workshop on OPACs and Gateways, University of North Carolina, Chapel Hill

Consultant, Demco Corporation

1995-97
Research Professor, University of Illinois at Urbana-Champaign

Summer 1995-96
Visiting Professor, School of Information Sciences, University of Tennessee, Knoxville

1995
Consultant, International Atomic Energy Authority

1994-1996
Consultant to Digital Library Initiative, University of Illinois at Urbana-Champaign, on matters relating to thesauri and users

Summer 1994
Visiting Professor, Graduate School of Library and Information Science, University of Washington

1991-1995
Visiting Professor, Graduate School of Library and Information Science, University of Illinois at Urbana-Champaign

1991-
Consultant, Library of Congress, Congressional Research Service

1991
Consultant, Walcoff and Associates, working on dissemination projects at the National Science Foundation

1990[1]
Consultant, U.S. Department of Education, Office of Educational Research and Improvement (OERI), Information Services

1989-90
Research Consultant, Catholic University, School of Library and Information Science, on distance learning strategies for library schools

1989
Program designer and instructor, U.S.I.A., short course on Social Science Reference Sources for Foreign Service Nationals–U.S.I.S. personnel from ten developing countries

1988-89
Consultant to National Library of Medicine Cataloging Department on the revision of NLM Classification

---

[1]In 1990 I went to Sri Lanka with my husband who was Chief of Party of a USAID Project until September 1991.

1989
Consulting editor, Learned Information, Inc. Assisted in publication of *Medline on CD-ROM*

1985-.[2]
Syracuse University, Professor Emeritus

1982-1986
Senior Staff Analyst, Automated Systems Office, Library of Congress (WAE status)

1982-1985
Consultant to OCLC, Inc., Research Division, on subject access developments and projects

1982-1983
Consultant to the H. W. Wilson Company on redesign of vocabulary control mechanisms once online

1966-1985
Syracuse University, Professor, School of Information Studies (teaching abstracting and indexing, thesaurus construction, cataloging, computer-based reference services)

1976-1984
ERIC/Information Resources Clearinghouse, Associate Director and Director, Special Projects Activities

Responsibilities included selection of articles for input, new descriptors for thesaurus, ERIC Course for Indexer-Abstractors; study impact of online searching on design of ERIC database, Vocabulary Improvement Project (major revision of ERIC Thesaurus)

1979-1980
Information Coordinator, Local Revenue Administration Project, funded by U.S.A.I.D.

Planned and implemented a specialized information service for forty faculty engaged in development projects in ten different countries

---

[2]In 1984 I went to Papua New Guinea with my husband who was a World Bank staff member seconded to the Papua New Guinea government. We took leaves from Syracuse University for two years and then retired from our tenured positions because we wanted to stay two more years. We returned to the Washington, D.C. area in November 1987.

1979-1981
Co-Principal Investigator, Pre-Search Interview Project, funded by the National Library of Medicine

Using video and audio tapes and special analytical tools, analyzed reasons for success or failure of professional intermediary before online searching

1978
Co-Leader, Workshop of Online Searching for Teachers of Library Science, University of Washington

1976-1978
Director, Subject Access Project, funded by the Council on Library Resources

Designed, implemented, and evaluated new online database for monographs in the social sciences and humanities using subject descriptions from contents pages and book indexes to augment library catalog records

1976-1981
Consultant to Cornell University School of Industrial and Labor Relations Library, funded by U.S. Department of Labor

Design, development, and evaluation of thesaurus, indexing procedures, and production of a machine-readable database; also comparison of coverage and indexing of relevant items in other databases

1974
Visiting Professor, UCLA Graduate School of Library and Information Science

1973
Visiting Professor, University of California, Berkeley, Institute for Library Research

Visiting Scholar, Danish Institute of Technology

1971
Visiting Professor, University of Washington

Visiting Lecturer in India and Ceylon (sponsored by Sarada Ranganathan Endowment)

1968-1971
Co-Director, S.U.P.A.R.S (Syracuse University Psychological Abstracts Retrieval Service), funded by the Rome Air Development Center (RADC)

First online retrieval system on a university campus designed for use by end users. Developed, revised, and evaluated system over two years of use

1967-1969
Director, LEEP (Library Education Experimental Project), funded by the U.S. Office of Education.

First use in a library school of MARC (Library of Congress Machine-readable Cataloging) records in the teaching of new technology and retrieval system design and evaluation; directed staff of system designers, programmers, and teaching assistants; developed computer-based reference and cataloging assignments; established LEEP-by-Mail service for other library schools; and experimented with online and batch retrieval systems for bibliographic searching

1961-1966
Assistant Director, Documentation Research Project, American Institute of Physics

Responsible for design and evaluation of new retrieval systems and journal indexes for physics; evaluated and suggested redesign of such abstracting and indexing services as *Physics Abstracts* and *Nuclear Science Abstracts.* Experimented with, and evaluated, citations indexes, automatic indexing, and author-aid-to-indexing. Projects funded by National Science Foundation

1960-1974
Consultant on indexing and library-related projects at Field Enterprises Educational Corporation

1957-1959
Cross Reference Editor, *World Book Encyclopedia,* during major revision, 1960 edition

Supervised staff of seven

1957-1961
Assistant Professor, Chicago Teachers College

1956-1957
Acting Reference Librarian, Chicago Teachers College

1954-1956
Librarian I, Chicago Public Library, Visual History, English, Science, Physical Education

1953-1954
Teacher, Seventh Avenue School, La Grange, Illinois. History, English, Science, Physical Education

1951-1953
Indexer, Central Files, Research Division, Corn Products Refining Company

Funded Research Projects
(see also Work Experience section)

1995-96
Digital Library Initiative, Graduate School of Library and Information Science, University of Illinois at Urbana-Champaign

Helped design hypertextual thesaurus browser

1986-87
Study Library Education in Papua, New Guinea, and Fiji. Grant from International Development and Research Center (IDRC)

1985-86
Unesco GIP Audio-Visual Project. Developed a slide-tape presentation of user-oriented information services in developing countries

1982
Entry Vocabulary Project. Developed routines for cooperative input to the Subject Catalog Division at the Library of Congress from four research libraries to effect subject access improvements. Funded by the Council on Library Resources

1975-76
Fellowship to study impact of online services on academic libraries. Funded by Council on Library Resources which resulted in a book, *Librarians and Online Services*, co-authored with Roger Christian

1974-75
Prepared and edited *UNISIST Handbook of Information Systems and Services*. Published in five languages and still popular. Funded by UNESCO

Prepared manuscript for *Guidelines for Seminars and Workshops* to assist workshop organizers in developing countries. Funded by UNESCO

1963-66
AIP/UDC Project to develop and evaluate AUDACIOUS, an experimental online system using the UDC classification as the retrieval vocabulary. Funded by the National Science Foundation

Professional Services in the Public and Private Sectors

1998
Workshop on Webcats and Gateways, University of North Carolina, Chapel Hill

1997
Organizer, 34th Annual Clinic on Library Applications of Data Processing, "Visualizing Subject Access for 21st Century Information Resources," sponsored by the Graduate School of Library and Information Science, University of Illinois at Urbana-Champaign, March 2-4, 1997, Urbana, Illinois

1994
Organizer, 36th Annual Allerton Institute, "New Roles for Classification in Libraries and Information Networks," sponsored by the Graduate School of Library and Information Science, University of Illinois at Urbana-Champaign, October 23-25, 1994, Monticello, Illinois

1993-94
Member, National Library of Medicine Panel on Training of Health Science Librarians and author of background paper for panel

1991-
Consultant to Congressional Research Service at Library of Congress. Improvements to legislative documentation databases, Legislative Index Vocabulary, and related CRS products, evaluating thesaurus maintenance and SGML electronic text programs

1991
Consulting editor on USAID project to produce a brochure entitled "Sri Lanka's Mahaweli Region"

1987-89
Consultant to University of Michigan Research Project on LCSH (Library of Congress Subject Headings in machine-readable form) (Karen Markey)

1987
Member of Advisory Committee on U.S.A.I.D. Research and Reference Services (a contract service of the Academy for Educational Development)

1979-1980
Member of Task Force on Public-Private Sector Information Policies, National Commission on Library and Information Sciences (NCLIS)

1975-1977
Member, Committee of International Scientific and Technical Information Programs (CISTIP), National Academy of Sciences. Since 1972, consultant to:

> Library of Congress
> UNESCO (General Information Program)
> United Nations Library (on UNBIS)
> U.S. Department of Labor
> Oak Ridge National Laboratory Information Division (on choice of online catalog)
> Minnesota Historical Society
> National Library of Medicine, Extramural Program
> Massachusetts Institute of Technology Library

1970-1971
President, American Society for Information Science

1961-1978
Member, FID/CR (Classification Research Study Group) (U.S. representative); on Organizing Committee for 1965, 1972 international conferences

1965-1966
Treasurer, American Documentation Institute (now ASIS)

Since 1962
Reviewer of research proposals and projects submitted to NSF, NLM, NIH, HEW, Canada Council, U.S. Department of Education, CLR, and UNESCO. Site team member for National Library of Medicine and American Library Association Committee on Accreditation

1960-1974
Co-founder with Phyllis Richmond, Classification Research Study Group, to encourage discussion and research on classification in the U.S.A. This group is now ASIS/SIG-CR

1979-1987
Editor, Wiley series on Information Science

1977
Consultant to EDUCOM on charging for library services

1974
Consultant to Westat (now King Research Inc.) on design of library surveys

1966
Consultant to System Development Corporation on preparation of national survey on abstracting and indexing services

Education

1957-1962
University of Chicago Post-master's study, Graduate Library School

1954
Rosary College, M.A. in Library Science

1951
Illinois College, B.A. in Social Science

HONOR
1999
Festschrift for 70th birthday, Graduate School of Library and Information Science, University of Illinois at Urbana-Champaign, Will Wheeler, ed.

1998
Pioneer of Information Science at Conference of the History and Heritage of Science Information Systems

1996
Award for Innovation for Education and Training, Syracuse University

1996
Distinguished Alumnus Award, Argo Community High School

1990
Award of Merit, American Society for Information Science "for pioneering and continuing work in several areas, including research and development efforts in the information sciences, the analysis and development of subject analysis tools, the active involvement in the development of improved communications within the profession, and her development and use of innovation instruction techniques"

1988
Jubilee Award for Outstanding Professional Achievement, Rosary College

1986
FID/CR Ranganathan Award for Classification Research

1981
Outstanding Information Science Teacher's Award from the American Society for Information Science

1981
Distinguished Visiting Scholar, OCLC, Inc.

1951
Phi Beta Kappa

Publications

Books

1998
Visualizing Subject Access for 21st Century Information Resources. Graduate School of Library and Information Science, University of Illinois at Urbana-Champaign, Editor (with Eric H. Johnson)

1986
Improving LCSH for Use in Online Catalogs; Exercises for Self Help with a Selection of Background Readings. 348 p. (Libraries Unlimited)

1985
Redesign of Catalogs and Indexes for Improved Online Subject Access; Selected Papers of Pauline A. Cochrane. 484 p. (Oryx Press)

1984
LCSH Entry Vocabulary Project; Final report to the Council on Library Resources and the Library of Congress. ERIC Ed. 234-780

1981
Basics of Online Searching (with Charles Meadow). 245 p. (Wiley)

1979
Online Searching of ERIC; Impact of Free Text on Controlled Vocabulary Searching on Design of the ERIC Data Base. (In five parts, 194 pp.) ED180431-180432

1978
Books are For Use; Final Report of the Subject Access Project, an experimental augmented online library catalog. 179 p. (Syracuse University Printing Services)

Design of Eric Usage Studies (ERIC/IR Special Project Report). 2vols. ED 167197-167198

ONTAP; Online Training and Practice Manual for ERIC (with Karen Markey) (ERIC/IR). 198 p. ED160108

1977
Handbook of Information Systems and Services. 299 p. (UNESCO, in 5 languages)

Librarians and Online Services (with Roger Christians). 124 p. (Knowledge Industry Publications)

1976
Guideline for the Organization of Training Courses and Workshops (UNESCO, in 5 languages)

1973
Putting Knowledge to Work (Lectures on library automation delivered in India and Ceylon.) 158 p. (Vikas, Delhi)

1965
Classification Research (editor, Proceedings of the 2nd International Study Conference of the International Federation for Documentation. 563 p. (Munksgaard)

1961
The Journal Literature of Physics (with Stella Keenan). 125 p. (American Institute of Physics)

1959
Cataloging for Elementary School Libraries. 105 p. (Chicago Teachers College)

Chapters in Books

1996
"Visual Dewey: DDC in a Hypertextual Browser for the Library User," in *Knowledge Organization and Change,* Proceedings of the Fourth International ISKO Conference, 15-18 July 1996, pp. 95-106. Frankfurt, Indeks Verlag

1996
"Interactive Term Suggestion for Users of Digital Libraries" (with B. Schatz, E.H. Johnson, and H. Chen) in *DL '96 (ACM International Conference on Digital Libraries)*

1994
"Improvements Needed for Better Subject Access to Library Catalogs via the Internet." In *Emerging Communities: Integrating Networked Information into Li-*

brary Services (Proceedings of the 1993 Clinic on Library Applications of Data Processing), edited by Ann P. Bishop, pp. 70-83. Urbana-Champaign, IL: Graduate School of Library and Information Science, University of Illinois at Urbana-Champaign

1993
"Warrants for Concepts in Classification Schemes," *Proceedings of the 4th ASIS SIG/CR Classification Research Workshop*, October 24, 1993, pp. 57-67

1992
"The Influence of Ranganathan upon Library and Information Science, Library Education, and Me" in *Ranganathan and the West*, edited by R. N. Sharma. Sterling

---

Periodical Articles
(in refereed journals)

(As the 1985 publication cited above contains the majority of my published papers on catalog redesign, the reader is referred to this source. Papers not on this topic are listed below)

1995
"New Roles for Classification in Libraries and Information Networks" (with Eric H. Johnson). *Cataloging & Classification Quarterly*, 21: 3-4 (Report of 36th Allerton Institute, October 23-25, 1994)

1992
"Information Technology in Libraries and Ranganathan's Five Laws of Library Science," *Libri*, 42, 235-241

1990
"Universal Bibliographic Control: Its Role in the Availability of Information and Knowledge." *Library Resources & Technical Services, 34* (October), 423-431

1980
"The Cultural Appraisal of Efforts to Alleviate Information Inequity" (with G. Cochrane). *Journal of the American Society for Information Science, 31* (July), 283-292

1978
"Standards for a User-System Interface Language in On-Line Retrieval Systems." *Online Review, 2*(Fall), 57-61

1977
"New Measures of User Satisfaction with Computer-Based Literature

Searches" (with J. Tessier and W. Crouch). *Special Libraries, 68*(November), 383-390

1976

"Knowledge Space, a Conceptual Basis for the Organization of Knowledge" (with P.P.M. Meincke). *Journal of the American Society for Information Science, 27* (January), 18-24

1976

"Research in Information Science; An Assessment" (with N. Van de Water, N. Supprenant, and B. Genova). *Information Processing and Management, 12* (March), 117-123

1975

"Views of the Communication Network of Scientific and Technical Information." *International Forum on Information and Documentation, 1,* 10-12

1972

"Putting Knowledge to Work in Today's Library Schools." *Special Libraries,* (January), 31-36

1970

"LC/MARC on MOLDS; An Experiment in Computer-Based, Interactive Bibliographic Storage, Search, Retrieval, and Processing" (with K. Miller). *Journal of Library Automation, 3*(June), 142-165

"Teaching with MARC Tapes" (with J. Tessier). *Journal of Library Automation,* (March), 24-35

1965

"Ranganathan's Classification Ideas: An Analytico-Synthetic Discussion." *Library Resources and Technical Services, 9* (Fall), 463-473

Index

✦ Compiled by Sandra Roe ✦